Routledge Revivals

Copyright

First published in 1980, *Copyright* offers an explanation and an analysis of the wider implications of copyright as an instrument for ordering the flows of information and culture within and among societies. The book traces the development of copyright and related rights with emphasis on the policy aspects and on how copyright was influenced by and in its turn influenced the users of new information technology.

Significant discussion is devoted to the international aspects of copyright, its unique position in international law, and its role in the relations between industrialized and developing countries. Having provided a basic understanding of copyright principles and their implications, the authors then analyse how well or badly copyright is coping with the various information and communication technologies that have developed primarily in the twentieth century. Finally, they discuss how copyright operates in a modern technological society, the existing challenges to copyright, and its prospects for the future.

Copyright

Intellectual Property in the Information Age

Edward W. Ploman and L. Clark Hamilton

Routledge
Taylor & Francis Group

First published in 1980
by Routledge & Kegan Paul Ltd

This edition first published in 2024 by Routledge
4 Park Square, Milton Park, Abingdon, Oxon, OX14 4RN

and by Routledge
605 Third Avenue, New York, NY 10017

Routledge is an imprint of the Taylor & Francis Group, an informa business

© The International Institute of Communications 1980

Publisher's Note
The publisher has gone to great lengths to ensure the quality of this reprint but points out that some imperfections in the original copies may be apparent.

Disclaimer
The publisher has made every effort to trace copyright holders and welcomes correspondence from those they have been unable to contact.

A Library of Congress record exists under LCCN: 80040493

ISBN: 978-1-032-85823-4 (hbk)
ISBN: 978-1-003-51997-3 (ebk)
ISBN: 978-1-032-85824-1 (pbk)

Book DOI 10.4324/9781003519973

Copyright

Intellectual property in
the information age

Edward W. Ploman
and **L. Clark Hamilton**

Routledge & Kegan Paul

London, Boston and Henley

First published in 1980
by Routledge & Kegan Paul Ltd
39 Store Street, London WC1E 7DD,
9 Park Street,
Boston, Mass. 02108, USA and
Broadway House, Newtown Road,
Henley-on-Thames, Oxon RG9 1EN

Set in 10/12 Compugraphic Times by
Malvern Typesetting Services Ltd, Malvern
and printed in Great Britain by
Redwood Burn Limited, Trowbridge & Esher

British Library Cataloguing in Publication Data
Ploman, Edward Wilhelm
    Copyright.
    1. Copyright
    I. Title   II. Hamilton, L Clark
    346.048'2   K1420.5   80-40493

    ISBN 0 7100 0539 3

Contents

Preface and acknowledgments

This study is offered as a contribution to the discussions about copyright in modern society; necessarily, if optimistically, it must aim at being of interest to the policy-maker, the expert and the layman.

The book has grown out of discussions on communications and law held by the International Institute of Communications, with which the authors are associated: Clark Hamilton, Director, Systems Development Office, Library of Congress, as a Trustee and Edward Ploman as Executive Director. It has had a long gestation; not surprisingly in view of its complex and controversial subject matter.

Certainly, the book could not have been undertaken without the encouragement and active assistance of Barbara Ringer, US Register of Copyrights, and the Copyright Office of the Library of Congress. Equally important has been the support of the Institute's Board of Trustees and numerous members.

The authors owe sincere thanks to many. In particular, we wish to thank experts in the US Copyright Office who contributed material for several sections – Kent Dunlop, Harriet Oler and Stephen Plichta.

Others have been kind enough to read and correct drafts of various sections. Our sincere thanks are due to Hassan Akrout, then Président, Comité Culturel National, Tunis; Dr Harry Bloom, University of Kent, Canterbury; Dr L. S. Chopra, Ministry of Education, New Delhi; Dr Ernst Fuhr, Zweites Deutsches Fernsehen, Mainz; Dr Francesca Klaver, University of Amsterdam; Mr Tokutaro Kurokawa, Nippon Hoso Kyokai, Tokyo; Dr Agne Henry Olsson, Ministry of Justice, Stockholm; Mr Vincent Porter, Polytechnic of Central London; Mme Annie Cerf-Weil, Avocat à la Cour, Paris.

For certain sections of the study we have drawn upon a seminar on copyright and new technology for which the IIC had been granted the use of the Rockefeller Foundation Research and Conference Centre at Bellagio, Italy. We have also benefited from a grant by the Swedish Bank Tercentenary Fund.

Even though we would not have been able to carry through this project without the encouragement and assistance so generously given, we are responsible for the views expressed, or rather for the questions asked. It is our hope that we have been able to ask the right ones.

Quotations from foreign-language sources have been translated by the senior author.

Edward W. Ploman
L. Clark Hamilton

London and Washington,.
May–June 1979

Introduction

Why is copyright important and why should anybody but the experts be concerned at all?

Valid answers are as varied as the purposes which copyright is made to serve. Copyright is used as a legal mechanism for the ordering of social and cultural life, or, put another way, copyright is one method for linking the world of ideas to the world of commerce. Just as many of the traditional assumptions for organizing and controlling the flows of information in society are called into question so too are the economic assumptions on which the law of copyright is founded. And these assumptions condition the patterns of our cultural and scientific life.

Copyright is also used to cope with the problem of how best to reconcile the partly shared, partly contradictory interests of 'authors who give expression to ideas; publishers who disseminate ideas; and members of the public who use the ideas'. Copyright is therefore expected to provide answers to another set of fundamental questions: How can intellectual creativity best be promoted? How is the livelihood of the author and artist best ensured and how is he integrated into social and economic life?

Different societies have given different answers to these questions. There is nothing universal about copyright. As any other social institution, it evolved in response to specific challenges in a specific environment. Its origin is Western and its parentage multiple: the invention of the printing press and the advent of the industrial revolution, the philosophy of the market place and that of natural rights, the rise of bourgeois society and the spread of literacy, the social attitudes towards art and the artist. The resulting notion of intellectual property is a European invention but is now used in diverse economic and social systems to structure the flow of information and cultural products.

At the present moment, copyright, as other branches of com-

1

munications law, is in a state of stress. The reasons for the current crisis are many and varied. Obvious is the impact of new technology, of new methods for the production, duplication, storage and dissemination of information and cultural materials. The flows of information within and between societies have reached new levels of density and variety. Communications both express and contribute to the transformations of the international system. Changes in economic organization affect the conditions of the intellectual worker. Changes in social and cultural values are reflected in new policies for culture, education and communications. The growth of the information sector has led to new ways of looking at national economies. In industrialized countries the concept of the information society is gaining ground. A new strand in development thinking emphasizes the need to integrate the cultural and information dimension into strategies for economic and social development.

How well do copyright and related rights perform their multiple functions in a situation where they have to respond to these new challenges and social requirements? And why have these questions not attracted greater public interest and why is there such limited understanding of the issues involved?

Clearly one reason is that copyright has become one of the most complex, technically difficult branches of law, an arcane area populated by experts hiding behind an almost impenetrable jargon. The legal complexities and the language of the experts make it difficult for the general public, for policy- and decision-makers, for technologists and even for practitioners in communication to understand the wider implications of legislation and practices in this field. The resulting failure to formulate coherent policies is serious in a situation where new technologies and changing social patterns alter the conditions for the ordering of cultural life.

The purpose of this study is to place copyright in a wide context and to discuss current copyright issues at the level of policy and underlying principles. Legal technicalities have been avoided as far as possible. The challenges to copyright will be seen mainly within the perspective of the emerging information society and the complex interlocking of issues and interdependence of countries.

Some of the questions will be hard and probing in the attempt to search for approaches in new circumstances where even hallowed precepts will have to prove their worth.

Creativity is vital for any time and any society, but present challenges require a premium on imagination and courage. Our responses must be turned towards the future in support of the creators and in aid of society.

Chapter I · **Origins and early development**

1 Origins

The nature of copyright is a favourite subject of doctrinal disputes, which are often conducted with great passion. Not surprisingly, therefore, the origins of copyright are equally hotly contested. When did the creator of an intellectual work gain a personal right over his creation, and how did the notion of intellectual property arise?

Some analysts seem to think that the longer the genealogy and the more impeccable the pedigree, the better is the case that can be made for copyright. However, it is a vain enterprise to look for signs of copyright in ancient cultures, where intellectual works did not belong to the creator but to the community and to society. 'Strikingly and significantly, early Indian history is the history of societies rather than of persons. Even the great literary and philosophical masterpieces are all anonymous. Not who said it, but what was said – this was what mattered' (Oliver, 1971, p. 21). Similar attitudes are found throughout history: although the artist may have been professional, his communication – the message – was conceived as expressing the sense of the community.

One example closer in time is the much admired and artistically lively culture of Bali. It has often been pointed out that there is no word in the Balinese language for 'art' or 'artist', no separate class of artists. 'The artist is in Bali essentially a craftsman and at the same time an amateur, casual and anonymous, who uses his talent knowing that no one will care to record his name for posterity. His only aim is to serve the community . . . the anonymous artistic production of the Balinese, like their entire life, is the expression of collective thought' (Covarrubias, 1972, pp. 162, 164). This attitude has two important implications. The Balinese did not permit the centralization of artistic knowledge in a special intellectual class and had evolved what in modern jargon would be called a participatory cultural model. In the community-oriented Balinese culture, artistic property cannot exist; the expression of any new idea is there to be used by all.

Consequently, the search for the origins of copyright has focused on the Western tradition. According to some experts, the rights of authors had already been recognized in classical Greek culture. In the sixth century BC, with the development of commerce and of urban society, 'a type of man appears on the scene who was hitherto practically unknown – the artist with a markedly individual personality. Neither in the prehistoric nor in the early Oriental epochs . . . was there anything like an individual style or personal ideals or ambitions – at any rate there is no sign whatever that the artist cherished any feelings of this sort' (Hauser, 1962, pp. 65–6). At about the same time, we find the first claims of the poet to be recognized as the author of his poems and the first signed works of visual art (ibid.). According to other analysts, the advent of copyright is to be located at a precise moment of time: the invention of printing in the West about 1436. Without the means to produce copies, there could be no right to copy. Other experts maintain that copyright did not exist until it had been regulated by law in the eighteenth century. Why these divergences? It is difficult 'to escape from the attitudes of the present when writing about the past' (Briggs, 1978, p. 448). Answers to questions about the origins of copyright often depend on the opinions held about the nature and function of copyright. 'The history of intellectual property was used as an aid in the polemics about the nature of authors' rights and studied by those who wanted to find in the past the confirmation of their own theories . . .' (Dock, 1963, p. 3).

Thus the perspective provided by legal doctrine alone is not enough. Copyright and its origins must be set in a larger context which encompasses the organization of cultural and economic life, the social attitude towards intellectual creations and their uses, and the position of the creator in society. Copyright has emerged as one method to cope with these issues and thus as a means of organizing and controlling the flow of information in society.

The concepts of organization and control are useful as a starting-point. All societies have evolved systems for the organization of information flows in society. These systems have many forms. An extreme example of ruthless control over intellectual works is the famous Burning of the Books in ancient China. In 213 BC the Chief Minister, Li Ssu, petitioned the first Ch'in Emperor:

> the Empire has been pacified and the laws of the country unified. May it please your Majesty to determine right from wrong, to proscribe all unorthodox opinions, to destroy by fire all historical records except those of the Ch'in, to rule that any man who possesses the writings of the Hundred Schools and the ancient literature must immediately surrender them to the Magistrates to be burned . . . Whoever shall not have burned their books within thirty days after the issuance of this ordinance shall be branded and condemned to forced labour on the Great Wall for four years (see Li, 1971, pp. 100–1; Legge, 1972, p. 256; Ching and Bloodworth, 1976, p. 30).

The petition seemed to please His Majesty, since the imperial decision was 'Approved.' The books were burned and, subsequently, 460 of the greatest scholars who were suspected of knowing the books so thoroughly that they could teach from memory were buried alive.

At the other extreme, control may be established through excessive protection. There is the story that the first and most effective protection for intellectual property was found in ancient Egypt. If persons other than the members of the priesthood were overheard reciting the sacred rituals, they were liable to immediate execution. It can be assumed that a similar prohibition applied to the replication of the hieroglyphs which described these rituals.

This story might be apocryphal but should not surprise, particularly when compared with very similar rules thousands of years later: according to a French ordinance of 1566, those who printed any matter without permission were liable to be punished by hanging or strangulation (Dock, 1963, p. 68).

A somewhat more lenient attitude has been revealed by studies of ancient Jewish law. The early prophets referred to the stealing of words from another. This concept was later expanded in Jewish religious law to the principle of 'reporting a thing in the name of him who said it'. In Talmudic law, the reporters who orally passed on principles of law from one generation to another were very careful not to express such principles without mentioning the author. Only when the reporter developed a principle that was original and unprecedented did he adopt it as his own (Hazan, 1970).

As they evolved over time, these Talmudic principles showed some remarkable similarities to modern concepts of copyright. In the body of legal literature developed by the rabbis over the centuries, a number of copyright principles evolved: the permission of the author or his heirs must be obtained to copy material published by the author; permission to copy from another's work should be paid for. Thus in these ancient principles we can already see the distinction between two basic concepts of modern copyright. In the earlier principle the stress was on the moral right of the author; i.e. 'to have that which was stated by the author reported in his own name'. The later principles introduced the concept of an author's economic or property right in his work, which could be passed on to his heirs and for the use of which compensation was due.

Much learned effort has been devoted to analyses of the possible existence and nature of authors' rights in Roman law. The written law was silent on the subject of copyright, but there are other indications. According to available evidence Roman publishing had developed into a well-organized industry and commerce. Thus the context for the emergence of copyright notions was right. In the writings and correspondence of Roman authors and public figures there are numerous statements which point to a recognition of certain concepts of intellectual property. In the texts, references are made to contracts between authors and publishers, and to authors selling their work for publication. Therefore the right of the author of a literary work to control the publication of his work seemed generally accepted. Also separate rights in the same work were distinguished; i.e. the right of the author in the integrity of the work versus the rights acquired by the purchaser of a manuscript, one of which would be the right to reproduce the work. It is assumed that the publisher obtained a percentage on the sale of copies of the work. Plagiarism was recognized as morally wrong, but there is no direct evidence that legal sanctions existed.

While opinions differ on the question of literary property and the right of reproduction, there seems to be general agreement about the existence of a right to public performance. There was extensive legislation which regulated the organization of games and plays down to the last detail. Playwrights sold the right for single or multiple performances of their works to the organizers of games. The contracts dealt with the right of the buyer – the games organizer – to show an unpublished play. In fact, the commercialization had gone far enough for Horatius to make nasty comments about the playwright Plautus: 'He wishes, in fact, to get money into his purse and then he is indifferent to the failure or success of his play' (quoted in Dock, 1963, p. 33).

After the decline of Rome and during the Middle Ages the religious institutions, in particular the monasteries, assumed primacy in the preservation and development of intellectual works. The monks functioned equally as copyists, scholars and authors. Among the major intellectual centres of this period were the Irish monasteries. Prominent among the scholar monks of this period was Columba, whose zeal in the pursuit of scholarship was renowned and apparently excessive. He visited his old teacher Abbot Finnian for the purpose of making a clandestine and hurried copy of Finnian's Psalter or Book of Psalms. Abbot Finnian upon hearing of Columba's deed contended that the copy Columba had made without his permission was a theft, because the transcript was the offspring of the original work. Columba refused to return the copy and the matter was referred to King Dermott, who ruled in favour of Abbot Finnian with the following words: 'To every cow her calf, and consequently to every book its copy.' This appears to be the first instance in early European history of the adjudication of a copyright issue (Putnam, 1962). In this case we see as the underlying basis for the decision the right of the author to the product of his creativity.

However, very few works during this period reveal the name of an author. Generally the work was not the product of one individual but of the religious and spiritual community represented by the monastery. Therefore the right to assign a manuscript to another was not a personal right but a right that belonged to the monastery as a moral person.

These early examples of control over intellectual works have been assimilated into modern concepts of copyright, but they were isolated instances and did not arise from a coherent doctrine concerning the rights of authors.

With time, literary activities spread in society. Not only monasteries, but also lay persons and establishments, undertook the reproduction of books, mainly by the classical authors. By the thirteenth century the literary life in countries such as France was highly organized. Those who dealt in manuscripts were protected by the University of Paris and divided into two classes: those dealing in existing manuscripts; and the stationers, who were the publishers of the day since they acquired manuscripts, who made copies and had them disseminated among the public. The scene is set for the arrival of printing.

2 Privileges and rights

Following Gutenberg's invention about 1436, the art of printing spread quickly all over Europe. Wherever it was introduced there was a proliferation of books – and of printers, who at the same time functioned as bookbinders and booksellers. Their number grew and they prospered. When they acquired from authors the right to print their works, and when they sold the printed products in the new-found 'markets', they became publishers. Very quickly they had to face competition in the form of unauthorized copies of their books. Publishing and piracy appeared almost simultaneously.

The complaints of the printers against piracy was one reason why the trade in printed materials attracted the attention of governments. There were others. The interest and subsequent intervention of governments in this trade was prompted by three principal concerns: the spread of knowledge, greed and control. The relative weight given to these concerns or motives changed over time depending on the circumstances of a particular government at a given time.

The mechanism adopted for controlling the printing trade was well known and had been used to regulate other commercial activities: the granting of 'privileges' or limited monopolies. The government granted to a publisher, for a specific work, individual privileges which contained a prohibition on anyone other than the beneficiary printing or selling the privileged work.

It appears that the first printing privilege was granted by the city of Venice in 1495 to the publisher Aldus Manutius.* Other countries followed suit. The oldest privileges in France date back to 1507 and 1508; in 1529 there followed the first law to regulate the right of publishing. This pattern was to prevail in Europe for the next 200 years.

*There are differences of opinion as to the exact date of the first Venetian privilege: some experts indicate 1469, others 1476.

Some analysts regard these privileges as the origin of authors' rights. However, most experts seem to agree that the functions of the privileges had little to do with protection of the author and his rights. They were based on a policy which exclusively focused on the uses of works and was expressed in the form of a private guarantee, with the purpose of regulating a trade and providing an industrial and commercial monopoly or safeguard. In addition to the economic function there was another, the political. Governments had often initially encouraged the new invention but soon discovered its dangers. They therefore tried to control printing by requiring prior authorization, but this control was not popular and was often circumvented. The solution was to combine the privilege and the authorization. Thus, 'the Crown was induced to use the only efficient means of enforcing the censorship: the granting of exclusive privileges to those who had obtained the authorization to publish' (Dock, 1963, p. 66). Thus, from having been an instrument for the protection of publishers, the privileges also came to serve as a tool for the maintenance of public order. Typically, the French Act of 1529 therefore regulated both publishing and censorship.

Even though there were no explicit rules protecting the author, it was taken for granted that the author had the right to decide over his unpublished work: whether to publish or not, whether to let his work be publicly performed or not. It was the rights in the published work which caused conflicts between the parties involved. In France, there were quarrels between the Parisian publishers, who had managed to get most of the privileges, and the publishers in the provinces who had received few, if any. The provincial publishers invoked what today would be called the public domain in support of their argument, while the Parisians found it expedient to use the concept of authors' rights to defend their privileged position.

The other major aspect of an author's rights was the right to public performance. There is evidence of early contracts between theatre groups and authors, and the right of the author to sell his play for performance was accepted in customary law even though not laid down in statutes. Later in France the creation of the Comédie Française (1680) established a monopoly in the theatre which lasted until the Revolution. The author was totally in the hands of the actors, since there was no control of costs, and often not only received nothing but found himself in debt to the Comédie Française. The conflicts between actors and authors became endemic during the eighteenth century.

Slowly, during the seventeenth and eighteenth centuries, the concepts of intellectual property and of authors' rights were articulated and formalized. The first country to adopt a 'modern' copyright statute was England.

In many respects, developments in England had been similar to those on the Continent. The religious struggles during the sixteenth and seventeenth centuries caused the government to adopt censorship as a regular policy. This policy was reflected in the Star Chamber Decrees of 1586 and 1637 and a series of licensing laws. The mechanism was the usual one: exclusive privileges. When the first Star Chamber Decree was issued, the instrument to enforce these acts was already at hand: the Stationers' Company. The Company consisted of members of the book trade – printers, bookbinders and booksellers. It had received its royal charter in 1557 and for the next 150 years had a monopoly on printing and publishing.

Copyright was originally used by the Stationers' Company to regulate the trade by protecting works published by one member from piracy by another. The right to print was literally the right to copy. This right was granted by the Company to one of its members, usually in perpetuity, and was protected by an entry in the Company's register. Copyright was a marketable commodity and members/publishers often sold or assigned copyrights to other members. In later times, the Company also enforced the various censorship rules of the government by printing only those works which were politically acceptable.

The right of the author during this period was implicitly, if not explicitly, recognized. There never appeared to be a question that the author should not be paid for his efforts. However, he had to sell the manuscript of a work to a member of the Company, as only the Company could issue the right to copy.

The author's right to have his work printed in its original and undistorted form was recognized by the publishers not so much on legal as on economic grounds. The best original copy for publishing tended to promote the value of the work, while distortions and variations of the original work would effectively dilute the market for the original work. In fact, there were instances where in the contract for the sale of the manuscript the author agreed not to make any subsequent changes to the original (Patterson, 1968a, p. 74). Other contracts between author and publisher conveyed the right to copy or print the original but reserved to the author the right to make 'additions, corrections and amendments' (ibid., p. 75). Underlying these relationships was the recognition by the book trade that the author by selling his manuscript did not divest himself of all of his rights, only the right to copy the manuscript of the original work. The author by selling his rights in the manuscript implicitly agreed that he would not object to its publication by the publisher. Later, this implicit right of the author was made explicit as the common law right of first publication (Patterson, 1968b).

During this period there were also instances where copyrights were granted directly to authors who were not members of the Company. The reason for the departure from normal procedure was apparently the desire of an author to publish a work in which the publisher/member was not interested because it lacked market appeal. In these instances the author agreed to underwrite the cost of all the printing in consideration of obtaining the copyright from the Company. This may be the origin of the practice of 'page charges' paid by modern authors to a scholarly journal in order to have the results of research published.

At the end of the seventeenth century the situation of the book trade in England was chaotic. The power of the Stationers' Company to regulate the book trade had been greatly diminished by the Civil War and the decline in the use of censorship by the government. Furthermore, the original practice of granting copyright in perpetuity had permitted the increasing monopolization by the booksellers/publishers of a great number of popular works. All of the worst aspects of monopoly were practised. In particular, artificially high prices were charged because the booksellers were able to control the number of copies that were printed of a particular work. These and other developments led the House of Commons to refuse the renewal of the Stationers' Company's privileges, which it found exaggerated. There followed a legal vacuum and pirated copies were published en masse.

Parliament undertook to pass legislation to deal with the situation. The law that resulted was the Statute of Queen Anne in 1709, which has been proclaimed as 'the first law on authors' rights in the modern sense of the word' (Recht, 1969, p. 22). The basic provisions of the Statute were directed towards resolving the problems and abuses of the book trade. To accomplish this, the framers of the Statute codified not only the Stationers' copyright but also the author's right to copy. This statutory copyright, unlike the Stationers' privilege, was limited in time but broadened in terms of those eligible to own the right. Any person who owned a current copyright had the right to print the work for a period of twenty-one years, after which time the work went into the public domain. New copyrights could be obtained by the author or his assignee for a period of fourteen years; the author, if living, had the right to renew the copyright for another fourteen years, otherwise the work went into the public domain. The Statute also provided that if the Stationers' Company were to refuse to enter a copyright on its register, copyright could be secured by advertisement in recognized official publications. Aside from the limitations of the copyright term, the Statute of Anne made it legal for any person, not only the authors and publishers, to acquire copyright. However, the Statute concerned the right to copy and no more. The protection afforded was against piracy of printed works. There was nothing in this Statute that touched upon the creative or moral rights of the author. The right protected was a property right.

Yet there was emerging during this period the concept of the rights of authors. In his *Two Treatises on Civil Government*, 1690, John Locke had postulated a theory of an intellectual property right in the author. The basis of the right was the labour that the author expended in the creation of the work. This theory corresponded to similar ideas on the Continent, and was amplified and expanded by European jurists in the late seventeenth and early eighteenth centuries. In its mature form the theory maintained that the author's rights are not created by law but always existed in the legal consciousness of man. In other words, copyright was a right growing out of natural law.

For the twenty-one years after the passage of the Statute of Anne there was no impact on the booksellers because the monopolies in existing works were secure. After the expiration of the statutory terms, the booksellers tried to circumvent the Statute by putting forward the legal argument that copyright was a natural right of the author under common law, and the right to print, publish and sell the work could be conveyed by the author in perpetuity to another; i.e. the bookseller. The other side of the argument was that copyright could be granted only by statute (Patterson, 1968a, p. 158).

The ensuing litigations culminated in the case of Donaldson *v.* Beckett decided by the House of Lords in 1774. The Lords decided that *one* of the rights that an author had under common law was the right to print, publish and sell his work and that this common law right could be assigned by the author in perpetuity to another. However, this common law right, the court further decided, was supplanted by the Statute of Anne. The House of Lords had to tackle the issue of the common law right of the author in copyright because the booksellers had prevailed in a case on the same issue some five years earlier (Millar *v.* Taylor, 1769); in addressing this issue, the Lords changed copyright from strictly a publisher's right to an author's right (Patterson, 1968a, p. 177).

Out of these two cases have developed two theories of copyright that have continued to influence Anglo-American copyright law until recent times. First, that copyright rests in the author at the time of creation of the work. This right is essentially that of control and dominion over the work – the right to publish or not to publish. Second, that after publication of the work the right of the author is qualified by statute. The qualification can range from donation of the work to the public to a limited monopoly for further exploitation of the work. What remains of the author's so-called natural right to maintain the integrity and content after publication has never been clearly resolved in Anglo-American jurisprudence.

The history of American copyright law is commonly believed to date from the passage of copyright statutes by twelve of the thirteen newly independent colonies in the years 1783 to 1786. These statutes were often patterned after the 1709 Statute of Anne. However, a statute enacted by the General Court (legislature) of the Massachusetts Bay Colony in 1672 anticipated the Statute of Anne by several years. The text is as follows:

> In answer to the petition of John Usher, the Court judgeth it meet and order, and be it by this Court ordered and enacted, that no printer shall print any more copies than are agreed and paid for by the owner of the said copy or copies, nor shall he nor any other reprint or make sale of any of the same, without the *said owner's consent* upon the forfeiture

and penalty of treble the whole charges of printing, and paper etc of the whole quantity paid for the owner of the copy, to the said owner of the copy, to the said owner or his assign (Crawford, 1975).

The significance of this statute is that although it reflected the English concept of the right to copy or a publisher's or printer's right, the right, unlike the prevailing English law, was not a monopoly or privilege, limited to a designated group of printer, publishers and booksellers (the Stationers' Company); it was given to all persons (the owner or his assigns). Also the requirement of the owner's consent to copy, as distinguished from a Stationers' Company licence to copy, was explicitly stated.

The early pre-constitutional statutes of the colonies are important to the study of the development of copyright because, unlike previous English statutes, they usually contained preambles which stated the purpose to be achieved by the laws. All these statutes sought to achieve the following purposes, in the order of importance listed:

(1) to secure the author's right;
(2) to promote learning;
(3) to provide order in the book trade;
(4) to prevent monopoly.

All except two of the statutes viewed copyright as essentially an author's right; South Carolina and Virginia provided copyright for the purchaser of copy or publisher. Protection was obtained by some form of registration. Although many of the statues were directly patterned after the Statute of Anne, the preambles indicated that the author might have rights not protected by the statute and that the right of the author to be secure in his profits was based on the idea of natural rights.

Although the underlying philosophy of the pre-constitutional statutes was the natural law rights, in actual form they resembled the Stationers' copyright.

It became obvious that a multiplicity of copyright laws could not be effectively enforced unless there were some central legislative source to provide for a uniformity in this and other laws that affected all of the States and the citizens thereof. In the Constitutional Convention of 1787, proposals involving copyright were to form the basis for the relevant clause of the United States

Constitution: 'The Congress shall have the power . . . to promote the progress of science and useful arts, by securing for limited time to authors and inventors the exclusive right to their respective writings and discoveries' (Art. I, Sec. 8). Although the dominant purpose of the clause appeared to be the promotion of learning, the protection of the author was stressed as the protection for a pre-existing material right based on common law. This position was not inconsistent with other powers of the US Constitution which were heavily influenced by the doctrines of natural rights.

Following closely on the adoption of the US Constitution in 1789 was the first Federal copyright law which was passed by the Congress in 1790. This law was significant for a number of reasons. It expanded the subject matter of copyright to include maps and charts as well as books; it contained a requirement that a copy of the work be deposited in the clerk's office at the Federal district court where the author or owner resided, to be followed by publication of the copyright registration in a newspaper for a period of four weeks; manuscripts were afforded protection for the first time; the pirating of foreign works was permitted. The concept of the common law right of the author is absent – the author and the copyright proprietor are considered essentially in the same light. In essence the Act of 1790 viewed copyright as the government grant of a monopoly limited to the citizens of the United States. It completely discarded the concept of the natural right of the author. Complete with the piracy provision it can be viewed as the action of a developing country to protect its burgeoning culture while exploiting the cultural products of more developed nations. In consequence, the copyright policy of the United States as reflected in the 1790 Statute was to be a source of strained relations with England throughout the eighteenth century.

Early copyright development in the United States culminated with the case of Wheaton *v.* Peters decided by the US Supreme Court in 1828. The basic law of copyright in the United States as it was to remain for the next 150 years was established with this decision – an author's property was to be protected for a limited time after he had complied with the terms of the Statute. The Supreme Court in the Wheaton case appeared to view the issue as essentially a resolution of the right of the author to enjoy the benefits of the fruits of his creative endeavour upon the publication versus the need to protect the public against the dangers of unlimited monopoly by the author (the denial of access by the public to knowledge). What the Wheaton decision failed to comprehend and foresee was that copyright would continue to be a publisher's right as well. Also, in rejecting the concept that certain authors' rights continue after publication, the Supreme Court created a legal structure for copyright in the United States that was to become increasingly inequitable and incomprehensible during the next century and a half.

As the preceding discussion has shown, the Anglo-American concept evolved in the eighteenth and nineteenth centuries as an exclusive economic or property right of the author to reproduce his work for a limited period. The right was based on the earlier practice of royal grants of privileges or monopolies to printers and publishers. Since it was a right granted by statute, it was a limited right which could be sold. And since the right was in the work and not in the author, the buyer of the work was free to exploit it as he saw fit. This exploitation could include changes to the work, adaptation of the work to another medium, and translation of the work to a foreign language.

John Locke's attempt to shift the rights in intellectual property from a statutory property right to a naturally given right meant in practical terms a shift of the right from the publisher to the author. Similar ideas emerged in the countries of continental Europe. Already in 1686 an ordinance adopted in Saxony recognized an author's right by protecting against piracy the books 'the property of which the publisher had acquired from the author' (Recht, 1969, p. 43). In France, the struggles between the publishers in Paris and in the provinces, between the publishers and pirates, led to the use of the concept of rights vested in the author as a supporting argument. The theory of authors' rights as enlarged by European jurists conceived of this right as being in the nature of things. Laws could have no other purpose than to recognize this naturally existing right and to give it a more precise formulation. In the name of this right the authors also fought against the actors of the Comédie Française for their rights to public performance. In the 1760s the authors combined against the actors and found a prestigious defender in the playwright Beaumarchais, who coined the famous phrase: 'However powerful the attraction of fame, if we are to enjoy it even for a year, nature condemns us to dine three hundred and sixty times.'

Beaumarchais' play *The Barber of Seville* has been regarded as one of the portents of the revolution to come. From the beginning, a major objective of the French Revolution was the abolition of old privileges in all areas. In the spirit of the natural rights theory, the concept of the author's rights was enshrined in two decrees: the right to public performance was recognized in 1791; the right to copy and reproduction in 1793. These two short, laconic laws provided the basis for copyright in France for over 160 years. And with the growing recognition of copyright also in other countries, relations between states in the area of intellectual property became a new issue.

3 International awakening

Before the nineteenth century, copyright was largely a matter of national concern. During the Age of Reason, copyright in the form of national statutory protection evolved with the growth of publishing. Because of the limited intercourse and communication between nations, works were distributed almost exclusively within the country of their authors, and the lack of international copyright protection caused little concern.

Interest in international copyright protection increased, soon after 1800, for a variety of reasons which affected the development of copyright generally. Social and political change meant that literary and artistic creation and consumption ceased to be the privilege of a ruling class. The changes in the social order were most clearly exemplified by the ascent of the bourgeoisie which demanded access to the cultural pursuits previously restricted to the aristocracy. Nationalism and national unity were reinforced by the pre-eminence given to national languages over separate vernacular languages or dialects. The spread of education extended literacy and the demand for reading materials to new social classes. Compulsory primary education had already been introduced in the seventeenth century in some of the German princely states and was adopted by other countries from the end of the eighteenth century. At the same time, the increased freedom of expression led to an unprecedented expansion of the press. Publishing was transformed from a craft into an industry through the advent of new processes for the manufacture and reproduction of literary and artistic works and through the wider circulation of books by the development of bookselling and the establishment of libraries.

Trade, communications and travel between countries increased, as did the learning of foreign languages. The more 'advanced' nations became concerned with the problem of protection abroad for their domestic works, as well as the related matter of their own protection of foreign works. Consequently, domestic copyright laws were revised and some treaties were negotiated to establish a basis for reciprocity under which eligible foreign works could enjoy the same copyright status as domestic works. Since there were strong conflicting interests, progress came slowly.

In fact, for a long time, what we would now call piracy had been a characteristic feature of the cultural scene. Intellectual property had not for long been an established concept. Shakespeare lifted plots, scenes and characters from the works of other authors, exactly as his were 'pirated' by rivals. The question has been put whether the flowering of Elizabethan literature would have been possible had there been effective copyright protection. Later, new countries, such as the United States, systematically pirated the property of European authors and publishers. In 1790 the Federal government of the USA for the first time introduced copyright protection, but only for American citizens to the exclusion of all foreigners, thereby fostering the piracy of foreign works. This was typical of the prevailing attitude. The sharpest disputes were between French authors and publishers in Belgium and Holland, the two 'hotbeds' of French piracy.

There were a few instances where protection was based on bilateral treaties negotiated between particular countries on the basis of strict reciprocity. In general, domestic printers and publishers were unwilling to surrender their established markets for unauthorized reprints. However, domestic authors found their economic position weakened by the great number of unauthorized foreign works published and sold at low prices. Foreign authors complained of the mutilation of their works and the loss of royalties in other countries.

As a result, demands for protection from pirating became more widespread. Because the countries of Europe were such close neighbours, the problem was most acute there. France took the lead. From 1840 to 1852, she attempted to secure copyright protection for French works by the conclusion of treaties granting reciprocal treatment. This effort failed to a large extent because it was not possible to reach agreement with Belgium and Holland.

Therefore France decided that negotiation was not the best method of achieving international protection of authors' rights. If, however, France began by declaring that piracy of foreign works in France was illegal, other governments might be more likely to adopt a similar measure. Accordingly, a Decree was issued on 28 March 1852, by which France extended copyright protection to all works, regardless of the place of publication or the nationality of the author. While this bold initiative did not set a pattern, it seemed to accelerate movement toward a multilateral copyright system. The French Decree of 1852 was a landmark of international copyright progress and has been called the genesis of international copyright protection.

This 'altruistic' granting of protection to all foreign works without condition of reciprocity was contrary to the view of most nations, who insisted on foreign protection for their works as a prerequisite to their protection of foreign works. France extended the protection of the law to foreigners as well as nationals. Piracy in French territory of works published in foreign countries was prohibited, as was the sale, exportation and transportation of pirated copies.

Thus piracy of any foreign work in France was declared to be a crime, regardless of reciprocity. This progressive declaration aided French authors by enabling France to conclude over twenty treaties for the reciprocal protection of authors' rights during the next ten years. Using to her best advantage the initiative taken by the law of 1852, France was even able to reach agreements with traditional 'pirate' nations such as Belgium and Holland.

From this time on, similar agreements for the mutual protection of authors' rights were concluded between other countries as well. However, this system of bilateral treaties appeared increasingly inadequate. The 'mosaic of treaties' then in force formed an embryonic system based on reciprocity, and the notion of a common international legal framework gained ground. It is interesting to note that, from the first, governments were not the only actors on the international copyright stage. The first international congress of authors and artists met in Brussels in 1858 and supported the ideal of worldwide uniform copyright legislation. And it was a nongovernmental organization, the International Literary and Artistic Association, which initiated the action which led to the first international copyright convention. This organization, established in 1878, prepared a draft convention text to serve as a basis for the intergovernmental meetings which the Swiss government had agreed to convene in Berne. The conferences held from 1884 to 1886 culminated in the formation of a convention and a union of countries adhering to this treaty, both named after the city where the agreements were concluded: the Berne Convention and the Berne Union. They provided the cornerstones for the present elaborate system of international treaties and structures in the copyright field.

Chapter II · **Modern systems and principles of copyright**

1 Systems of copyright

In overall terms, copyright is a method for organizing economic and cultural life. It is not the only one. Throughout history, societies have evolved different systems for the organization of cultural life. The emergence of copyright is conditioned by a set of specific attitudes and circumstances. The distinctive character of copyright is well encapsulated in the concept of 'intellectual property' which seems to be a uniquely Western idea conditioned by two main interlocking features: the socio-cultural attitude towards intellectual and artistic creation and the industrial revolution.

The industrial revolution is an oft-quoted and easily understandable condition for the emergence of intellectual property concepts. The other aspect is often neglected. However, in comparison with other cultures, the Western system for the organization of cultural life and the attendant position of the artist in society appears to be the exception rather than the rule.

One of the prerequisites for copyright is a tradition of individual creation and art in which one goal of the artist is to attain recognition and fame. It is in a climate of competition for public acceptance with the attendant system of direct economic benefits that a class of professional authors and artists can be established.

This market-oriented attitude is directly related to the second prerequisite for modern copyright: the industrial revolution. The printing press was the forerunner and new technical methods transformed publishing into an industry for mass production. Together, these two circumstances combined in the concept of immaterial rights, of intellectual property that could be bought and sold. It is significant that intellectual property has been divided into two main branches: industrial property and copyright. The area of industrial property concerns the protection of inventions, patents, trade marks and industrial designs, and also the restraint of unfair competition. Copyright encompasses the protection of cultural works in all media: literature, music, arts, architecture, audio-visual productions. Industrial property protection and copyright are similar in that in their modern form they have originated with the industrial revolution in some Western countries but still have come to be widely accepted as methods to regulate the orderly exploitation of intellectual works. Each branch, though, has developed a specific legal regime with partly similar, partly different, rules and objectives.

It may appear as a surprise that copyright has gained such widespread acceptance. Even though the countries of the world are organized under a variety of political and economic systems, the majority of nations possess statutes which establish policy and regulation in the area of copyright. The nations which have adopted systems of copyright represent a broad spectrum of political, social, economic and cultural ideologies; thus the popularity of copyright cannot be accounted for simply by a meeting of minds on this subject. Instead a contributing though underrated factor would appear to be the ability of copyright to be integrated flexibly into a wide variety of economic structures and to be moulded in a way which advances differing national priorities. 'The underlying arguments in favour of copyright contain elements of thought which appeal to governments and legislators of almost every political complexion. Copyright can be seen as beneficial both to public policy and to private profit; as a boon to individual freedom and as an aid to State intervention; either as an expression of natural justice or as an assertion of property rights' (Freegard, 1977, pp. 42–3). Thus the flexible nature of copyright allows it to serve different functions and combine with other methods for the financial support of intellectual creation. While most countries would maintain that they apply basic principles of copyright, the results may vary considerably from one to another. The high degree of international co-operation in this field has fostered a greater uniformity among national copyright laws than would otherwise be the case. But since the international conventions have been drafted so as to achieve a maximum agreement on common principles, these principles yield different results when they are applied in various economic and social systems.

Which then are the different functions that copyright is supposed to perform, and what are the reasons advanced on its behalf? From within the copyright community, the traditional grounds in favour of copyright have been summarized as follows:

First, there are reasons of common social justice: the author should be able to benefit from the fruits of his labour; the royalties function as the intellectual worker's salary.

Second, on the grounds of cultural progress. Through copyright protection, the author will be encouraged to create new works and thus enrich his country's store of literature, drama, music and science.

Third, on economic grounds: the investment that is necessary for the creation of works (e.g. film-making or architecture) or for their exploitation (book publishing, record manufacturing) will be more easily obtained if protection exists.

Fourth, on moral grounds. The work is the personal expression of the author's thoughts, so he should be given the right to decide whether, when and how his work may be reproduced or performed in public, and also the right to prevent mutilation or changes.

Fifth, for reasons of national prestige. Without protection, the cultural heritage of a country would be meagre and the arts would not flourish (Masouyé, 1974, 1977).

A further point made is that protection would be incomplete and illusory if it were confined within the boundaries of the author's own country. It is a characteristic of intellectual works that they can easily cross frontiers. In this respect, three main factors are mentioned (ibid.):

—the desire of every nation to export its works, either for reasons of spreading knowledge of its culture, to influence the cultural development in other areas or for economic considerations;

—the desire of every nation to have access to the works of other nations, frequently in order to improve its own cultural development;

—the resulting interchange of ideas which makes feasible the creation of an international intellectual community.

At a more practical level, the following reasons have been advanced for the expectation that copyright will enjoy a secure long-term future. The copyright system ensures that the remuneration to the author is borne by and equitably shared among the ultimate 'consumers'; i.e. the purchasers of books and records, or the paying customers of the cinema, theatre or concert hall. Works of the mind, especially those such as musical works which are not structured in language, transcend national boundaries. The practical problems of remunerating authors for the exploitation of their works in foreign countries by means other than copyright are seen as defying reasonable solution. Finally, 'copyright represents a delicately poised balance between the legitimate needs of society for access to material of importance for the enjoyment of a full and rich life and the equally legitimate needs of the creators of that material' (Freegard, 1977, p. 43).

As will be seen later, all these grounds and their assumptions have been questioned. In a wider perspective, a number of basic dimensions of the nature and function of copyright may be distinguished. In an overall cultural perspective, the stated purpose of copyright is to encourage intellectual creation by serving as the main means of recompensing the intellectual worker and to protect his moral rights. In an economic sense, copyright can be seen as a method for the regulation of trade and commerce. Copyright thus serves as a mechanism by which the law brings the world of science, art and culture into relation with the world of commerce. In a social sense, copyright is an instrument for the cultural, scientific and technological organization of society. Copyright is thus used as a means to channel and control flows of information in society.

In another perspective, copyright can be analysed in terms of the different interests involved. In the first instance, it is possible to distinguish four major interests: those of the creator, those of the publisher, distributor or other user of works, those of the ultimate consumer (i.e. the public at large) and finally those of society as such. The essential character of copyright is thus founded upon the author's prerogative to control the use of his work by granting or withholding his consent for its utilization.

While varying greatly in detail and emphasis, most national laws on intellectual property deal with copyright under two distinct aspects: property or economic rights and personal rights. Among the property rights are the rights to authorize the publication, reproduction, performance, exhibition, translation or dissemination of a work. Included among the author's personal rights, or what in many countries are called moral rights, are his right to prohibit distortions, mutilations or modifications of his work and a right of 'paternity' which is a right to prevent some other person being named as the author. These moral rights are taken to exist independently of and even after the transfer of the economic rights.

The relative emphasis given to these two aspects indicates differences in the philosophy of copyright which have been the subject of doctrinal controversies and debates often conducted with great passion. Since the end of the eighteenth century numerous legal theories have been advanced. Of more immediate relevance are the attempts that have been made to describe and categorize the different copyright systems used in the world.

According to one doctrine which was dominant until some twenty years ago, a distinction was made between three main copyright concepts:

(1) the essentially individualistic European approach;
(2) the essentially commercial Anglo-American approach;
(3) the essentially societal approach in socialist countries.

Under the first approach, the protection a creator receives over his creation is a natural right expressed in the concept of an author's right (droits d'auteur, Urheberrecht, etc.) which is absolute in the sense that it cannot be restricted in theory but necessarily is subject to limitations in practice. The Universal Declaration of Human Rights embraces this concept by providing: 'Everyone has the right to protection of the moral and material interests resulting from any scientific, literary or artistic production of which he is the author' (Art. 27 (2)).

As implied by the expression 'copyright', the second theory starts from the concept of a right to copy; i.e. to print and reprint a work. Copyright thus depends upon a work existing in material form, whereas an author's rights, particularly his moral rights, can be seen to exist immaterially. In an extreme form, copyright would be the right granted to authors of works in order to make possible the transfer of exclusive rights to publishers, without the author having any inherent rights in the intangible property he has created.

In principle, the nations of mainland Europe tend to emphasize the natural rights approach which gives their legislation a distinctly individualistic slant. Other nations, in particular the English-speaking countries, treat copyright as a privilege granted to authors or their assigns as successors in ownership.

In a more modern approach, the differences between the

European and the Anglo-American concepts are not of primary importance, since they are expressed less in the level of protection provided than in the formulation of rights. The theoretical basis for this approach is the social role of intellectual property rights. One version provides for a distinction in three other groups: legal regimes in countries with a market economy, in countries with a socialist economy and in developing countries (see Dock, 1974).

In this perspective, the legal regimes in all countries with a predominantly market economy share certain basic guiding principles. In the 'market-place of ideas', the relationship between the author and society is regulated mainly by economic factors. The major feature of copyright is thus the exclusive character of the author's rights which provide for a 'property' in the technical sense of the term. The creator thus has a monopoly with regard to the use and exploitation of his work, whether this monopoly derives from a recognition of a natural right or from a legally defined privilege. It follows that the author may dispose of his work as he wishes through the right to grant exclusive contracts or licences by which he can authorize a third party to exercise all or part of his rights.

However, the ideal market-place is no more a reality in the copyright field than in other economic relations. The ideal of the individual creator being able to sell his work to the highest bidder in the market-place was probably always more the exception than the rule. With the exception of the few famous creators, the author would generally be in a weak position in the negotiations with publishers or other users of his work and would thus benefit only imperfectly from the results of his intellectual labour. Moreover, in present circumstances, when to a very large extent works are produced in an employment situation or as the result of teamwork, the adaptation of traditional copyright concepts poses a series of new issues. Since copyright in this sense is based on an abstraction, countries with a market economy now experience great difficulties in evolving concepts and methods to adapt copyright to rapidly changing economic and social circumstances.

In countries with a socialist system, which in this context refers mainly to those of Eastern Europe, the principles underlying copyright legislation are based on a different conception of the interrelationship between the author and society. This approach has been expressed in terms of harmonizing the general interest and the special interests of the author. The creation of an original work depends upon the individual creative activity of the author, but only within the given social framework which provides the sources of insight and experience expressed by the author. It is in the general interest to stimulate creative activity which contributes to the improvement of cultural life and the building of a socialist society. The relationship between author and society can therefore not be ruled by economic aspects only, but as much or even more by the cultural policies pursued by a socialist society. Copyright has thus been described as 'an instrument for the management of cultural processes' (Püscher, 1976, p. 19).

Copyright is only one method of achieving the objectives of those policies and must be seen in relation to other means for giving, through employment, subsidies, prizes and otherwise, an economic status to cultural workers which, at least in principle, is different from that applied in countries with market economies. Copyright transactions are by nature dependent on contemporary social reality. Thus, in a socialist society, the activities related to the dissemination of works are placed in the public sector. The corresponding cultural institutions such as publishing houses, theatres and film companies are the property of society or subject to state planning. The state in principle takes the responsibility for the dissemination of creative works: generally, therefore, there is no right of exploitation outside the network of state-owned or public and semi-public cultural institutions and enterprises.

It follows that, in contrast to the copyright concepts applied in the market economies, the socialist approach provides for a different treatment of personal and economic rights. Thus, a basic idea in the Copyright Act of the DDR (German Democratic Republic) is the unity of personal copyright and the right of society. Copyright is conceived as a 'socialist personal right' (sozialistisches Persönlichkeitsrecht). As a personal right, the moral rights of authors are generally recognized in that the law protects the author's right of paternity, and the integrity of the work. As a socialist right, the author's exclusive commercial rights which are universal in market economies do not exist in socialist countries. The author may dispose of the work only under the conditions laid down by law, and for a remuneration which is regulated by statute. It follows from the socialist approach to copyright that the copyright laws recognize a broad range of uses in the general interest which go beyond the limitations to copyright accepted in market economies and include uses for which compensation is not granted.

Within this overall framework, the national legislation of each of the socialist countries differs considerably. This is proved by the differences in adherence to the international conventions, which reflect variations in the levels and nature of copyright protection provided in the various socialist countries.

Even less homogeneous as a grouping is the large number of developing countries. Here the distinction between domestic and foreign copyright policy is of even greater importance than in the other two groups. The major reasons are the special requirements of economic and social development and the fact that developing countries in most cases are net importers of intellectual property. Since these countries, therefore, have to design copyright policies suited to their particular and varied needs, it might appear surprising to note the large participation of the developing world in the multilateral copyright conventions that have originated in the industrialized world.

Several explanations would seem to account for this high degree of international co-operation. First, many of the developing countries were former colonies of European powers which introduced the principles of copyright into their domestic laws.

Second, although most developing countries must import a large portion of the intellectual property they utilize, they all are anxious to promote indigenous intellectual production. A widely accepted means of achieving this goal is the establishment of a copyright law which is intended to provide the necessary incentive for authorship to flourish, and also to protect fledgling cultural industries.

Third, in order to bridge the economic gap between themselves and the developed countries, it is important for. the developing countries to have access to the intellectual property of the developed world at costs which they can afford. However, a rejection of copyright protection for foreigners might jeopardize the progress which appears possible; such action would undoubtedly produce a backlash in the developed countries, particularly from private enterprises in the intellectual property field. In addition, technological developments in the communications field such as satellites and computer data networks offer the possibility of much faster assimilation of intellectual property than had been possible in the past. The basic objectives are therefore two-fold: to encourage domestic production of intellectual works and to gain access on reasonable conditions to foreign works.

The governments of the developed countries have, to a certain extent, been sympathetic to the needs of the economically disadvantaged nations. The unions of intellectual workers and the commercial enterprises of the developed countries engaged in the exploitation of intellectual property have been less generous. While not opposed to the advancement of developing countries, they object to an economic burden being shifted onto them through a dilution of copyright protection. Despite the conflicts which have arisen, compromises have been made which, while not completely satisfying any one interest group, have at least preserved large-scale international co-operation between the developing and the industrialized countries.

2 Principles of copyright in modern legislation

Copyright concerns a wide range of activities and interests in society and is used to perform an increasing number of different and not necessarily concordant functions. From its origin in the print media it has been extended and stretched to cover totally new situations. In the words of the recent United Kingdom Committee on Copyright and Designs: 'The first Copyright Act was enacted in 1709 and dealt only with books. This Act may be likened to a modest Queen Anne house to which there have since been Georgian, Victorian, Edwardian and finally Elizabethan additions, each adding embellishments in the style of the times' (Department of Trade, 1977, p. 3).

The crucial issue in theory and practice is therefore the definition of copyright, the delimitation of what can and should, cannot or should not, be included in copyright protection.

If one starts with the question: what is copyright?, the easiest answer would be: copyright is basically the individual right of an author to dispose of his work in return for remuneration. This might sound simple enough but in fact copyright has become one of the most complicated and esoteric branches of law.

It should already have become clear that many expressions are used in the copyright field with a meaning different from that in ordinary language. This is true for the expression 'work' as the object of copyright, for the concept of 'author' as the beneficiary of copyright, for the concept of 'publisher' as the user of protected works.

The object of copyright is the protection of 'works'; that is intellectual creations in the field of literature, music, art and science. The protection covers the expression of an idea, not the idea itself. The Pygmalion theme or an explanation of how to build a radio receiver cannot be monopolized through copyright protection, but the particular play or article which expresses the idea is protected. In general, the 'work' must thus have a tangible form to qualify for protection.

The 'work' must also be an original creation to qualify for protection. But originality should not become confused with novelty: when two artists paint a picture of the same landscape each creates a work, each being original since it reflects the personality of the maker. It is left to the courts to determine whether a sufficient degree of originality exists. Nor should originality be confused with the merits or intrinsic value of the work or even with the purpose of the work; these factors seem immaterial to the protection obtained.

What should be regarded as a 'work' appears with some stretch of the imagination reasonably clear in respect of traditional forms of expression. Often the legislation of a country provides long catalogues of the 'literary and artistic works' which are to be protected, even though they include objects no ordinary person would classify as either literary or artistic.

In some national laws, a monolithic approach is used through such expressions as 'intellectual works' (e.g. France, Italy); others use a binary concept, 'literary and artistic works' (e.g. Belgium, Denmark) or different trinary variations: 'literary, scientific and artistic works' (West Germany, USSR) or 'literary, dramatic and musical works' (UK, Ireland).

The situation is not made easier by the variations of terminology and definition in both international conventions and national laws. The Universal Copyright Convention* includes only a very general description: 'literary, scientific and artistic works, including writings, musical, dramatic and cinematographic works, and paintings, engravings and sculpture' (Art. 1). The Berne Convention* is more explicit and includes among literary works not

*For explanation of these Conventions, see chapter III.

only books, pamphlets and other writings but also lectures, addresses and sermons. The legislation in some countries has in some cases gone further to include even street directories, football pool coupons and mathematical tables which, according to some experts, are examples of an exaggerated extension of the original concept. Other categories are dramatic and dramatico-musical works, choreographic works and 'dumb shows', musical compositions with or without words, cinematographic works; drawing, painting, sculpture, engraving and lithography; photographic works; works of applied art; illustrations, maps, plans, sketches and three-dimensional works relative to geography, topography, architecture or science.

In modern national legislation such as the most recent law in a major country, the US Copyright Act of 1976, it has been found necessary to start with a definition at another level of generality: 'original works of authorship fixed in any tangible medium of expression, now known or later developed'. This definition is then followed by a listing of seven categories:

1 literary works;
2 musical works, including any accompanying words;
3 dramatic works, including any accompanying music;
4 pantomimes and choreographic works;
5 pictorial, graphic and sculptural works;
6 motion pictures and other audio-visual works; and
7 sound recordings.

However, with each advance in new technical production methods, the more confusing become the problems and the more elusive the 'work'. Most national laws protect 'works' in the classical categories but vary widely with regard to other, new, forms. Motion pictures have presented a series of thorny problems. Some countries have chosen to view the production of broadcasting and sound recording material as authorship and have incorporated such works within the copyright law. Other countries, while recognizing that the production of such material requires skill, have not viewed the broadcaster or record manufacturer as being the equivalent of an author. These countries have preferred to protect such material under a theory of 'neighbouring rights' – a term originating in the French expression 'droits voisins' – to indicate rights that are neighbours to, but not part of, authors' rights strictly speaking. In the case of broadcasting material recourse is sometimes had to a public service concept based on a public monopoly over the transmission and a neighbouring right in the broadcast (e.g. France). Finally, there are some countries which offer the record manufacturer or broadcaster protection not under private law in the form of copyright or neighbouring rights legislation but rather under unfair competition laws. And recent international conventions have admitted various legal approaches or moved the protection required out of the traditional private law sphere into public law.

Nor is it a simple matter to define the 'author', the originator of a work and supposedly the main beneficiary of the protection; i.e. he who is entitled to enjoy the benefits flowing from the work. The archetypical author is of course an individual who unaided produces the finished work by actually putting the paint on the canvas, the letters on the paper or the notes on the stave. Intermediaries such as the typist or compositor do not share the quality of authorship. The position is less clear when the intermediary uses more than mechanical skills as when the master provides the creative matrix and leaves it to his apprentices or collaborators to fill in the detail.

This case approaches collaborative works in which several independent and each fully creative talents are used in combination to create the finished work. The typical example is a feature film. This situation has been dealt with in different ways. One possibility is to give each or some of the participating originators (scenario, dialogue, music, director) a share in the authorship (France). Another is to assign the authorship to the person whose overall conception is embodied in the work or to the entity which organizes the production of the work (West Germany, UK, USA). In this case, the collaborators have no share in the authorship of the film itself but retain authorship in their individual contributions.

Of a different nature is the work of joint authorship; for example, a book written by two authors, each collaborating on a basis of equality. In such a case, each co-author has full rights in the work and the agreement of both is required for any dealings in it.

There are also different approaches to the nature of the 'author'. In countries which have adopted the individualistic natural rights approach, the author must be a natural person, an individual who may transfer by contract his economic rights but whose moral rights are inalienable. In countries where the Anglo-American system is followed, the author may be a physical person or a legal entity, particularly in the case of collaborative works. Significantly, the English copyright law changes the terminology and refers to the 'maker' of a sound recording or film and not to the 'author'.

Another set of problems has arisen with the changes in the working conditions of the 'author'. Today, the author more often than not is an employee of a legal entity, whether it be government, university or company. The question then arises of who should own the copyright in works produced in the course of employment and, similarly, who owns the copyright in works produced on commission.

It would seem that, in socialist countries, the issue of copyright in works produced in an employment situation would logically follow from the premises of socialist attitudes to cultural policy and authors' rights: the copyright, with the exception of the moral rights, would be vested in the employer.

In market-oriented countries, the situation is more complex and contradictory. According to one attitude, copyright can, even in an employment situation, be vested only in the creator who by contract assigns all or part of his rights to the employer. On the other side it is maintained that employers or commissioners would normally and not unreasonably expect to own the copyright in works which they have caused to be created. The matter is complicated in another respect. In countries where the legislation transfers the copyright in the works of employees to their employers, an underlying assumption is that the interests of the author and the employer/publisher coincide and together are in conflict with the interests of the public. However, this assumption has been challenged since the interests of the employer/publisher may well conflict with both those of the author and those of the public (see chapter VI).

Examples of these conflicts of interests would include the case when the employer deliberately withholds from the market information or products produced by an employee in order to promote other products.

Not only the 'author', however defined, may be the beneficiary of copyright. The majority of copyright laws provide that copyright will devolve upon the heirs of the author or may be bequeathed by testament. However, by far the most important means of transferring copyright to another person, physical or legal, is by contract. The transfer may be total in the sense that the assignee acquires all the economic rights and is entitled to exercise them as if he were the author. Usually, the transfer concerns only one or more specific rights as stated in the contract. The ownership of copyright is almost infinitely divisible. In the case of an author, he can sell the copyright completely, or sell the publishing rights to a book publisher, the film rights to a film company, the broadcasting rights to a broadcasting organization, the right to adapt a story to a drama society or a television company.

The more elusive the definition and nature of the 'work', the more difficult it becomes to locate the 'author'. New technologies make possible new ways of producing works so that neither 'work' nor 'author' has more than a vague resemblance to the classical definitions and situations. An extreme example is the case of works which have been produced, edited or given their final form through the use of electronic equipment, including computers.

Similar difficulties have arisen over what is to be understood by 'publisher' and 'publication'. When copyright applied only to books and other printed matter it was fairly simple to decide the meaning of these words. New means of production and forms of expression have made it necessary to extend these concepts. Thus, 'publication' in the case of literary, dramatic, musical and artistic works is defined to mean the distribution of material reproductions to the public. A sound recording is 'published' if records are issued to the public. The 'publication' of a film may include the sale, hire or offer for sale or hire to the public. Since publication involves the availability of the work in some tangible form, the performance, public recitation, broadcasting or exhibition of a work do not constitute publication. The right to public performance is a special right that generally concerns dramatic and musical works but includes both live performance and 'performance' by means of a recording. For this purpose there is no difference between a dance hall with an orchestra and a café with a juke-box. Further steps into this thicket of new uses had to be taken with the arrival of new technical means of distribution. Thus, the right to performance further includes 'communication to the public' of the 'performance' of a work (cable television, public loud-speaker systems etc.). No wonder that difficulties have arisen with regard to the distinction that has to be made between 'publication' in the sense of making the work in a physical form available to the public and 'performance' of the work in public.

Thus, the term 'performance' covers both the individual performance and the performance of a copy of the work. The margin between the concept of supplying copies and the concept of providing a performance – which is crucial for the economic exploitation of such works as films – also leads to questions concerning the relationship between the protection of authors and the protection of performers; i.e. between the protection of a 'work' and the protection of a 'performance'. The protection of 'works' taken to include the right to public performance and that of 'performances' varies considerably in legislation around the world. However, in one international convention and in the legislation of several nations, the two concepts are linked in that protection is provided for the rights of performers in their performance, the rights of broadcasters in their broadcasts and the rights of record producers in their records. The difficulties are even more complex when the 'works' – or should it be 'performances' – are 'published' electronically. New methods such as the electronic recording, storage and retrieval of images, computer-originated works, the distribution of 'works' by cable television do not easily fit into concepts drawn from the practices of the print media.

An area where approaches vary widely from country to country concerns the recognition of the rights of a performer in his performance. At this time no country appears to extend statutory copyright to the performer. However, a number of countries have established protection for the performer under the neighbouring rights theory so as to give performing artists legally protected claims when their performances are used. In other countries, performers may be protected under a variety of general principles of law such as unfair competition, equity or unjustified profit-making.

In a historical perspective, the scope of copyright consisted originally in the privilege or right accorded to the printer or publisher, and to the author, of being able to reproduce a printed work, and to authorize the public performance of a dramatic or musical work. Finally, the idea gained ground that the creator should not only be associated with specific methods of using or exploiting his work but should be able to benefit from any kind of use, with some few exceptions in the public interest. Thus the author should be able to exercise exclusive rights for the exploitation of his work, whether by himself or by third parties.

The resulting 'bundle of rights' has been described and analysed in many ways. In a recent study (Dietz, 1976), the following categories are proposed:

(a) The author has the exclusive right to exploit his work in a material form; this right comprises
—the right of reproduction;
—the right of dissemination;
—the right of exhibition.

(b) The author also has the exclusive right to communicate his work publicly in a non-material form (right to public communication) which comprises
—the right of recitation, performance, and presentation;
—the right of broadcasting;
—the right of communication through visual or sound recording;
—the right of communicating broadcast transmissions.

Even such an attempt at an exhaustive classification would not capture all shapes of works and methods of using them. It would still cause problems of interpretation in the sense that certain expressions would have to be stretched beyond any normal use to include new technological possibilities.

The nature of copyright and neighbouring rights is based on the formulation of exclusive, more or less absolute, rights granted to the creator and his assignees. However, social reality is not abstract and social intercourse is not conducted in absolute terms. Therefore, in actual fact, whether copyright is constructed as a natural right or as a privileged monopoly it cannot be dealt with in these abstract, absolute terms. Copyright finds itself in a measure of opposition to other social objectives and requirements: the requirements of cultural life and of the collectivity, the needs of information in modern society and the protection of privacy.

In order to satisfy these other requirements in the face of exclusive copyright demands, it has been necessary to resort to the awkward procedure of 'limiting' copyright or to the equally awkward idea of 'depriving' the author of the control over certain uses.

One such limitation is the duration of copyright which does not extend indefinitely. In general, the duration of copyright and neighbouring rights is regulated in terms of minimum periods of protection which may vary with the object of protection and with national laws and international conventions. In general, for literary and artistic works, this period is the lifetime of the author plus twenty-five or fifty years.

Further, copyright is limited in terms of certain types of uses. The methods adopted are either to declare that certain uses of protected works are 'admissible' or 'free' or that certain uses do not constitute an infringement of copyright or, in another version, that they cannot be prohibited by the author. Such 'limits' or 'exceptions' are found in the majority of national legal systems and also in international conventions. In general terms, these situations include cases such as reproduction of protected works for personal use, right of quotation, reproduction of public speeches and newspaper articles, uses of works for educational and religious purposes, etc. (see chapter VI, section 4).

The author's exclusive right to decide over the use of his work may also be limited through a system of compulsory or legal licences. In order to serve the interests of the public and simplify procedures for the acquisition of rights, a number of countries have introduced into their laws provisions which make it possible to use, in certain cases, protected works without permission of the holders of rights but against remuneration.

The rights granted to copyright-owners would be ineffective if the law did not include means for preventing infringement and remedies when infringement has occurred. In some countries the law includes preventive measures which allow copyright-owners to resort to administrative, police or judicial authorities if they have reason to fear that their rights are about to be violated. Specifically, laws provide for the suspension of unauthorized public performances, prohibition on the sale of pirated copies or importation of unlicensed copies from abroad. If the violation is deliberate, most laws provide for criminal sanctions and the payment of damages to the injured party. Further possible measures are seizure, confiscation or destruction of the instruments for and products of the infringement.

Changes in technology and thus in the production and dissemination of 'works' constitute one major set of reasons for the current difficulties in intellectual property rights. The same holds true with regard to the use of works. The introduction of various methods of video-recording and playback for private use has raised new problems and requires new solutions. The pressure on the traditional copyright concepts is also shown in the need to adopt rules to cover an increasing number of special cases: library deposits and public lending rights, archives, protection of titles and fictitious names, classic works, photocopying, cable distribution, official documents and anonymous works (as in the case of folklore).

A further major set of reasons for what is called the present crisis in copyright is even more difficult to explain in a few words.

In one perspective, the problem can be expressed in terms of the conflict between public and private interests, between the rights of the author or copyright-owner and the rights of the users. Both of these fundamental principles are expressed in Article 27 of the Universal Declaration of Human Rights.

(1) Everyone has the right freely to participate in the cultural life of the community, to enjoy the arts and to share in scientific advancement and its benefits.

(2) Everyone has the right to the protection of the moral and material interests resulting from any scientific, literary or artistic production of which he is the author.

It is not only a matter of preserving these two principles but of finding an adequate reconciliation. A balance between them has to be attempted exactly as there is a balance to be struck between the interests of the creator, the 'publisher' and the public. This series of balances will have to be based on an analysis of the social role of copyright and neighbouring rights. The legal policies which condition the norms applicable to copyright and neighbouring rights are intimately linked to political, economic and social structures. These rights, as any other field of human rights, cannot be seen only in static terms. In most countries, social and cultural developments have resulted in an increased need to use protected material for information and other forms of public service such as education, research and administration. Policies in the field of intellectual property rights must, therefore be defined in relation to policies for education, culture, information and communications generally. This wider perspective is required at the national, as well as at the international, level.

3 Administration of rights and collective concepts of copyright

In the copyright field, the law provides the foundation for a large and complex constantly changing edifice of practices, negotiations and contracts, public and private organizations. The administration of rights is as complex as law and technology combined.

In the first instance there is a series of problems that require the involvement of governments: the administration of the law itself, participation in the continuing work of the international organization, and the need for systematized information on copyright matters. Many countries have found it necessary to establish government offices to deal with copyright matters. Both attitudes towards copyright and administrative traditions are revealed in the location of these bodies, which varies considerably: in Ministries of Education (Austria, Belgium, Bolivia, Cuba, Finland), Ministries of Culture (USSR) or Ministries of Justice (Indonesia, Netherlands, Sweden). Some countries have attached copyright to patent offices (Honduras, Hungary), while others have locked on to the trade aspect (Board of Trade, UK; Ministry of Commerce, Zambia). Another solution is attachment to the national library (Brazil, Egypt, Ireland, Poland, USA).

An interesting light on the present-day needs for government involvement in copyright administration is shown by the organizational structure set up in the USA, following the 1976 revision of the copyright legislation.

As early as 1870, Congress adopted legislation providing for copyright registration and legal deposit activities to be centralized in a Copyright Office within the Library of Congress. Later laws added significant new responsibilities in the areas of compulsory licensing and the review of the administration of existing rules. One of the principal activities of the Copyright Office concerns the registration of works: yearly total copyright registrations recently amounted to half a million. Whereas the Copyright Office is charged with the administrative and recordation aspects of the law, a special organization was created in 1976, the Copyright Royalty Tribunal, to assume tasks that were new to the government activities in the copyright field. The Tribunal determines which copyright-owners will share in the proceeds collected from the compulsory licences affecting cable systems, juke-boxes and mechanical recording. Furthermore, the Tribunal has the authority periodically to review and adjust the rates of royalty payments. Some observers feel that the creation of the Tribunal reflects a disturbing trend of leaving difficult problems to be solved by complex bureaucracies instead of by individual initiative. Other parties have argued that the adjudication of these matters has become so complicated that a more formal mechanism is needed. The 1976 Act also provided for the creation of the American Television and Radio Archive. The Library of Congress is allowed to record off the air, without copyright liability, radio and television programmes in order to preserve them as historical and cultural records. Finally, the uses of copyrighted works in computer systems and the issues of photocopying were studied and reported on by the National Commission on New Technological Uses of Copyrighted Works (CONTU).

Not all countries have set up such a complicated government machinery. Many, though, have established centralized copyright offices (Canadian Copyright Institute; All-Union Copyright Agency (VAAP), USSR; Artijsus in Hungary, etc.). In recent years, under the auspices of Unesco, several countries have set up or are in the process of creating national copyright information centres located in the public or private sector. One of the main tasks of such centres is to facilitate copyright relations between developing and developed countries. Thus some of the duties of these centres are: to obtain information on copyright-owners of protected works and on publishers and producers so that they may be located in the shortest possible time, to obtain from copyright-owners as favourable terms as possible for all copyright permissions for which the transferee is a user in a developing country, and to provide guidelines or models for the drafting of contracts authorizing the use of copyright works.

These official institutions represent only one species among the varied organizations active in the copyright field. These organizations group holders of rights, publishers and producers, beneficiaries and users. Seen from the outside there appears to be a dichotomy between the legal constructions of copyright and the application of these rights. From a strictly legal point of view, copyright is constructed as a 'bundle of rights' attached to the creator who controls the exploitation of his work through the contractual freedom which is an essential aspect of these rights. In reality, the situation looks quite different, since increasingly 'authors' and 'publishers' act not individually but through a variety of organizations for negotiating the transfer of rights and conditions of use and for administering royalties and fees.

The active copyright organizations vary widely, and have diverse purposes and mandates. Four different kinds can easily be discerned:

—trade organizations of 'producers' and distributors generally established in keeping with traditional categories: publishers, film producers, record companies, cinema owners, broadcasting organizations;

—professional organizations which in certain cases may overlap with the trade associations but include groupings based on professional categories ranging from authors to copyright lawyers;

—'collecting societies' as a generic term for a variety of associations sharing at least one major purpose: the administration of royalties on behalf of their members who assign certain of their rights to the societies;

—trade unions, particularly those grouping performers (actors and musicians) and employees in large media enterprises in the theatre, cinema and broadcasting.

These organizations represent a wide range of partly complementary, partly overlapping, partly opposing, interests which in many respects fall outside the strict copyright domain. For instance, the relevant legal framework for these organizations includes not only copyright law but also legislation regulating labour conditions, and the contractual relations of the author and the societies that manage his rights.

An underlying factor in this area is the general attitude in a given society to what can and should be regulated in law and what can and should be left for negotiation and contract. In one approach to these issues, reference is made to the historical development of the protection for authors' rights. It is maintained that the legislator only at a relatively late stage was concerned with regulating the internal copyright conflict between the 'author' and the 'publisher': 'this has, in various periods, led to considerable complaints and protests from the authors who did not hesitate to declare in clear terms that copyright was finally only a publisher's right and that under its present aspect copyright was no more than a form of exploitation or expropriation of the authors by the publishers or other users' (Dietz, 1976, pp. 210-11). This argument rests on the perceived weakness of the author in his negotiations with publishers or other distributors. It has even been maintained that freedom of contract is prejudicial to the author as the economically weaker partner in any negotiations.

The perceived solutions to these problems seem to fall into three categories:
—legislative measures in favour of the author;
—collective administration of rights;
—solutions outside of copyright through such mechanisms as social security.

Among the legislative measures that might be introduced in favour of the author, particular attention has been paid to regulations binding the contractual rights of the author. The basic issue concerns to what extent the transfer by contract of copyright can be so structured that the legitimate interests of the author are protected and maintained without ignoring the equally legitimate rights of publishers and other distributors. In fact, such legislation exists in a number of countries such as Denmark, Germany and Italy. Generally, France is regarded as having the most complete regulations in this respect. The French Act of 1957 includes a series of general binding rules concerning the majority of copyright contracts with specific rules concerning the most important kinds; i.e. those for performances and publishing.

The need for legal rules regulating the contractual rights of authors also depends on whether the interested parties have managed to negotiate satisfactory arrangements through standard contracts which are collectively adopted. In most countries such standard contracts are applied in publishing and other sectors.

Another method of defending the interests of the author and of strengthening his bargaining position is the collective administration of copyright through societies or associations of authors. Such societies were first created by composers and librettists with regard to musical performances* and have since been established by other categories of authors. Since the individual author is generally in no position to supervise all the uses

---

*The first authors' society in the world was the Société des Auteurs, Compositeurs et Editeurs de Musique (SACEM) established in 1776 in France.

made of his work, it seems agreed that only when authors have combined in a society for the administration of rights and collection of royalties can they effectively obtain the revenues due to them. By concluding reciprocal contracts of representation with societies in other countries, such a society may also ensure protection abroad. Furthermore, such societies also render services to the users. If they did not exist, users would have to identify the copyright-owners and negotiate individually with each owner – which in many cases would pose almost insuperable problems.

The development of such societies has taken different routes. In some countries, a large number of such societies were established for specific defined areas, as is the case, for example, in France. In other countries only one or a few multi-purpose societies were created, which were responsible for various domains. However, even in countries where several societies coexist, they work on the basis of a functional monopoly for certain uses and a certain repertoire of works in order to avoid conflicts. In some countries, like Italy, such *de facto* monopolies have also been regulated as legal monopolies.

Copyright as a 'bundle of rights' sometimes seems infinitely divisible so that different societies may administer different rights. A 'performing right society' may be responsible for the collection of royalties in respect of the public performance of copyright music, which, as in the case of the UK, would include royalties from juke-boxes, background music contractors, clubs, pubs, cinemas, industrial premises, hotels, restaurants and cafés, non-commercial halls, commercial dancing halls, local authorities, bingo clubs, popular concerts and variety shows, holiday camps and caravan parks, shops and stores, Post Office 'Dial-a-Disc', and miscellaneous (PRS, 1977, p. 14). This is still relatively straightforward. Often a distinction is made between 'grands droits', which include theatrical performing rights including the rights of broadcasting and cinematographic adaptation of an entire work, and 'petits droits', which may include musical performing rights, or, in another version, the right to perform less important works such as poems, songs, parts of major works and choreographic works. To these categories should be added 'droits mécaniques', the 'mechanical rights' which cover sound and audio-visual recordings and 'droits littéraires', the rights to literary works as long as they do not fall under 'grand droits' or 'petits droits'. Each category of rights may, by itself or in various combinations, be administered by a special collecting society.

The status and efficiency of a collecting society depends on the size of the repertoire of works assigned to it by owners of rights: ideally these assignments should cover all works and authors in its area of operation. With regard to the works assigned to it, a collecting society will be in a monopoly situation in negotiations with users and in reciprocal agreements with other societies. This kind of administrative structure has obvious practical advantages but might be contrary to public regulation on competition, monopolies, trusts or other restrictive practices. A clash between copyright administration and trade law has occurred within the European Economic Community (EEC). The EEC Commission has investigated the statutes and agreements of certain collecting societies in member states to establish whether their *de facto* monopolies would contravene the Treaty of Rome.

On the basis of both theory and practice it has been argued that the existence of several competing societies in the same domain would be harmful to all interested parties – to the authors as well as to the users of works. Various, somewhat contradictory, reasons have been advanced in support of this attitude. In the case of several competing societies, the users of works can supposedly gain the upper hand by playing one society against the other or by being able to avoid payments. Other reasons appear more solid. The entire system for the transfer of rights, the control of the uses of works and the collection of royalties and other payments would become even more complex and expensive both for the users and for the societies. The monopoly situation is obviously to the advantage of the societies; it is intended to serve the authors and has been perceived to be of advantage also to users of works. There are cases where, for example, broadcasting organizations have refused to negotiate certain rights unless they had clearly identifiable contracting partners with clearly identifiable mandates.

The relationships between authors, societies and users have been seen to be very complicated, and some countries have introduced legislation or other mechanisms to regulate the collecting societies. The most detailed regulation seems to have been introduced in West Germany through a special law on the administration of copyright and neighbouring rights.

In the view of some experts such legislation constitutes the only possibility of counteracting certain risks inherent in the monopoly of the societies. Apart from arguments of efficiency and expediency, an interesting and controversial argument has been advanced by Adolf Dietz in his study of copyright in the Common Market countries. He maintains that the collective agreements concluded between associations of authors and associations of users should be considered as analogous to collective bargaining agreements. Thus, authors' societies are seen as being similar to labour unions, or at least having a quasi-union character. This view form part of a general approach which seems to discern – and approve – a trend implying that copyright should be detached from the domain of property rights and be brought into the area of labour law. Thus, according to this concept, the rules of individual and collective labour law should also encompass copyright and neighbouring rights, at least partially. This argument is supported by references to what has been called the 'relativization' of copyright. Writers and artists might look for solutions to their precarious situation outside copyright, for example through social security arrangements; one procedure might be for users of works to be responsible for the payment of social security fees on behalf of the creators, similar to the contributions paid by employers on behalf of their employees. In this view, such practices undermine the bases of traditional copyright by shifting the problems from the area of authors' rights to the area of labour law. To some extent, this line of reasoning seems to bring the market-oriented approach closer to the principles that have been adopted in socialist countries.

Chapter III · International agreements and structures

Some of the earliest steps towards a modern system of international law and organization were taken in the field of communications. Thus the first genuine international conventions were concluded in the 1860s for telecommunications and postal services. These were quickly followed by the two treaties that provide the basis for the development of rules governing the relations between states as regards the protection of intellectual production: the Paris Convention for the Protection of Industrial Property of 1883 and the Berne Convention for the Protection of Literary and Artistic Works of 1886.

These two sets of early modern international law-making are similar in certain respects but also show interesting differences. In both cases the agreements were concluded primarily at the initiative of a number of European countries. In telecommunications the starting-point was – and still is – a clearly emphasized national sovereignty. The International Telecommunication Convention still begins by 'fully recognizing the sovereign right of each country to regulate its telecommunications' (Preamble). It is on this basis that the contracting governments agreed to establish the Convention as the basic instrument of the International Telecommunication Union (ITU), the object being to facilitate relations and co-operation between peoples by means of efficient telecommunication services. Thus, in contrast to current practice which endows international organizations with a permanent Charter or Constitution, the ITU Convention must be re-adopted by each Plenipotentiary Conference of the Union.

In this respect, both the Paris and Berne Conventions have a more modern flavour. These Conventions were designed to provide a permanent legal framework subject to amendments and revisions if required. The countries which adhere to the Berne Convention constitute themselves into a Union. This organization was intended to be not merely a contractual agreement between a number of countries but a genuine 'society' of states, a kind of association open to all states that wished to protect the rights of authors.

It has often been pointed out that the Berne Convention has known a permanence and relative stability which few international agreements can match. Even though the ideal held by many of one universal treaty did not prove feasible, it still constitutes the foundation for the elaborate international structure that has grown up in the area of copyright and related rights. This structure is both complex and complicated in the eyes of those who do not spend their professional lives mapping and adding to the intricate web of international rules in this area. We now face a series of interlocking international conventions and structures with partly similar, partly different, intentions, and varied membership.

As in national legislation, this international structure is subject to increased stress caused by technical developments and by changing policy attitudes in the communications field. A major reason for the evolution of the international system of conventions and organizations has been the impact of new communications and information technologies, new ways of producing, reproducing and exploiting intellectual works. The creators and performers of these works, the enterprises that publish or otherwise use and disseminate protected works, and the legislators, have attempted to keep pace with these developments by extending the scope and adapting the nature of copyright rules. The revisions of existing international conventions and the adoption of new treaties prove the dynamic nature of intellectual property rights. However, the tension between the changing interests of the copyright-owners, of the public and of society is still with us and probably always will be, as one of the key issues in copyright. Another major question is to what extent amendments and additions to the existing edifice are adequate to deal with the new challenges, which to an increasing number of observers herald not only a quantitative but also a qualitative change in man's information environment.

The following survey of international conventions and structures will cover copyright in the strict sense as well as neighbouring rights and related issues. The focus will be on the evolution of basic approaches and on the attempts to find solutions to new social and technical challenges rather than on the details of current provisions.

1 Copyright conventions

(a) The Berne Convention

The Berne Convention or, to give the full title, the International Convention for the Protection of Literary and Artistic Works was concluded in 1886 and is thus the oldest of the international treaties dealing with copyright and related rights. Even though some non-European countries participated in the preparatory diplomatic conferences, the Convention was mainly the result of agreement between a number of European countries. Even today, after more than ninety years of existence and a series of revisions, it is still far from being universal; on 1 January 1979 seventy-one states had adhered to the Convention, notable exceptions being the USA and the USSR. However, the Berne Convention still acts as the starting-point and the touchstone for international relations in the copyright field.

The Berne Convention is clearly based on a continental European approach. The basic purpose of the Convention is 'to protect, in as effective and uniform a manner as possible, the rights of authors in their literary and artistic works' (Preamble). The establishment of a common system of international copyright rules implied for adhering countries that 'they would have to sacrifice, in some measure, their rigid national conceptions and bend their internal legislation to general rules that were internationally recognized. Two problems demanded solution: conflicts of laws had to be adjusted and differences between national legislation bridged, if not eliminated' (Masouyé, 1968, p. 11).

The first issue was solved by introducing the principle of national treatment or assimilation: foreign works and foreign authors are protected in each member country in the same manner as national works and authors. The second issue was settled by adopting the principle of a minimum standard of protection with regard to the content of copyright, its scope and duration. States which are parties to the Convention must grant protection at a level not below that provided for in the Convention. In addition to these principles of national treatment and minimum standards, a third basic principle provides for automatic protection without any formalities such as registration or notice.

The characteristic features of the Berne Convention as it has evolved through a series of revisions have been variously described.

Four features appear particularly important. First, the Convention focuses on the exclusive rights of authors, although these are conditional, in some cases, on exceptions and limitations. The Convention is primarily intended to protect the interests of the originators of literary and artistic works and does not make reference to other aspects or dimensions of copyright. Second, the Berne Convention is designed to provide a high level of protection and to give authors the most comprehensive set of rights it seems possible to grant. It is thus no exaggeration to speak of 'the severity of Convention law' (Masouyé, 1968, p. 17), which requires certain relaxations in response to both social requirements and technical developments. Third, the major trend in the development of the Convention is towards a continuous increase in the scope of protection provided. Finally, the primacy of Convention rules over national legislation has been reinforced: in earlier versions, the adhering countries were required to guarantee the protection of works, but since 1948 the Convention itself explicitly grants the enjoyment of this protection.

The provisions of the Berne Convention fall into two classes: those of substance which deal with what is known as the material law, and those clauses which cover matters of administration and structure. As regards the substantive provisions, a distinction is often made between two sets of rules. The so-called 'conventional' rules seek to resolve international copyright problems by imposing uniform rules on each member country: member countries must thus ensure that the rule in question forms part of their national law. The other set of rules, 'which refer back', do not provide such uniform solutions: they seek to achieve agreement by allowing each country where protection is claimed to formulate its own rules within the limits laid down in the Convention. The rights provided in the Convention are usually obligatory in the sense that each member country must grant all of them, but in a few cases optional clauses make it possible for member countries to refuse to implement them or to modify their effect.

The original Berne Union consisted of fourteen nations. The present membership comprises seventy-one countries that have adhered to one or more of the seven successive revisions of the Berne Convention. The original Berne Convention of 1886 was amended and supplemented in Paris in 1896 by an additional Act and an 'Interpretation Declaration'. A further revision took place in Berlin in 1908. In 1914 an 'Additional Protocol' was signed in Berne. The Berlin text was revised in Rome in 1928. The next revision took place in Brussels in 1948. The two most recent revisions are those of Stockholm (1967) and Paris (1971).

An interesting – and complicating – feature of this system is that not all member countries have accepted all the revisions, so that there is a complex structure of adherence by the various member states. Thus, some countries have stayed with the level of protection provided in the Rome version, others with the Brussels version, while still others have adopted the more recent Stockholm or Paris versions. The result is a situation which has been described by an expert from a non-Berne country in terms of 'complete confusion as to the relationships and mutual obligations of countries adhering to different texts, whether there is a common text or not' (Ringer, 1977, p. 45).

The most important aspect of the evolution represented by this series of revisions concerns the changes in substantive rules and what they reveal of changes in underlying concepts. In general terms these changes may be characterized as a continuous expansion of the rights enjoyed by authors.

According to the original Berne text of 1886, enjoyment of any rights was 'subject to accomplishment of the conditions and formalities prescribed by law in the country of origin'. The successive revisions of the Berne Convention finally abolished formalities altogether, making protection automatic upon the creation of a work by an author who was a national of a Berne Union nation, regardless of the existence of protection in the country of origin.

The duration of the protection granted has also been greatly extended. Originally, the duration of protection abroad was limited to the period of protection in the country of origin. Protection against unauthorized translations lasted until the expiration of ten years from the date of publication of the original work. In the present version, the minimum term of copyright has become the lifetime of the author plus fifty years. Similarly, with some exceptions, translation rights have been extended to the full duration of copyright.

A vital aspect concerns the definition of protected works, of what is to be understood by the expression 'literary and artistic works'. In the first instance, it should be noted that the Convention speaks of 'works' but nowhere defines what is to be meant by the word. It is, however, clear from the general tone of the Convention that a work must be an intellectual creation, and that it should be 'original' in the sense of possessing creativity and be clearly distinguishable from so-called derivative works; i.e. those based on another, pre-existing work.

Of more immediate interest in this context is the meaning of the expression 'literary and artistic works'. In Article II the Convention asserts, first, the principle of protection for all productions in the literary, scientific and artistic domain and, second, the principle of protection regardless of the form and mode of expression. In order to illustrate this, para. 1 of Article II gives a non-exhaustive list of examples which is intended to include all the main categories of works. This list in its present form covers not only such traditional categories as written works ('books, pamphlets and other writings'), and oral works ('lectures, addresses, sermons and other works of the same nature'), but also dramatic, dramatico-musical works, and musical compositions. Also included are works created by new methods, such as cinematographic and photographic works. In both cases the appearance of new technical means has led to the addition of the expression 'to which are assimilated works expressed by a process analogous to' cinematography or photography. However interpreted, this list obviously stops short of a variety of new methods, particularly those associated with computer-based production.

The revisions of the Berne Convention have also extended the scope of the rights granted to authors and thus of the protection granted. Specific minimum requirements have been established with respect to the protection of exclusive rights, among which the most important are: the right of translation, the right of reproduction, the right of performing dramatic, musical and dramatico-musical works in public, the right of broadcasting, the right of recording musical works, cinematographic rights and the right of adaptation.

The Convention explicitly recognizes the moral rights of authors. These provisions (which were introduced in the 1928 Rome revision) lay down two of the author's prerogatives: to claim the paternity of his work and to claim a 'right of respect' for his work. Accordingly, even after assigning his work to another, the author may proclaim his authorship and object to any distortion, mutilation or other modification of the work that would injure his reputation. The legislative means of guaranteeing these 'moral rights' are left to each Berne nation.

The only exceptions to the extension of the author's rights concern changes in the rules concerning limitations of protection and the 'fair use' principle: a limited freedom to use protected works. In the first case, the Convention admits the possibility of national legislation excluding from protection certain specified works such as political speeches or the reproduction or broadcasting of public lectures and addresses. National legislation may also permit the reproduction of literary and artistic works in certain special circumstances. The 'fair use' principle applies in three cases: the freedom to make quotations, the use of works for teaching purposes and the use of works in connection with reporting current events. The provision concerning the freedom to use works for teaching purposes was introduced as late as 1948 through the Brussels revision. In its present form, it lays down similar conditions as for quotations: the use must be compatible with 'fair practice', a concept which was introduced in the Stockholm revision (1967) and 'fair use' is admissible only to the extent that it is 'justified by the purpose' (teaching, information) – another new idea. In both cases, the 'fairness' and 'justification' of such free use is a matter for national legislation and for the courts to decide. In a larger sense, the freedom to use protected works became a controversial issue between developed and developing countries or, seen from another angle, between mainly exporting and mainly importing countries. This issue will be further discussed in section (d), p. 61.

As regards other substantive provisions, the Stockholm Conference maintained the general framework of the Convention but adopted a number of clarifications and additions. With regard to eligibility criteria and the country of origin, the nationality of the author was accepted as the single and universal test. A comprehensive right of reproduction was introduced, while, at the same time, the 'fair use' principle was extended to include reproduction of articles on current economic, political or religious topics in broadcasting and other news media. 'Fair use' for teaching purposes was broadened to include broadcasts and sound and visual recordings. The most complex and controversial features of the new text were the provisions governing cinematographic works.

In view of the differences between the Anglo-American approach and the European continental approach, the determination of ownership of copyright (in terms of pre-existing works used for a film, contributions specially made for the production of a cinematographic work, and the film itself) is a matter for national legislation; however, without prejudice to the copyright in any pre-existing work, a cinematographic work is to be protected as an original work. Further minor changes were made in the provisions concerning the reproduction of speeches, lectures and addresses by the press; moral rights; terms of protection and works of joint authorship; rights of translating, public performance and recitation, 'mechanical' production rights and the protection of folklore.

Apart from the controversial Protocol Regarding Developing Countries, the major change adopted at the Stockholm Conference concerned administrative and structural changes in the Unions associated with the treaties. These changes were designed to modernize and rationalize the administration of the various Unions through the creation of a new organization, the World Intellectual Property Organization (WIPO), which replaced the earlier administrative structure. This organization, located in Geneva, became a specialized agency within the United Nations system in 1974 (see section 3 below).

(b) Inter-American copyright conventions
As stated earlier, although the Berne Convention of 1886 was successful, it did not receive universal acceptance. In fact, in the Western hemisphere only Brazil and Canada acceded to the original Convention. On the other hand, from 1889 onwards, a series of purely American conventions was completed. Simultaneously with the successive revisions of the Berne Union, six multilateral copyright conventions were drafted in the Western hemisphere: (1) the Montevideo Convention, 1889; (2) the Mexico City Convention, 1902; (3) the Rio de Janeiro Convention, 1906; (4) the Buenos Aires Convention, 1910; (5) the Havana Convention, 1928; and (6) the Washington Convention 1946. These conventions, with the exception of the Montevideo Convention, are open to adherence only by Western hemisphere republics.

Although not, strictly speaking, a Pan-American agreement, the

Montevideo Convention of 1889 is generally considered to be the first instrument in the development of the Pan-American copyright system. Unlike later agreements it was open to non-American states. Like the Berne Union it established certain minimum rights irrespective of national law. Unlike the Berne Union, however, it followed the principle of *lex loci* rather than *lex fori*; i.e. the rights of an author are determined by the laws of the country of first publication and not by the laws of the country where an infringement has taken place.

The first truly Pan-American copyright convention was signed at Mexico City in 1902. It provided for a Union to protect nationals of the contracting parties, but it adhered to the principle of *lex fori* in that the nature and extent of protection were determined by the law of the nation where protection was sought. The protection to be given to foreign works under the Mexico City Convention of 1902 was clearly the concept of national treatment as found in the Berne Convention.

The Third International Conference of American States, held at Rio de Janeiro in 1906, affirmed the provisions of the 1902 Convention and provided further for the creation of a copyright bureau for international registration. However, too few nations ratified the agreement, and the bureau was never established.

The most notable of the inter-American copyright conventions was that at Buenos Aires in 1910. It is still in force and requires that an eligible work, protected in one of the member nations and bearing a notice reserving the property right, be protected in all others. Here too, as in the Berne Convention, the principle of *lex fori* as to the nature and extent of protection was established. This Convention has been ratified by seventeen Latin American nations and the United States. It specifies that authors of any contracting country who have secured copyright in their own country will enjoy in each of the other member nations the rights that that nation accords to its own works.

In effect, this agreement provides for reciprocal national treatment and recognition of copyright if appropriately marked with a reservation of rights. The words 'Copyright Reserved', 'All Rights Reserved' or the equivalent in any other language should be sufficient to meet the notice requirement.

The terms of the Buenos Aires Convention became binding on each country as that country ratified; thus, the date of ratification is important in deciding the status of the works of each nation. Under this agreement, the duration of copyright protection need not exceed that of the country of origin, but otherwise is governed by the laws of each country. There is one important right which this Convention does not expressly cover, namely the right of mechanical musical reproduction by means of sound recordings.

The Buenos Aires Convention of 1910 remains the basic Pan-American copyright instrument even though an attempt was made at Havana in 1928 to revise the agreement, by requiring that the notice should include the name of the copyright proprietor and the year and country of first publication. However, this revision was not well received and has been ratified by only five states.

In 1946, delegates of all of the members of the Pan-American Union signed at Washington, DC, a new Inter-American Convention on the Rights of the Author in Literary, Scientific, and Artistic Works. The agreement was intended to replace the 1910 Buenos Aires Convention and its 1928 Havana revision and all earlier inter-American conventions on copyright. Rights granted under the earlier conventions would not be affected by the agreement.

Since it approaches the principles of the Berne Convention, the Washington Convention is much more far-reaching than any previous inter-American agreements. This Convention establishes, without regard to the domestic law of the contracting nations, a group of enumerated substantive rights in literary and artistic works. It requires each signatory state to grant these rights without any formality to all persons, other than its citizens or domiciled aliens, who are nationals or resident aliens of any contracting state and have procured copyright in accordance with the law of that state. Fourteen nations have adhered to this Convention, but not the United States: the non-adherence of the United States was because of the absence of any formalities in the Washington Convention as required by US national legislation.

Critics of the Pan-American copyright conventions cite the lack of general ratification and the multiplicity of conventions among the countries of America, which have resulted in what they term confusing and ineffective protection. Even if the Pan-American conventions are viewed as having been fairly successful in governing copyright relations in the Western hemisphere, by definition they are not truly international in scope and effect.

Therefore, during the past twenty years there has been a clear trend away from regional copyright conventions in favour of worldwide arrangements. Consequently, in many instances, the Universal Copyright Convention has replaced the Pan-American conventions as the operative agreement.

(c) Universal Copyright Convention
By the 1940s, countries could be divided into three categories according to the position they had adopted for the regulation of their international relations in the copyright field:
—countries that were parties to the Berne Convention;
—countries that were parties to one or several of the inter-American copyright conventions;
—countries that had not adhered to any international copyright protection system.

Even though some countries belonging to one or another of these categories had established bilateral relations with others, there was a growing recognition that international copyright relations were anything but satisfactory. Thus, the copyright relations of the United States have been described as 'a complex mixture of bilateral treaties, proclamations and regional agreements' (Ringer, 1977, p. 47). It was also becoming increasingly doubtful whether a number of countries, including the United States, would ever adhere to the Berne Convention. After the Second World War, efforts were again made to unify international relations in the copyright field through a new multilateral convention acceptable to a majority of states. For obvious reasons, this work had to be undertaken outside the Berne Union and came to be centred in Unesco. In 1947 the General Conference of Unesco resolved that the Organization 'shall with all possible speed and with due regard to existing agreements, consider the problem of improving copyright on a worldwide basis' (Resolution 2.4.1).

Following the work of a number of expert committees, Unesco in 1952 convened an international conference to seek a workable unity in copyright law. Any agreement reached would have to meet a number of criteria before it could be accepted. It had to be flexible enough to cover a wide range of situations. It had to be acceptable to the authors and proprietors of protected works. Since it was not intended to supplant existing agreements, it had to find a basis for conciliation between countries with widely different cultural, legal and administrative traditions. It was also intended to establish stable treaty relationships between the countries of the Berne Union and those of the American continent and provide a system acceptable to the countries which had not yet acceded to any international copyright convention.

The necessary compromises were made and the Universal Copyright Convention (UCC) was the result. This landmark agreement was signed by forty nations at Geneva on 6 September 1952 and, following the required twelve ratifications, came into effect in 1955.

The Universal Copyright Convention represents a compromise between the European concept of copyright protection, as expressed in the Berne Convention, and the American view. Under the Berne Convention, intellectual works are regarded as an extension of the personality of the author and protection is granted automatically upon creation of the work, without regard for formalities. Conflicting with this broad theory of protection was the view prevailing in the United States and some Latin American nations. Under this latter approach the intention is to balance the copyright-holder's interest with the user's interest by the requirement that copyright protection in published works be subject to compliance with prescribed formalities.

In comparison with the Berne Convention, the general purpose of the UCC has been given a wider scope. In the Berne Convention there is no other purpose than the protection of the rights of authors. While this objective is also emphasized in the UCC, it has been supplemented by two other considerations which set copyright in a larger context: copyright protection is seen as a means to ensure respect for the rights of the individual and to encourage the development of literature, the sciences and the arts as well as the dissemination of works of the human mind.

The text of the UCC is brief and couched in general terms. Like the Berne Convention the fundamental principle of the UCC is national treatment; i.e. foreign authors are treated like national authors and foreign works like national works. The Convention thereby solves the conflicts arising from the differences between the domestic legislation of contracting states. However, unlike the Berne Convention, the UCC makes no allusion to the concept of reciprocity. There is no restriction on the principle of assimilation in cases where the level of protection established by the national legislation of a contracting country results in little protection for foreign authors. In other words, there is no minimum level of protection within the UCC for a foreign author to rely upon, neither can he claim the level of protection from his country of origin in another contracting country. This situation clearly favours those countries which import works.

The Berne Convention expressly provides that the exercise of copyright shall not be subject to any formality. This abolition of all formalities for the establishment of copyright was one of the reasons why many countries, particularly in the Western hemisphere, felt unable to accede to the Berne Convention. In order to secure unanimity, the UCC adopted a compromise solution. Formalities are not totally abolished but considerably simplified. Any formalities which might be required by a country as a condition for the protection of foreign works are replaced by a single notice of claim of copyright. This notice consists of three inseparable elements: the symbol ©, the name of the copyright proprietor, and the year of first publication.

There are four substantial benefits which accrue to authors through the UCC. The most important is that an author's works are protected in other nations to the same degree as the works of authors native to that country. Second, the author is relieved of the burden of formalities except the notice of claim. Third, he is assured a minimum term of protection. Finally, the author has control over translation rights.

As mentioned earlier, the UCC is based on the principle of national treatment; i.e. foreign authors are afforded the same protection as national authors. There are, however, three important exceptions to this principle in the form of internationally binding standards set by the UCC. First, the maximum formality admitted is the UCC copyright notice. The second exception to the national treatment principle concerns the establishment of the minimum term of protection which, as a rule, consists of the lifetime of the author and twenty-five years (in contrast to the Berne Convention's fifty years). In certain specified cases referring to photographic works and works of applied art, contracting states are, however, not obliged in their relations to other states to accord more than ten years' protection. The third deviation from national treatment concerns the guarantee of minimum translation rights. On this point there were considerable differences of opinion: some countries were in favour of an author's exclusive right to authorize translation of his works during the whole term of protection, while other countries held the view that his exclusive right should be limited to a relatively short period. The compromise solution adopted in the Convention attempts to ensure a balance between the rights of authors and the interests of the dissemination of culture. The exclusive right of the author is recognized, but is restricted by a system of compulsory translation licensing.

One of the most controversial issues in the preparation of the UCC concerned the relation to the Berne Convention. Many of the principal members of the Berne Union feared that the UCC might give countries that wished to restrict copyright protection an opportunity to leave the Berne Union. They therefore made their acceptance of the Universal Copyright Convention conditional on provisions safeguarding the Berne Convention. The text adopted in 1952 contains a safeguarding clause which states that the UCC shall in no way affect the provisions of the Berne Convention, and also a penalty clause: any country which withdraws from the Berne Union is to be deprived of the benefit of both the Berne and the Universal Conventions in its relations with other members of the Berne Union. This provision, which was seen as being against the interests of developing countries, became one of the key issues during the work on the revision of both Conventions in 1971.

Most of the countries that were members of the Berne Union joined the UCC although they regarded it as a retrogression from the level of desirable protection and from the ideal of a unitary worldwide regime of copyright protection.

From the point of view of a developing country, the situation looked different:

> on the one hand we have the Berne Convention which above all grants considerable advantages to the creators of literary and artistic production and hence clearly enjoys the backing and support of countries exporting works of the mind, as it involves a considerable source of revenue for these countries and their nationals, and, on the other hand, we have the Universal Convention which, while firmly protecting the same creators, realistically allows for the economic, social and cultural situations of the various countries in today's world (Chakroun, 1969, p. 51).

(d) Paris revisions of 1971

In the late 1960s the world of international copyright was shaken by a serious crisis. This crisis concerned international copyright relations between industrialized and developing countries. In 1966 the General Conference of Unesco concluded that 'the conventions at present governing international relations in the matter of copyright should be partially revised to take account of the economic, social and cultural conditions obtaining in the developing countries'. The Director-General of Unesco was invited to take the necessary steps for an examination of the possibility of revising the UCC for the benefit of developing countries. The main issues concerned the demands made by these countries for access to protected works for teaching, study and research, and their demands for a change in the safeguard and penalty clauses linking the Berne Convention and the UCC.

The relations between industrialized and developing countries also became the most controversial issue at the 1967 Stockholm Conference for the revision of the Berne Convention. The idea of including in the Convention special provisions in favour of developing countries was first put forward at an African copyright meeting in Brazzaville in 1963. It was pursued in the preparatory meetings for the Stockholm Conference. The basis of the developing country position can well be exemplified by the following statement:

> whilst the author has certainly a right to benefit by his intellectual creations, it is quite another thing to claim that he should have the exclusive right to control the use of his creations without considering the rights of users. It should not be forgotten that, however gifted an author may be, he stands on the shoulders of those who have gone before him and he, in his turn, has an obligation to posterity. An author can claim no more than the right to receive equitable remuneration. To endeavour to constitute intellectual creations into a monopoly for exploitation would be unbecoming. The more civilized a nation, the less ought to be its desire to exploit another nation not so fortunately placed (Krishnamurti, 1967, pp. 60–1).

After long, arduous and often heated negotiations, agreement was finally reached on a special Protocol Regarding Developing

Countries, which was attached as an Annex to the Convention. It represented a departure from the high level of copyright protection traditionally given within the framework of the Berne Convention. It thus provided an opportunity for any developing country which adhered to the Convention to make reservations in respect of a number of specified matters which would have the effect of providing a lower level of protection in that country than was afforded in other countries of the Berne Union. This lower-level system of protection in favour of developing countries concerned a reduction of the maximum terms of protection (from fifty to twenty-five years), a right of translation and a right of reproduction in the form of a statutory licence in return for equitable payment, special provisions for a right to broadcasting and, most important, a possibility of restricting protection with regard to uses of protected works intended exclusively for teaching, study and research in all fields of education.

However, the agreement reached at the Stockholm Conference did not prove capable of solving the controversy. In the eyes of the developing countries, the Protocol bore the stamp of the industrialized world since everything had been done to incorporate the changes suggested by the industrialized countries so as to make the Protocol acceptable to them. Even with the Protocol, the representatives of developing countries felt that the invitation to non-member countries to join the Berne Union looked dangerously 'like the spider's invitation to the fly to walk into its parlour' (Krishnamurti, 1967, p. 67). In the developed countries, there were even stronger reactions against the Protocol. The Protocol was said to permit legalized piracy, to single out one section of the public – i.e. authors and publishers – for sacrifices on behalf of the developing countries and so to dilute the level of protection that the result would be a dissolution of the Berne Union.

The result was that those countries which mainly produced and exported literary and artistic works – i.e. the most important countries for the purposes of the Protocol – refused to ratify the new version of the Berne Convention. Thus, in order to obtain the required advantages, the only line open to the developing countries was to work for a revision of the UCC, particularly concerning the link with the Berne Convention.

In order to avert the crisis in international copyright relations resulting from the dispute over the demands by the developing countries, it was decided to convene simultaneously in Paris diplomatic revision conferences for both the Berne and the Universal Copyright Conventions. Following this joint conference a compromise revision of both Conventions designed to stabilize international relations in the field of copyright was signed in July 1971. The revised Conventions came into force in 1974.

The revision of the Berne Convention did not cover the Stockholm Act as a whole but only the Protocol Regarding Developing Countries and related provisions. In the Paris Act of the Convention, this Protocol was replaced by an Appendix which forms an integral part of the Act. The revision of the UCC was more comprehensive. The author's rights of reproduction, public performance and broadcasting were firmly formulated. The concession to the developing countries included not only the same substantial provisions as accepted in the Berne Convention but also the suspension of the Berne Union safeguard clause.

Thus certain basic similar changes were made in the two Conventions in favour of the developing countries, but to a lesser extent than had been provided in the Stockholm Protocol. One of the central goals of the revision conferences had been achieved: the establishment of an international mechanism for permitting the developing countries a greater degree of access to protected works while respecting the rights of authors.

The relaxations of copyright provided for in both Conventions are reserved for developing countries; i.e. those countries which are regarded as developing in accordance with the established practice of the United Nations. In contrast to the Stockholm Protocol, the possibility of introducing exceptions is allowed only in respect of the rights of translation and reproduction.

This relaxation of the protection of translation and reproduction rights can be affected through a system of compulsory licences which, however, is surrounded by a series of conditions and preconditions. A developing country which so wishes may provide for a regime of non-exclusive, non-transferable licences which make it possible to translate and reproduce printed works after consultation with and upon fair payment to the copyright-owner. These licences must be issued by the competent national copyright authority.

In the case of translation the compulsory licence may only apply to works published in printed or analogous forms. The licence may be granted only for specified privileged purposes: teaching, scholarship and research, including adult education. There are provisions for the period that must have elapsed from the first publication of a work and for an additional waiting period before the licence can be issued. The reproduction licence concerns the reproduction and publication of a particular edition of a work. Also, in this case, the possibility of issuing a licence is surrounded by a series of conditions with regard to length of time from first publication, the purpose of the reproduction, etc.

The various conditions surrounding the possibility of granting compulsory licences were agreed upon at the insistence of the industrialized countries in order to safeguard the interests of authors and their publishers. The new provisions ensure waiting periods which are intended to allow authors and publishers to satisfy the needs of developing countries by publishing the works or translations themselves. The requirement of prior consultation with the holder of rights is presumed to result in negotiation on a contractual basis, since the availability of compulsory licensing might increase the willingness to negotiate.

With regard to the link between the Berne and Universal Copyright Conventions, the abolition of the safeguard and penalty clause in the UCC provides a choice for developing countries. Those which belong to the Berne Union can withdraw and adhere only to the UCC without incurring the sanctions laid down in the safeguard clause. If they should choose to remain with or adhere to the Berne Convention, they will also be able to relax the rights of translation and reproduction as provided for in both revised Conventions.

The result of the revision conferences has been described as 'a balance of interests which has regard to the legitimate concerns of developing countries, without expecting unjust sacrifices from authors and publishers. The need to arrive at compromises, even wholly new questions, has resulted in more complex arrangements than those originally contemplated' (Ulmer, 1971, p. 98). It is an open question whether there is universal agreement on the first statement, but there is no doubt about agreement on the second.

Despite the differences that remain between the two Copyright Conventions, the Paris revisions brought them closer together. However, it also became clear that a merger between the Conventions – which many, particularly in Europe, would like to see –

would remain impracticable. Thus the situation of having two international Copyright Conventions existing side by side will remain, at least for the time being.

Apart from the relaxation of certain rules concerning translation and reproduction, a number of other steps have been taken in order to facilitate access to protected works by the developing countries. In 1970 the Unesco General Conference approved the establishment of an International Copyright Information Centre (ICIC). The main functions of the Centre include the following: to collect copyright information on books that can be made available to developing countries on terms as favourable to them as possible, to arrange for the transfer of rights to developing countries and to help in the development of simple model contracts for translation, reprint and other rights required by developing countries.

In order for a country to become party to the Berne or Universal Copyright Conventions, it must be in a position to give effect to their provisions under domestic law. In order to assist states in the drafting of national copyright legislation, it seemed useful to provide them with a draft model law to which they could refer if they so wished. This work has been carried out jointly by Unesco and WIPO. Under their sponsorship a committee of governmental experts met in Tunis in the early part of 1976. The committee drafted a Model Law on Copyright for Developing Countries which is compatible with the 1971 revisions of both Conventions. The Tunis Model Law also takes into account both the Anglo-Saxon and the civil law approaches and is intended to serve as a clear and simple framework for drafting – or amending – national copyright laws, taking into account the individual interests of each country.

Moreover, in 1976 WIPO adopted a 'permanent programme for developing co-operation related to copyright and neighbouring rights'. The objectives are to encourage in developing countries intellectual creation in the literary, scientific and artistic domains, to facilitate the dissemination of intellectual creations protected by copyright or neighbouring rights 'under fair and reasonable conditions', and, finally, to assist in the development of legislation and institution in this field. This programme is directed by a permanent committee composed of forty-two states, both developing and industrialized.

2 Neighbouring rights and related conventions

The Copyright Conventions were designed to regulate the international protection granted to authors of literary and artistic works. The most important forms of utilizing works were book publishing, art exhibitions, concert and theatre performances. Consequently, the two most important rights of the author concerned reproduction and public performance. With the introduction of new communications media – photography, film, sound recording, broadcasting – the protection of authors' rights were extended to cover these new forms of expression and of utilization of works.

The new media affected other categories of intellectual workers and brought about the emergence of new sets of 'producers' and media institutions, neither of which was covered in traditional copyright. In the 1920s the performing artists had already started to raise claims for the protection of their performances because of the increasing use of recording devices. These issues were expressed in a number of bodies, and particularly in the International Labour Organization (ILO). The ILO was concerned with the impact of sound recording and broadcasting on the economic and social conditions of performers and other intellectual workers.

The changes in the situation of performers has been described as follows:

> Until rather less than a hundred years ago, the work of performing artists . . . had not changed in its essentials for centuries. The performer's performance was ephemeral and local; it could be seen and heard only by those persons who were actually present, and it had no afterlife, except in the memory of the audience. This situation began to change towards the beginning of the present century, and became something quite different in the years between the First and Second World Wars as a result of three major inventions: the gramophone or phonograph, the cinema and sound radio . . . With the development of 'talking pictures' the cinema had also become a medium of mass entertainment throughout the world . . . Two other developments – the long-playing gramophone record and nation-wide television – became important after the Second World War. It was by

then possible to fix the performances on all kind of materials – records, films, tapes, wire, etc. – and also to transmit the sounds and images comprising these performances to millions of people at one and the same time, even across national frontiers (Thompson, 1973, p. 304).

The effects of these developments on the performers have been far reaching. They have changed the relationship between performers and their audiences and therefore also the direct link between performers and their income. The greatest fear concerned the risk of technological unemployment which is seen as affecting the majority of performers who are not recording or film 'stars'.

Later other concerns were added. The manufacturers of 'instruments for the mechanical reproduction of musical works' – i.e. the record producers – started to claim protection against illicit exploitation of their products, and particularly against the unauthorized duplication of their records (or 'phonograms' according to the expression used in this context). A third group comprised the broadcasting organizations which in their turn demanded protection for their broadcasts against unauthorized use. In view of the close relationship between copyright and these sought-for new forms of protection, and the possible incidence of any new international arrangement on authors' rights, the Berne Union and Unesco became involved in the work on an international agreement regulating these neighbouring rights. Similarly, all the major international associations representing the various interests concerned took an active part.

The preparation of international rules covering these neighbouring rights which could be accepted by all the parties concerned proved to be a difficult and lengthy procedure. Intensive work took place through the 1950s. In the early 1960s it resulted in the first international agreement in this area which was later followed by other conventions designed to respond, by international regulation, to the challenges and problems created by the new communications media.

(a) The Rome Convention
All the laborious preparatory work involving national authorities, the international associations of performers, record manufacturers and broadcasting organizations and the three most directly con-

cerned intergovernmental organizations (the Berne Union, Unesco and the ILO) finally resulted in a draft convention text which was submitted to a diplomatic conference convened in Rome. In October 1961 agreement was reached on the International Convention for the Protection of Performers, Producers of Phonograms and Broadcasting Organizations which, for obvious reasons, became known as the Rome Convention. It came into force in 1964.

The preparatory work for this strange 'menage à trois' had clearly shown the very real problems to be solved. There was a variety of legal theories and doctrines which were often in conflict as to the nature of the protection to be granted and therefore also as to its scope and content. These diverse theories were reflected in the differences in national laws and practices; the diversity of attitudes also accounted for the absence of any regulation in many countries. The three international organizations concerned pursued different objectives: the Berne Union and Unesco wanted to attach the new rights to copyright, while the ILO sought pragmatic solutions to specific economic and social problems and preferred a clear distinction between copyright and the new rights.

The interests of the three parties concerned might at first glance seem to be common or at least reciprocal, since they would all be protected by the Convention. However, the underlying economic factors and the impact of new rules on the relative strength of their bargaining positions gave rise to disagreements and they split into opposing camps. In fact, proposals were made at the diplomatic conference that it might have been better to regulate these matters in two different instruments: the protection of performers concerned the rights of persons whereas the protection of phonograms and broadcasts would be granted to large enterprises. This solution was not accepted and the notion of a single convention maintained. The compromises finally agreed to might be described in terms of 'a balance to which the concerned parties contributed by abandoning certain rights which they felt entitled to claim and by recognizing other rights which they would have preferred to avoid' (Straschnov *et al.*, 1958, p. 31). In any case, the Rome Convention seems to have caused more passionate reactions, for or against, than any other agreement in the field of intellectual property.

The Rome Convention, like the major copyright conventions, establishes national treatment as the basic principle of protection. There is, however, a strong element of reciprocity with regard to certain forms of remuneration. The second basic principle is the guarantee of minimum rights for the three protected groups which a country must provide for in order to be in a position to adhere to the Convention.

A new convention means new definitions. The definition of performers does not at first seem to present any difficulties, as meaning 'actors, singers, musicians, dancers and other persons who act, sing, deliver, declaim, play in or otherwise perform literary and artistic works'. But what about the awkward expression 'phonogram', which is taken to mean any exclusively aural fixation of sounds of a performance or other sounds (which, in fact, refers to bird-songs and other sounds of nature!). Most important, broadcasting is defined as 'wireless transmission' and does not include cable television. In order to provide for the required distinctions in the Convention, the concepts lying behind the definitions of expressions such as 'performance', 'publication', 'communication to the public', 'fixation'* seem to have become increasingly esoteric and a lawyer's paradise.

The minimum rights which are granted to the performers are expressed as the control over: the broadcast and public communication of their previously unfixed and unbroadcast performances; the fixation of their unfixed performances; and the reproduction of a fixation of their performance, if the original fixation was made without their consent or for a purpose different from the one originally envisaged.

The minimum standards of protection for broadcasters provides that the use of broadcasts, including rebroadcasts, fixations, reproductions and communication of television broadcasts to the public, for profit can be made only with the consent of the originating broadcasting organization. However, broadcasters are not protected against wire distribution, which became one of the reasons for their negative attitude to the Convention.

The unauthorized commercial reproduction of phonograms – i.e. mainly gramophone records and sound cassettes – is prohibited. The playing of a phonogram either in a broadcast or by any other performance requires the payment of 'equitable remuneration'.

---

*To 'fix' a work is to embody a work in a medium which is sufficiently permanent or stable to permit it to be perceived, reproduced, or otherwise communicated for a period of more than transitory duration.

With regard to formalities for protected phonograms, the Convention stipulates that, if a contracting state's domestic law requires formalities, they are considered to have been fulfilled if all authorized and published copies or their containers bear a notice containing the symbol ℗, accompanied by the year of first publication, and, unless it appears elsewhere on the copies of their containers, the name of the producer, his successor in title or exclusive licensee, and the name of the owner of performers' rights in the country of fixation. The notice must be located at a site which gives 'reasonable notice of claim of protection'.

The Convention establishes a minimum term of twenty years for the protection of intellectual property rights in performances, phonograms and broadcasts. Like the copyright conventions, it also permits contracting states to legislate for or regulate exceptions to Convention protection as regards the private use of works, the use of excerpts in reporting current events, 'ephemeral' fixations by broadcasting organizations for their own broadcasts and use exclusively for teaching or scientific research.

One of the most difficult problems before the diplomatic conference concerned what the Convention should provide in connection with the so-called 'secondary uses' of phonograms. 'Secondary uses' is a general expression, not found in the Convention, which designates the use of phonograms in broadcasting or other communication to the public. The main issue was whether the Convention should impose an obligation to grant secondary use rights; i.e. the principle of obligatory payments for secondary use. The final outcome was that, if a phonogram which had been published for commercial purposes was used for broadcasting or any other public communication, a single equitable remuneration must be paid by the user to the performers, to the producers of the phonogram, or to both (Art. 12). However, one of the permitted reservations involved the provisions on these secondary use rights: any contracting state had the right not to apply these provisions at all or not in respect of certain uses. Even so, these provisions on secondary use rights were one of the main reasons for the refusal of many states to adhere to the Rome Convention.

There were also other reasons for the resistance to the Convention. In many respects, the true story of the origin and development of the Rome Convention would offer fascinating insights into the skirmishes between the various interests involved, the reversals of positions, the compromises and horse-dealings, the play of personalities.

A major problem concerned the relationships between the three parties directly invoved which represented very different interests and social institutions. Under the auspices of the ILO, the performers appear in this context both as claimants of an individual right and as labour unions anxious to ensure adequate opportunities and conditions of work for their members through strengthened bargaining positions. There is no doubt that their bargaining power has been increased by the rights conferred under the Rome Convention. Their associations have therefore always strongly supported the Convention and have been active in trying to ensure its wider acceptance.

The 'producers of phonograms' correspond to what in normal language would be called the 'record companies'. In all countries that adhere to the Rome Convention they are private enterprises with a direct interest in the widespread adoption of the Convention.

The broadcasters represent a more mixed group, ranging from state undertakings to public service corporations and commercial enterprises. They have also shown more mixed reactions to the Rome Convention, in particular those most immediately concerned in Western Europe. After having been actively involved in the framing of the Convention, the European broadcasters represented by the European Broadcasting Union (EBU) changed their attitutde and offered the most determined opposition to the Convention. Even though broadcasts are protected by the Convention, the broadcasters maintained that the Convention demanded too high a price to secure these rights. In particular they opposed Article 12 which would oblige them to pay record companies for the right to play records over the air; this, to many, represented an obligation to recompense the record companies for publicizing their records. Thus, for these and similar reasons, the broadcasting organizations in many countries have preferred the *status quo* to acceptance of the Convention.

There are also problems involving other parties. Authors did not initially favour the Rome Convention since they feared that the value of their own creations might be reduced by greater compensation to performers and record companies. In fact, the interests of performers and authors need not always coincide and may even be contradictory. An exclusive right granted to performers to prohibit the use of phonograms in broadcasting can be used to the detriment of authors, in this case mainly composers and songwriters. The income of authors whose works are recorded on phonograms depends to a considerable extent on the broadcasting of records; their legitimate interest to have their recorded works broadcast would be violated if the performers by virtue of an exclusive right were to prohibit such use of phonograms.

It has been admitted by all concerned that the Convention itself is unclear and ambiguous on many points. Thus one of the reasons given for the plight of the Convention is the multiplicity of criteria for eligibility for protection (nationality, fixation or publication). In particular, it is said to create imponderables with regard to the principle of reciprocity through the adoption of the notion of simultaneous publication. Also, in the opinion of many experts, it included a series of provisions which worked to the disadvantage of developing countries both in their international relations and in the domestic arrangements they would have to make in order to adhere. Here again, though, opinions differ depending on the particular interest group represented.

The Convention came into force in 1964 when seven states had adhered. Thereafter the pace of ratification slowed considerably: two countries in 1965, one in 1966, none in 1967–9 and one in 1970. To date only twenty-one states have adhered. Some analysts have seen this as a failure of the Convention. Although it has received strong support from West Germany, the United Kingdom and the Scandinavian countries, it has so far been able to attract neither other European nations such as Belgium, France and the Netherlands nor industrialized non-European countries such as Australia and Canada. It is also significant that neither the USA nor the USSR – although for different reasons – have adhered and do not seem to have any intention of doing so. So far, only a few developing countries have adhered to this Convention. In its defence, it is pointed out that since its adoption a large number of states have legislated in matters relating to it. Thus it is seen as having had a great indirect impact on national legislation.

Until recently, there was doubt as to whether the Rome Convention would ever achieve sufficiently wide acceptance to have a significant impact on international intellectual property law. In the early 1970s it was therefore decided by the intergovernmental organizations concerned to take active steps to promote the

Convention, including the preparation of a draft Model Law in order to facilitate its application or accession to it.

As could be expected, the drafting of the Model Law proved to be a tough undertaking. First, since the intention was to provide as simple a text as possible, it was necessary to clarify a number of the provisions of the Convention. Second, for one text to be valid generally, different legal traditions had to be accommodated and alternatives presented whenever necessary. Third, and this was the most difficult aspect of all, agreement had to be reached among the three immediately concerned parties, all of them represented in the negotiations by their international associations: the performers, the producers of phonograms and the broadcasters. The performers and producers of phonograms were relatively easy to satisfy because of their general support for the Rome Convention. The position of the broadcasters was different altogether. The EBU admitted that there had been organized opposition to the further ratification of the Convention. The basic reason was that in the opinion of the broadcasters the Convention no longer offered protection of real interest to the broadcasters. It did not deal with satellite transmissions and cable television – which were of major concern to broadcasters – but included provisions which the broadcasters perceived as against their interests and public service mandates. The broadcasting organizations, in particular the EBU, took the position that they would change their negative attitude to the Convention itself only if common agreement could be reached on the draft Model Law. However, their opposition to Article 12 remained unchanged and they wanted clarifications on a number of other substantial points such as the problems of performers who are permanent employees of a broadcasting organization, the problems arising when performers have previously ceded their rights to a trade union, collecting society or another third party and the problems of exceptions and their conformity with copyright legislation.

The outcome of all the difficult and sometimes acrimonious negotiations can be described as a swap. Once the major problems of the broadcasters had been solved, they agreed to the Model Law and to the termination of their active opposition to the Convention, on condition that the other parties would not oppose the proposed satellite convention which will be mentioned below.

Compared with the Convention text, the Model Law is often

more specific and provides, together with a commentary, clarifications on the options open to states. The Model Law provides for definitions of expressions which are used in the Convention without explanation. Another important example of clarification concerns the administration of the equitable remuneration for the secondary use of phonograms. The Model Law and the commentary describe in detail the issues involved and possible ways of dealing with them.

The commentary cites five possibilities. The remuneration is paid (1) to the performers alone; (2) to the phonogram producer alone; (3) to the performers and the producers, both of whom would be represented by a single organization; (4) to the performers, with a provision requiring them to pay a share to the producer; or (5) to the producer, with a provision requiring him to pay a share to the performers. The Model Law opts for the fifth method, with the payment equally divided between the two parties. The commentary makes it clear that this seemed to be the simplest solution, but draws attention to the fact that the Convention itself leaves open both the question of the recipient and the proportion of the benefits to be paid to the parties. Moreover, the commentary also mentions a further option, drawn from Norwegian law. It involves the establishment of a national fund into which the remuneration would be paid for the benefit of performers, record producers or both. Under Norwegian law, a fund has been established to be used as a support for Norwegian performing artists and their heirs. A certain part of the fund is allotted to the producers for phonograms actually used in public performances and broadcasts. It has been suggested that should developing countries adhere to the Rome Convention and accept Article 12, the establishment of such a fund might be of particular practical advantage, since otherwise the bulk of the remuneration might have to be paid to foreign performers and producers.

The negotiations over the Model Law clearly show the interdependence of issues concerning legally defined rights and the application and exercise of these rights. During one of the preparatory meetings, complaints were raised about the mixing of juridical concepts and industrial relations. There is reason to recall a statement made in a similar situation: 'The obscure language frequently used in this field must not let us lose sight of the real facts: economic interests are at stake' (Chakroun, 1969, p. 54).

The general unease about the Rome Convention and in particular the allegations concerning the difficultues of application have caused the administering intergovernmental organizations (Unesco, WIPO and the ILO) to undertake, in conjunction with the non-governmental associations, a major study of the problems involved. Particular attention has been paid to the administration of rights under the Convention rules. A number of regional seminars have also been organized in the developing world in order to promote national legislation on neighbouring rights and adherence to the Convention.

(b) European regional agreements

With the advent of television, the national broadcasting corporations of Western Europe established close co-operation for the exchange of programmes and the organization of joint transmissions of major events (Eurovision). These activities had to face a series of new problems of a technical, programme and legal nature. Since some of the legal issues required action at intergovernmental level, they were placed before the Council of Europe.

Under the auspices of the Council of Europe, two regional agreements were concluded. The first of these, the European Agreement Concerning Programme Exchanges by Means of Television Films, dates back to 1958. A major purpose of this Agreement was to alleviate the difficulties with regard to copyright ownership in television films which confronted those countries where copyright can be vested only in individual creators and not in a legal entity. In order to solve the practical problems of negotiation and contract, the Agreement provides that a broadcasting organization which has made a television film has the right to authorize its exploitation on television in the other member countries.

The other Agreement of 1960 concerns the protection of television broadcasts. This Agreement was originally intended as a temporary arrangement pending widespread European adherence to the Rome Convention. Since a number of countries like France have not yet adhered to this Convention, the European Agreement has been given a longer lease of life than expected.

The Agreement, as modified by a Protocol of 1965, accords television broadcasters the power, within the territory of member states, to control rebroadcasts, distribution of broadcasts to the public by wire; public communication of broadcasts 'by means of any instruments for the transmission of signs, sounds, or images'; fixations and reproduction of fixations of broadcasts; rebroadcasts, wire distribution or public performances with the aid of fixations or reproductions.

Broadcasters organized in the territory of a member state or transmitting from such a territory enjoy national protection in another contracting state's territory. And as in the Rome Convention, the Agreement, as modified, provides for a term of twenty years to run from the year in which the first broadcast is made from a contracting state's territory.

Again, as in the Rome Convention, parties may, as regards their own territory, legislate exceptions to minimum protection with respect of broadcasts by wire, broadcasts for private use or for educational purposes, still photographs, and broadcasts otherwise protected under the party's domestic law. Exceptions may also be legislated for the use of excerpts of broadcasts, and ephemeral fixations by broadcasting organizations for their own broadcasts. Finally, parties may restrict the operation of the Agreement to broadcasting organizations both organized in and transmitting from their territory.

In contrast to the Rome Convention, the European Agreement thus responds to a major and real preoccupation of the broadcasters: distribution of television transmissions via cable. However, as will be discussed in a later section, the Agreement has not prevented a relatively chaotic situation from arising in Europe with regard to the cross-frontier transmission of television programmes via cable. This, together with the relatively small membership of no more than nine contracting states and the broad powers to legislate exceptions, renders it of little moment for the wider international community.

(c) The Geneva Phonogram Convention of 1971

1971 was a busy year for international copyright lawyers and the government departments responsible for intellectual property rights. The diplomatic conferences in Paris for the revision of the Berne and Universal Copyright Conventions were followed later that same year by yet another diplomatic conference in Geneva with the task of legislating against piracy of gramophone records and sound tapes.

Modern piracy is mainly technological in nature and takes many forms: in this case the illicit duplication of records and sound tapes obviously without the consent of the original producer. Since the advent of the sound cassette, such duplication has become one of the most successful forms of modern piracy. The technical procedure is simple and the market is vast. According to recent figures, the pirate market concerns some 250 million copies a year at a value of $500 million, or approximately some 15 per cent of the total market.

The pirate copies are sold much more cheaply than the original legitimate recordings. The availability of these cheaper copies constitutes a threat to the recording industry and by cutting the producers' return from record sales the piracy also deprives of royalties authors, composers and performers. The piracy strikes at the interests of producers of phonograms in all countries, including those developing countries which have their own record industries.

In principle, protection against this kind of piracy was already provided through the Rome Convention. However, the limited acceptance of the Convention and the unlikelihood of its fast growth ruled it out as a possible remedy. The urgency of the problem – or, as some have put it, the clout of the record industry – was such that a new international treaty was drafted and adopted in less than eighteen months, which is exceptional in international law practice.

Some fifty states participated in the Geneva diplomatic conference which was convened jointly by the Directors-General of Unesco and WIPO. The resulting convention, which bears the title of 'Convention for the Protection of Producers of Phonograms against Unauthorized Duplication of their Phonograms', came into force in 1973 and has been ratified or acceded to by thirty-two states as of 1 January 1979.

In order to avoid the problems that had arisen in the case of the Rome Convention, the goal of the Geneva Conference was to establish an international instrument which should be as simple as possible and open to all states, so as to receive quickly a wide acceptance. Thus, the Geneva Convention provides minimum standards, while leaving it to adhering states to flesh out, through domestic legislation or regulation, the skeletal framework.

As in other intellectual property rights conventions, definitions are essential and much time was spent on the somewhat arcane expressions adopted.

The Convention adopts the Rome Convention's definitions of 'phonogram' and 'producer of phonograms', thereby delineating phonograms as 'exclusively aural fixations', and raising questions about how far recordings made from the sound tracks of cinematographic or other audio-visual works can be protected. Clearly, the protection of such recordings is within the intended scope of the Convention, which, however, provides only for minimum standards of protection so that 'it is within the competence of each contracting state to protect recordings produced from sound tracks as phonograms under its national legislation, if it wishes to do so.' It is also left to national legislatures to determine who is entitled to the Convention's protection by virtue of being 'the person who first fixes the phonogram as such'. Ephemeral recordings may be considered to be phonograms, and broadcasters may be producers, for purposes of the Convention.

A 'duplicate' of a phonogram is defined as 'an article which contains sounds taken directly or indirectly from a phonogram and which embodies all or a substantial part of the sounds fixed in that phonogram'. This rather broad definition brings acts of successive piracy and 'substantial', as well as complete, duplication of the sounds of the original phonogram within the bounds of the Convention. It leaves to domestic legislation or courts to determine when a substantial taking constitutes an infringing duplication.

Finally, there was the question of what is to be understood by 'distribution to the public' of pirated copies. The Convention provides for minimum standards by the definition of distribution to the public as 'any act by which duplicates of a phonogram are offered, directly or indirectly, to the general public or any section thereof'. Thus adhering states are free to go further and to prohibit the broadcasting of pirated records or to legislate the conditions of permitting broadcast programmes containing such duplicates.

Against the backdrop of these minimal and flexible definitions, the remaining articles establish criteria of protection against phonogram piracy. Eligibility for protection is determined by the phonogram producer's nationality, with contracting states bound to protect producers who are nationals of the other contracting states. Such producers are protected against three specified acts: the manufacture of duplicates of their work without their consent, the importation of such duplicates and the distribution of unauthorized duplicates to the public.

By the Convention, the producers are not vested with a new individual right but adhering states are required to grant protection by the legal means of their choice. Thus, the Convention leaves it to the contracting states to choose among four legal means of applying the protection. This may be done by granting an individual right under copyright or neighbouring rights legislation, by ordinary laws on unfair competition or penal laws.

The Convention empowers domestic legislature to set the terms of protection (provided it endures for a minimum of twenty years), and to decide whether the term should run from the time of first fixation or first publication of the phonogram. Individual contracting states are thereby free to adopt the Rome Convention's starting-point as the year of first fixation of the sounds embodied on the recording.

The Convention adopts the Rome Convention's approach to formalities; that is, the publication of authorized copies with a reasonably placed notice consisting of the symbol Ⓟ accompanied by the year of first publication and the names of the proprietor.

The Convention also deals with the difficult problem of limitations, exceptions and compulsory licences which arises in all cases where states have not chosen to rely exclusively on regulations governing unfair competition.

In the first instance, the Convention allows states to subject the protection granted to phonogram producers to the same kinds of limitations as those applied to authors of literary and artistic works. In order to avoid some of the difficulties which had arisen in connection with the Rome Convention, no protection is afforded against secondary uses of phonograms; i.e. public performance or broadcasting. Moreover, no compulsory licence is permitted, apart from one exception intended especially for developing countries. A compulsory licence may be introduced if three conditions are met: the duplication must be only for teaching or scientific research, exportation must be prohibited and the original producer must be 'equitably' compensated. Thus this provision permits limited compulsory licences, especially for developing countries who would duplicate the work for teaching purposes.

With regard to the relations of the new Convention with other existing agreements, the Convention specifies that it shall be supplemental to, and in no way limitative of, or prejudicial to, the protection 'otherwise secured to authors, to performers, to producers of phonograms or to broadcasting organisations under any domestic law or international agreement'. States that are parties to both the Rome and Geneva Conventions will be bound by the obligations of both Conventions, and, if provisions overlap, states will apply whichever provision affords the greater protection.

However, it is left to the domestic law of contracting states to determine the rights of performers whose performances are fixed on protected phonograms. Thus, states are free to regulate performers' rights, but they are under no obligation to do so. This provision is similar to others designed to provide only minimum protection and make possible a wider adherence than in the case of the Rome Convention.

Finally, the Convention has no retroactive effect, and need not be applied to phonograms fixed before the Convention came into force with respect to that state.

At the Geneva Conference long discussions were devoted to the administrative provisions. It was finally agreed that there was a need for secretarial functions which should be entrusted to a single organization and it was decided that this organization would be WIPO, which had been set up by the Stockholm Conference of 1967.

The effectiveness of the Geneva Convention will evidently depend on ratification not only by those countries which are major producers but also by countries where piracy is a particularly well established practice. This Convention might manage to restrict one kind of piracy, but both technology and its legitimate and unauthorized uses have already gone beyond the piracy of mere gramophone records or sound cassettes. During the last few years, a flourishing market in illicit copies of feature films and television programmes has arisen. So, there is more work ahead . . .

(d) The Brussels Satellite Convention

In many respects the Geneva Phonogram Convention represents a relatively straightforward response to a specific problem in a limited area of intellectual property protection, a problem which, moreover, was amenable to solution by the application of traditional legal concepts in this field. Other new technologies create problems which are more difficult. Certain issues of protection of rights cannot be dealt with in isolation but only in relation to other areas of law, and to the mandates of other organizations than those specifically concerned with intellectual property rights.

One new technology which created unrest in the intellectual property field was that of communications satellites. In the early discussions of the technology and its possibilities and constraints, the implications of different patterns of use were not well understood by the non-technologists. There was great confusion over the applicability of existing national and international regulations and the possible need for new kinds of protection in relation to the transmission of television programmes and materials. At the same time, the issues of 'rights' and 'protection' could not be isolated from the development of general international law applicable to satellite communication; in the context of space and telecommunications law, work was undertaken by the United Nations and the International Telecommunication Union (ITU). Concurrently, the battles about the Rome Convention and the draft Model Law continued.

All these issues came to a head over a question that in itself might be seen as being of relatively minor importance. With the increased use of satellites for the transmission of television programmes, particularly from one continent to another, there were cases of programmes having been 'poached', in the sense that the satellite signal was picked up by earth stations and then broadcast, without any authorization or contractual arrangements, to audiences for whom the signal was not intended. In itself, this kind of poaching might have been regarded as no more than an irritating irregularity had it not also created a real difficulty for the broadcasters. In their contracts not only with owners of intellectual property rights but also with sports promoters and other contractual partners, the area for which the broadcasts were intended had to be specified as a basis for the negotiated price. If a programme designed, financed and produced for a particular area could be intercepted and distributed in other areas not covered by the contracts concluded by the originating organization with the parties concerned, there could be no possibility of guaranteeing the distribution as originally negotiated and agreed.

When discussion of this issue began in the early 1970s, opinions differed even as to whether this problem should be dealt with as an intellectual property right at all or should be regulated by telecommunications law. One of the solutions envisaged was thus an amendment of certain provisions in the International Telecommunication Convention and the Radio Regulations annexed to it. The other solutions discussed were a revision of the Rome Convention, the elaboration of a new multilateral treaty, or some other method such as reliance on existing international agreements.

Reliance on the ITU Convention and the Radio Regulations would have had the advantage of wide acceptance, since with very few exceptions all countries of the world adhere to the ITU instruments. However, it was felt that these instruments do not include satisfactory sanctions procedures. Moreover, the ITU was hesitant since at that stage in the discussion it seemed that the Union and the national telecommunication administrations might have to concern themselves with matters of content which would have constituted a major departure from the existing scope of telecommunications regulation.

To nations adhering to the Rome Convention, that Convention appeared to be the logical choice for protecting broadcast material transmitted through communications satellites. It was argued that if the Convention were more widely ratified, unauthorized uses of satellite signals would be effectively controlled. The major problem with this argument was that the lack of widespread international support for the Rome Convention made universal treatment impossible. In addition, some believed that the Rome Convention would not cover broadcast material sent through a satellite, because of the technical definition of the term 'broadcast' given by the Convention.

As the preparatory work advanced, a consensus emerged in favour of the third option: a new treaty to prevent retransmission of satellite signals by unintended distributors. However, it proved unusually difficult to find agreement on the content and wording of such a treaty.

One of the main difficulties concerned the issue of a balance between the rights of broadcasting organizations and those of contributors to programmes; i.e. authors, performers and other holders of rights. There was a feeling in favour of a simple, globally acceptable instrument that would give adhering countries wide discretion as to the legal means for implementing it. However, many countries, particularly those adhering to the Rome Convention, stated that they could accept an independent treaty only if it safeguarded not only the broadcasters but also the interests of authors, performers and producers of phonograms and did not prejudice the future of the Rome Convention. Provisions to this effect were, as could be expected, vehemently opposed by the broadcasting organizations, who feared the adoption of new rights or an extension of existing rights.

When finally the preparatory work had proceeded far enough for a diplomatic conference to be called in Brussels in 1974, one of the major controversial issues was the relationship between the proposed new convention and the Rome Convention. This issue, in turn, was related to the attitude of the broadcasters to the Rome Convention. In fact, statements were made to the effect that unless the broadcasters manifested a substantial change in approach to the Rome Convention, some governments would be unlikely to consider signing or adhering to the new treaty.

The solution which was ultimately agreed was the result of a third meeting of governmental experts which had been convened in 1973 in Nairobi. The proposals put forward by the Moroccan delegation and adopted at Nairobi have been described as a breakthrough and a turning-point (Unesco/WIPO, 1974, para. 12). They implied a fundamental change in the philosophy and legal framework of the draft Convention. Previous agreements in the area of intellectual property generally concerned the recognition and protection of certain exclusive rights vested in the private individual (or in certain cases producers of works). Thus international agreements in this field fall in the category of international private law. The Nairobi draft proposed to shift the Convention from the field of international private law to international public law. This was done by eliminating any mention of private rights and leaving the states free to decide the most appropriate means of suppressing piracy of satellite signals in their territory. Instead of making states enforce individual property rights, this approach requires them to take all appropriate measures against distribution on their territory of satellite signals by distributors for whom these signals were not intended. Since the Convention would therefore not confer any new rights on the broadcasters, there was no longer any corresponding need to create additional new rights to safeguard the interests of programme-contributors.

This solution was adopted. In order to avoid the problem of

private rights in programme content, the Convention protects 'programme-carrying signals' rather than the programme content *per se*. Contracting states are left free to implement the basic requirement of the Convention as they see fit. 'While the obligation of the Convention might well be undertaken within the legal framework of intellectual property laws, granting protection to signals under theories of copyright or neighbouring rights, a contracting state could just as rightly adopt administrative measures, penal sanctions, or telecommunications law or regulation on the subject' (Unesco/WIPO, 1974, para. 74).

Despite the general requirement that adhering nations prohibit the piracy of satellite signals, several provisions substantially limit the scope of the obligation. The duration of protection is unspecified and rebroadcasting activities are generally outside the scope of the Convention. Adhering nations are permitted to recognize fair use exceptions, such as reports of current events or quotations for information purposes, and the developing countries are allowed to distribute programme-carrying signals for the purpose of teaching. Finally, states are permitted to make a reservation excluding cable operations from the provisions of the Convention which recently entered into force.

3 International organization

The international organizational structure which has been established in the field of intellectual property presents a number of distinct and also unusual features. Generally, modern international organizations follow certain common patterns. In summary, they are based on a charter or constitution and provide for an assembly of all adhering states, and in most cases also for an executive body and an international secretariat which is headed by the chief executive of the organization (Secretary-General or Director-General). International agreements concluded under the auspices of these organizations do not generally provide for the establishment of special new organizational structures; if there is a need for administrative functions, they are entrusted to the most immediately concerned existing organization.

The organizational structure is very different in the area of intellectual property. When the two first Conventions in this field were concluded – i.e. the Paris Convention for the Protection of Industrial Property of 1883 and the Berne Convention of 1886 – the adhering countries constituted themselves into two unions, each with an international bureau or secretariat. These were united in 1893 and functioned under various names; the last was the United International Bureaux for the Protection of Intellectual Property, known as BIRPI (the French acronym of the name).

With time, there was an increasing need to modernize this machinery for the administration of the Paris and Berne Unions and of other new treaties regulating various aspects of industrial property. An administrative and structural reform was adopted by the Stockholm Conference in 1967.

The result is the present two-tier structure: the various intellectual property unions and the new World Intellectual Property Organization (WIPO).

For each Union there is an Assembly of member states which meets every three years. The two principal Unions (Paris and Berne) each elects an Executive Committee which meets annually. The Assemblies act as the principal organ for their Unions. The Executive Committees decide on the programmes and the annual budgets and provide continuity between the sessions of the Paris and Berne Assemblies.

The other tier is represented by WIPO, established by a special Convention which came into force in 1974. WIPO then succeeded BIRPI and was admitted as a specialized agency of the United Nations. BIRPI legally continues to exist for the purpose of those countries which are party to the Conventions but have not yet become members of WIPO. For all practical purposes, however, BIRPI is indistinguishable from WIPO.

WIPO's structure consists of three organs: the General Assembly which meets every three years; the Conference in which WIPO members who are not yet members of at least one of the Unions may also participate; and a co-ordinating committee comprising those states that are members of the Paris and/or Berne Union Executive Committees.

The objectives of WIPO are to promote the protection of intellectual property throughout the world and to ensure administrative co-operation and co-ordination among the intellectual property unions. When WIPO became a specialized agency of the United Nations, it acquired new responsibilities, which go beyond the traditionally defined objectives. Thus WIPO has the duty to take appropriate action to promote creative intellectual activity and to facilitate the transfer of technology related to industrial property to the developing countries.

In contrast, the overall administration of the UCC is provided by Unesco, which provides the Secretariat of the Intergovernmental Copyright Committee, which is the governing body of the UCC.

The main duties of the Intergovernmental Committee are: (1) to study the problems concerning the application and operation of the UCC, (2) to study any other problems concerning the international protection of copyright, and (3) to prepare for periodic revisions of this Convention. These revisions are to take place at inter-governmental conferences. The Intergovernmental Committee consists of the representatives of eighteen contracting states to be selected with due consideration for fair geographical representation. The Committee must 'inform the Contracting States as to its activities'. In view of the fact that Unesco provides the Secretariat of the Intergovernmental Committee, the Committee's communications reach the governments of the contracting states through Unesco's Director-General, who is also permitted to attend meetings of the Committee in an advisory capacity.

The administrative structure set up by the Rome Convention is similar to that of the UCC: an Intergovernmental Committee which has the duty to study questions concerning the application and operation of the Convention and to collect proposals and prepare documentation for possible revision. The Secretariat of the Committee is held jointly by officials of the ILO, Unesco and WIPO. The secretarial functions of the Geneva Phonogram Convention are entrusted to WIPO, but otherwise no specific administrative structure is foreseen. The Brussels Satellite Convention has no provisions concerning administration; since it was concluded under the auspices of Unesco and WIPO, either or both of these organizations will be responsible for the administrative functions once it comes into force.

This complicated structure, which involves governments differently according to their adherence to the various conventions, demands close co-ordination and co-operation among the inter-governmental organizations concerned. This is particularly true about WIPO and Unesco being the guardians of a copyright convention each, and jointly involved in the major neighbouring rights conventions, with the addition of the ILO in the case of the Rome Convention.

As could be expected, this co-operation is not without its problems in view of the interlocking and partly overlapping mandates and the partly common, partly different, constituencies. The approach of each of the three organizations also differs, since each deals with copyright issues in a different context. For WIPO this context is the entire field of intellectual property, including both industrial property and copyright. For Unesco, the wider context includes education, culture, science and communications. The ILO in turn places the issues of performers' rights in the context of industrial relations and labour law.

The overall picture is even more complicated, since there are other intergovernmental organizations directly concerned with intellectual property. In the UN context, issues of copyright in relation to satellite broadcasting have been raised in the Committee on the Peaceful Uses of Outer Space, which wisely enough has chosen to avoid any discussion of substance. In connection with the issues concerning the transfer of science and technology from industrialized to developing countries, the main focus has so far been on patents and other forms of industrial property, but copyright problems arise with regard to the transfer of scientific and technical information which is of concern to several UN agencies (e.g. UNCTAD).

The organizational complexity is most pronounced in Western Europe. Most of the countries in this area have adhered to international copyright and neighbouring rights conventions, administered by WIPO, Unesco and the ILO. The regional European agreements concerning television fall under the Council of Europe. Moreover, the European Economic Community (EEC) has through both the Commission and the Court of Justice of the European Communities had occasion to deal with copyright issues in relation to cable television and the status of collecting societies. Interestingly enough, the EEC seems to be moving deeper into this field which would not, at first glance, appear to be included in its mandate. However, there are questions concerning the application of the Treaty of Rome with regard to the possible harmonization of copyright legislation among the member states, the working conditions of performing artists and the flow of cultural goods between member states (see Commission of the European

Communities (1978), also the report on the Conference on the EEC and the Arts (ICA, 1979)).

Finally, organizations concerned with computerized data systems, informatics and transnational data flows have to deal with copyright problems as part of policies and regulation in this field. These organizations include the OECD (Organization for Economic Co-operation and Development) and the Intergovernmental Bureau of Informatics (IBI).

One peculiar feature of international co-operation and structure in the copyright field is the important role played by nongovernmental organizations. Generally in the context of the UN and its agencies, governments are all-important, and nongovernmental entities play a minor role and are associated with on-going work often under strictly circumscribed conditions. The practice is altogether·different where copyright is concerned, particularly in the context of WIPO. This is clearly revealed by a look at who is represented at what meetings. It seems typical that at a recent meeting of the subcommittee on cable television established by the Intergovernmental Committee of the Rome Convention, there were five national delegations making up the Committee itself but twelve nongovernmental organizations. At a similar meeting on video-cassettes, the ratio was about the same: seven governmental representatives and twelve nongovernmental organizations.

These nongovernmental organizations are mostly federations or associations of national organizations representing various groupings of authors, performers, publishers and other producers of works. To a large extent they reflect national organization structures involved in copyright. Some of these private international organizations have been in existence for about a century, such as the International Literary and Artistic Association created in 1878; others represent such recent areas of activity as broadcasting, cable television or videograms.

Since these organizations reflect the national interest groupings, they represent a series of complementary, overlapping and opposing interests. To a large extent, work at the international level consists of efforts to reach agreement not only among governments but also among the contending interest groups. Often the governments that make up the intergovernmental organizations appear reluctant to decide on current issues unless the various concerned nongovernmental organizations have agreed to, or at least do not oppose, a given course of action.

The prospects for the future imply an increase in complexity and thus an increase in the need for co-ordination. It is a fair assumption that the greater the attention which the international community pays to issues of communication and information, the greater will be the number of organizations with a stake in copyright issues.

Chapter IV · **Representative national copyright systems**

Moving from the international to the national level, this chapter summarizes a selected number of national copyright systems. The intention is not to give a detailed, technical description but rather to capture salient and distinctive features in each case. The selection has been done so as to include major examples of different copyright systems: the Anglo-American system (UK, USA), the European continental (France, West Germany), the Nordic (Sweden); the socialist (USSR), developing countries (Tunisia, India) and finally two contrasting examples from Asia (Japan, China).

1 United Kingdom

The concept of copyright as developed in the United Kingdom was essentially a publisher's right. In 1694 the Act granting the Stationers' Company, that is the publishers, a monopoly in the right to copy printed material expired, and there followed a statutory void. Anyone could print and publish books and not only new books but also those already published by others. It was not the authors but the stationers – i.e. the publishers – who requested Parliament for protection of their 'copies' of books. They obtained this protection under the Copyright Statute of Queen Anne in 1709. This Act vested the right to copy in the author or the purchaser (owner) of such copies for a period of fourteen years. Since the publishers had lost the monopoly in publishing and the Act provided protection only for a limited period, it was in their interest to establish that authors had a common law right in their works. Thus the United Kingdom traditionally had a dual system of copyright: statutory copyright for published works and common law copyright for unpublished material. This tradition was abrogated by the 1956 Copyright Act which abolished common law copyright so that the scope of copyright protection in the United Kingdom is determined solely by statute.

The 1956 Copyright Act is now up for review, following the report of the Committee to Consider the Law on Copyright and Designs (named after its chairman, Justice Whitford). The Whitford Committee in an interesting description of the 1956 Act has also indicated one major reason for the desirability of a revision: 'The Act of 1956 is a remarkable feat of draftsmanship but, even if it is a draftsman's dream, it has proved a nightmare to those who have to understand it whether as laymen for their own purposes or as lawyers seeking to guide their clients' (para. 16).

The subject matter of copyright in the 1956 Act is expansive. Copyright is dealt with in three different categories: (1) literary, dramatic and musical works, to which are often assimilated (2) artistic works, and in a special section (3) sound recordings, cinematograph films and broadcasts. In comparison with the law of other countries, the material which is protected under the British Act covers a broad range of cultural products. In all categories of works, unpublished as well as published material is covered by the statute.

However, the Whitford Committee found that 'the present system of definition has been said to be inexplicable even to the extent to which it is comprehensible' (para. 32). The Committee therefore has recommended that in any new Copyright Act there should be one comprehensive definition section, a system found or proposed in legislation in many other countries.

In order to obtain the right to claim copyright, an author merely needs to create a copyrightable work. There are no formalities such as notice, or deposit. Although registration is not required by law, it can help to establish evidence in case of dispute. For published works, a publisher is required to deposit free copies with certain national libraries, although noncompliance does not affect the copyright or the ability to enforce rights established by the Copyright Act.

The United Kingdom participates in the Berne Union, which obliges its member nations to recognize the 'moral rights' of an author, but the concept of a 'moral right' has never existed in British law. Instead, in the United Kingdom, the integrity and paternity of an author's work are protected under a variety of alternative remedies including legislation covering contracts, breaches of trust, defamation and passing off. When the Berne Convention was amended in 1928 to require its member nations to recognize the moral rights of authors, the British delegation was assured that remedies available in the United Kingdom in equity and at common law (law of defamation) were sufficient to meet the new obligation. Since that time, however, copyright authorities have occasionally criticized the British copyright law for not specifically enumerating the moral rights of an author. The Whitford Committee, in recommending that the UK should ratify the Paris text of the Berne Convention, stated that this would involve the adoption of special provisions for moral rights under copyright law.

The specific form of legislation proposed by the Committee is based on the Netherlands Copyright Act. According to the proposed drafting, the moral rights of the author would focus on a right of paternity while keeping the possibility of permitting reasonable modifications to be made to the work.

It has been pointed out, though, that the Committee has not considered the crucial difference which exists between the concept of the author in Anglo-American legal practice and that in continental Europe on which the Berne Convention is based (Porter, 1978). This point has interesting implications. The continental European concept which has been taken over by the Berne Convention is based on the theory of the author's rights: the relationship between an author and his work is thus not only economic but also personal or moral. It follows that the author can be only an individual, a physical person. The distinction has been clearly expressed in the French law of 1957: the author of an intellectual work shall, by the mere fact of its creation, enjoy an incorporeal property right in the work, effective against all persons. This right includes attributes of an intellectual or moral nature as well as those of an economic nature. Thus the moral rights are inalienable, while the economic rights may be transferred. The position in Anglo-American law is quite different. Not only does the theory of copyright as opposed to the theory of the author's right locate the concept of copyright in the completed work in a tangible form. By locating copyright in the work, it follows that the 'author' can be not only a physical person but also a legal entity. The introduction of the concept of moral rights in the UK system would imply giving legal entities a moral right which, by definition, can be assigned only to a person. An analysis of these issues arrives at the following conclusions, which probably will surprise many fighting in good faith for the extension of authors' rights:

> Copyright defines the border between classical market economies which regulate the flow of cultural goods and the political economy which is concerned with the informational and cultural needs of society. By concentrating exclusively on protecting authors' rights and ignoring the cultural progress of society, the United Kingdom and the whole of the European Community are in danger of stunting cultural growth . . . What is needed is an overall policy which can integrate both commercial and cultural needs (Porter, 1978, p. 108).

Rights secured under the 1956 Copyright Act are freely transferable, either by assignment, partial assignment or by licence. In making a partial assignment the author may limit his transfer as to time, locality and/or means of reproduction. In addition, copyright in works created by commission is vested in the employer or the commissioner. This provision proved to be a contentious issue in the work of the Committee. As could be expected, representatives of the authors and other copyright-holders pleaded for the repeal of these provisions, leaving a simple rule that copyright is vested initially in the author of a work. Other submissions to the Committee supported the view that employers whose employees create works in the normal course of their employment and those who commission an author for the purpose of creating a work normally expect to own the copyright in works which they have caused to be made. The Committee did not reach unanimity on this difficult issue. In summary, the recommendation is for a first principle of copyright-ownership vested in the author, subject only to an agreement to the contrary or specific statutory exceptions. At the same time, there should be a general provision that rights in a work produced by an employee in the course of his employment should be vested in the employer, subject to certain rules in favour of the author. In the case of commissioned works, the majority of the Committee recommends that the copyright should belong to the author unless there is an agreement to the contrary, subject to certain rules – this time in favour of the commissioner. Among the more radical proposals for solving this issue is one that tries to deal with the possible abuses of the employer's copyright through non-publication or restriction of availability of a published work: it is proposed that five years after publication the copyright should automatically revert to its author (see Porter, 1974).

In the United Kingdom, essentially two ways are established for enforcing the Copyright Act. First, there are the so-called 'summary remedies' which establish criminal sanctions against the knowing infringement of copyright. Second, there are the civil remedies available to the copyright-owner, namely injunction and damages. The measure of damages in the United Kingdom is frequently large, since the copyright-owner not only receives damages for the depreciation of his copyright but may additionally receive special damages for wilful infringement and damages for conversion. As an alternative to damages, a copyright-owner may seek an account of profits which is an equitable remedy incidental to the right to an injunction.

In the United Kingdom only one type of use is subject to compulsory licensing – the mechanical reproduction of previously recorded musical compositions. In order to obtain a licence, a manufacturer must intend to sell the record by retail, must notify the owner of the copyright of his intention to record, and must pay the owner the prescribed royalty. The normal standard royalty is $6\frac{1}{4}$ per cent of the retail price.

The UK copyright legislation, like the law of other countries, has always accepted that certain dealings in protected works in the public interest do not infringe copyright, under the theory of 'fair dealing' or 'fair use'.

Under the 1956 Act, fair use is dealt with under a number of different headings related to the various categories of protected works. In the case of literary, dramatic and musical works, fair dealing is permitted for the purpose of research and private study, criticism and review, the reporting of current events in certain specified media (newspapers, magazines and periodicals; broadcasting, cinematograph films). Special provisions cover fair dealing in the case of artistic works including such uses as the reproduction of sculptures and other works situated 'in a public place or in premises open to the public'. There are no general fair dealing exceptions covering other protected works, but a number of specific exceptions cover public performances of sound recordings and broadcasts in certain circumstances. Other provisions deal with exceptions in respect of libraries, education and diffusion by wire.

The Whitford Committee, in order to clarify the law, proposed an exception provision, covering all classes of works and subject matter, in favour of 'fair dealing' which does not conflict with normal exploitation of the work and does not unreasonably prejudice the copyright-owner's legitimate interests. In addition to these general exceptions, a number of specific exceptions in the 1956 Act should be retained.

On the matter of performance, the law in the United Kingdom is substantially different from those of many industrialized and developing countries. In addition to giving authors performing rights in literary material, musical compositions, films and dramas, the United Kingdom establishes copyright in the recording and performance of sound recordings as well as separate broadcasting rights and diffusion rights. Under the 1956 Act the broadcasting of literary material, music, dramas, artistic works, films and sound recordings gives rise to a royalty. Furthermore, the distribution of signals through a diffusion system gives rise to an additional royalty where the works reproduced are literary, dramatic, musical, artistic or cinematographic. No royalties are created, however, for the owners of sound recordings which are distributed through a diffusion system.

Only the recording of musical compositions is subject to compulsory licensing, but the United Kingdom exercises considerable control over licensing systems in general through its Performing Right Tribunal. Since the 1956 Act broadly extended performing, broadcasting and diffusion rights in much of the intellectual property in the United Kingdom, a danger was created of authors establishing performing right societies which would have a monopolistic control over the exploitation of such property. The British answer to this problem was the creation of the Performing Right Tribunal, which has regulatory authority over 'licensing bodies' of copyrighted works. Essentially the Tribunal serves two functions. First, it either confirms or varies licensing schemes established by the regulated organizations. Second, it deals with applications from aggrieved parties unable to obtain a licence from an organization regulated by the Tribunal.

The functioning of the Performing Right Tribunal is a unique feature of the British approach, which, in practice, appears to achieve many of the advantages of compulsory licensing while avoiding some of the disadvantages. The major advantage of compulsory licensing is that it ensures public access to valuable intellectual property. The main argument against it is that it denies an author control over the manner in which his creations are exploited. Under the British approach, the copyright-owner of material containing performing, broadcasting and diffusion rights has complete discretion over the manner in which his property is exploited until he chooses to affiliate himself with a performing right society. Once he has accepted the commercial convenience of such an association, the licensing schemes which that organization advances come under the scrutiny of the Performing Right Tribunal.

Under the present Act, the jurisdiction of the Tribunal is limited to the exercise by licensing bodies of public performance, broadcasting and diffusion rights. A number of the Whitford Committee's proposals involved new functions for the Tribunal, including arbitration of rates and other terms with regard to the proposed licensing to deal with reprography and educational recording, review of royalty rates for the statutory recording licence, and the exercise of recording rights.

Unlike performers in many countries, those in the United Kingdom have been protected against unauthorized exploitation of their performances for many years. The first statute protecting performers was the Dramatic and Musical Performers' Protection Act of 1925 which was repealed and re-enacted in 1958.

The 1958 Act has been several times modified and supplemented by further legislation, *inter alia* to implement the Rome Convention. The nature of the protection afforded to performers is to make certain unauthorized acts connected with performances criminal offences. A summary criminal remedy is thus provided unauthorized recording, filming, broadcasting or wire diffusion of a work. The Whitford Committee recommended a number of specific changes in the existing statutes, and also a general consolidating Act covering all the current provisions for the protection of performers.

Other recommendations of the Committee concern reprography, audio- and video-recording, performing and performers' rights, diffusion by wire, computers, ownership of copyright, term of protection, exceptions to copyright and fair dealing, remedies and related matters, and extensions of the jurisdiction of the Performing Right Tribunal. The recommendations of the Committee were intended to serve a number of purposes: to revise the structure of the Copyright Act of 1956 'in order that the law may be placed on a plain and uniform basis', to make it possible for the UK to ratify the Paris text of the Berne Convention, to accede to the Brussels Satellite Convention and to permit the cancellation of certain reservations with regard to several international agreements and, in general, to update a number of the current provisions.

2 United States

Until 1976 the United States had one of the oldest copyright laws in existence. Now the country has one of the most up-to-date laws: in October 1976 President Ford signed the new copyright Act which as of 1 January 1978 completely abrogated the old Act of 1909. The 1909 Act still applies to copyrights subsisting prior to 1 January 1978.

The campaign for a new law lasted for about twenty years. During this period every aspect of US copyright law and practice had been under debate with the forceful participation of the many powerful contending interests. As stated by the Register of Copyrights, Barbara Ringer:

> Except for the most prescriptive and technical of its provisions, practically everything in the bill is the product of at least one compromise, and many provisions have evolved from a long series of compromises reflecting constantly changing technology, commercial and financial interests, political and social conditions, judicial and administrative developments and – not least by any means – individual personalities. The bill as a whole bespeaks concern for literally hundreds of contending and overlapping special interests from every conceivable segment of our pluralistic society. It was not enough to reach compromise on a particular point; all of the compromises had to be kept in an equilibrium so that one agreement did not tip another over (Copyright Office, 1977, pp. 1, 2).

The new law makes sweeping changes in the old legislation in order to establish a firm foundation on which modern copyright can rest. It recognizes the broad rights to which creators are entitled while at the same time trying to tailor those rights to fit the technological environment prevailing in industrialized societies. The full implications will emerge only in the light of the inevitable litigation which characterizes the application of copyright in the United States. In one interesting comment on the American approach to the legislative expression of copyright, a comparison is made with the recommendations of the English Whitford Committee. The Whitford Committee proposed that a new UK copyright law should be framed on a plain and uniform basis, with a comprehensive definition section and using words of description which relate closely to the meaning those words have in common use.

> The intellectual property principle is, of course, a more sophisticated concept than the idea of ownership of physical property: and copyright legislation is bound to be complicated to a certain extent; but like all legislation, it should as far as possible be reasonably comprehensible to the average layman. To a reader who is not an American it does seem that parts of the new US copyright law may not be reasonably comprehensible even to an average lawyer (de Freitas, 1977, p. 58).

Copyright protection in the United States is written into the Constitution, which empowers Congress to grant authors exclusive rights in their writings. However, the system has been dual in the sense that Federal statutory protection was extended to published material while common law protection under State law existed for unpublished works. To a large degree the 1909 Act had departed from this tradition by making it possible to secure Federal protection for many types of unpublished material. One of the most significant changes in the American approach to copyright brought about by the new Act is the elimination of this dual system in favour of a unified Federal system. The 1978 Act completes the Federal dominance by pre-empting State common law copyright in works falling within the subject matter of the Federal statute, whether published or unpublished.

The subject matter of Federal copyright protection according to the 1909 Act was established by a provision listing broad categories of works. A strict adherence to these broad classes was not required, causing such anomalies as treating computer programmes as books, choreographic works as dramas, dolls and fabric designs as works of art and video-tapes as motion pictures.

In general, the subject matter of copyright under the new law is intended to encompass all 'original works of authorship fixed in any tangible medium of expression'. This includes seven broad categories of material: (1) literary works, (2) musical works, including any accompanying words, (3) dramatic works, including any accompanying music, (4) pantomimes and choreographic works, (5) pictorial, graphic and sculptural works, (6) motion pictures and other audio-visual works, and (7) sound recordings. The major forms of expression receiving Federal statutory protection for the first time are unpublished literary and sound recording materials, and even computer-readable data bases and other works fixed on electromagnetic tape, although they are not 'eye-readable'.

Excluded from copyright protection are ideas, systems, methods, processes or principles, no matter how unique the concept. Other areas denied copyright protection under the new law include standard works which include information that is common property, such as calendars, height and weight charts, devices and forms such as those used for measuring or printed material designed to record rather than convey information, works where the creative authorship generally is too slight to be worthy of protection (such as names, titles and slogans) and works of the US government.

Under the former copyright law, there were many ambiguities regarding the exclusive rights of the copyright-owner. The new law attempts to clarify this matter through a general provision establishing the broad, exclusive rights of copyright proprietors, followed by special provisions setting forth various limitations, qualifications and exemptions. Under the new law, the five fundamental rights of the copyright-owner are reproduction, adaptation (including translation), distribution, performance and display. Limiting these rights are twelve specific provisions dealing with a great variety of issues. Some of these provisions delineate specific rules regarding certain kinds of works such as sound recordings, artistic works and computer works. Others primarily involve certain kinds of uses such as fair use, library use, broadcaster use of ephemeral recordings and certain public performances and displays. Finally, each of the four compulsory licensing systems limits the exclusive rights of copyright-owners through the establishment of an elaborate licensing mechanism.

One of the most important and well-established limitations on the exclusive rights of copyright-owners is the fair use provision (Sec. 107). Under this provision it is provided that the fair use of a copyrighted work for purposes such as criticism, comment, news reporting, teaching (including multiple copies for classroom use), scholarship or research is not an infringement. Four factors are to be considered to determine the applicability of fair use. They are:

(1) the purpose and character of the use, including whether such use is of a commercial nature or is for nonprofit, educational purposes;

(2) the nature of the copyrighted work;

(3) the amount and substantiality of the portion used in relation to the copyrighted work as a whole;

(4) the effect of the use upon the potential market for, or value of, the copyrighted work.

The section dealing with library uses of copyrighted works is one of the first efforts to define in statute the scope of permissible library photocopying. In general, the provision attempts to exempt isolated and unrelated reproductions of a single copy or phonorecord on separate occasions. Excluded from the exemption, however, is concerted reproduction of multiple copies or phonorecords and systematic reproduction of articles or other contributions to periodicals or collections. Interlibrary loan arrangements are exempt from liability so long as the aggregate copies reproduced do not serve as a substitute for a subscription or purchase of the work. Guidance as to the extent libraries can seek copies through interlibrary arrangements is given by the National Commission on New Technological Uses of Copyrighted Works (CONTU).

Of all the rights generally extended to authors, probably that which is the most complicated and involved is the performance right. Under the 1909 Act, nonprofit performances of non-dramatic literary materials, lectures and musical compositions were generally exempt from copyright liability. In drafting the new law, the requirement that such performances be 'for profit' was considered too broad in light of the growth of the public sector of the economy, and accordingly it was eliminated. In order to ensure that undue hardships would not be imposed, certain educational and religious performances of copyrighted materials are exempt from liability. Included among the exempted uses are performances and displays pursuant to face-to-face teaching activities, limited instructional broadcasting of non-dramatic literary or musical works for classroom use, religious performances in certain instances, and non-commercial, non-broadcast performances of non-dramatic literary or musical works.

One issue which was not completely resolved by the new Act was the advisability of establishing a performance right for sound recordings. While the revision Bill was pending before Congress, some sentiment was expressed in favour of recognizing such a performance right in the new law. Its inclusion in the revision Bill, however, might have jeopardized the passage of the entire law, and as a result consideration of the proposal was deferred. The new Act did authorize a comprehensive study on the issue to be conducted by the Register of Copyrights. On 3 January 1978, this study, along with proposed draft legislation, was submitted to Congress, generally recommending the recognition of a performance right under a compulsory licensing system for the benefit of copyright-owners of sound recordings and performers. Legislative proposals advancing such a right are now before Congress. If enacted, the performance right in sound recordings would affect businesses which use sound recordings in their operations, such as broadcasters, juke-box operators and entertainment clubs.

In order to give broadcasters the flexibility necessary to transmit works that they are entitled to carry, the new law establishes a limited exemption for so-called 'ephemeral recordings'. Essentially, this provision allows the limited reproduction without liability of copies of phonorecords of a copyrighted work solely for transmitting purposes. Interestingly enough, the rules for commercial broadcasting and educational broadcasting are different: the commercial broadcaster may reproduce one copy or phonorecord of a copyrighted work provided it is destroyed within six months; an educational broadcaster, on the other hand, is permitted to make up to thirty copies of phonorecords so long as the copies or phonorecords are not retained for more than seven years after the initial transmission.

Under the 1909 Act the moral rights of an author generally protecting the integrity of a work and proper designation of credit were not recognized. The copyright revision Bill maintains American policy on this issue. However, rights protected in countries under the doctrine of moral rights are frequently protected in the United States under alternative legal theories, particularly contract law. Despite the Federal pre-emption of State common law copyright, protection under alternative legal doctrines should be unaffected, since the theory of protection is not based on copyright.

One trend which is clear under the new law is an increased reliance on compulsory licensing to settle differences between copyright-owners and certain user groups. The new copyright law retains the compulsory licensing system established under the 1909 Act for the mechanical reproduction of musical compositions, although in substantially altered form. Three additional uses, moreover, are made the subject of compulsory licensing schemes by the new law: cable television uses of certain broadcast material, juke-box performances of musical compositions and performances of published non-dramatic musical works and published pictorial, graphic and sculptural works by public broadcasters.

The extension of compulsory licensing by the new Act forced the creation of an entirely new agency of the government – the Copyright Royalty Tribunal. Administratively supported by the Library of Congress, the Tribunal consists of five commissioners appointed by the President and confirmed by the Senate. The Tribunal is empowered, according to certain statutory criteria, to adjust the rate of royalty payment for cable uses, juke-box performances and mechanical reproduction of musical compositions. In addition, the Tribunal is to determine reasonable terms and rates of royalty payment applicable to public broadcasters. Finally, disputes over the distribution of royalties collected from the cable television industry and juke-box operators are to be adjudicated by the Tribunal.

The provisions establishing the operational mechanics of the four compulsory licensing systems are among the most complex of the entire law. Each system has its own unique character and can be understood only through an overview of the industries they were tailored to foster.

In 1909 the United States had established the world's first

compulsory licensing system through a compromise provision dealing with the mechanical reproduction of musical compositions. In essence, the 1909 Act permitted a recording company to use a musical composition once that composition was embodied in a first recording.

Despite the availability of compulsory licensing to recording companies, in practice commercial relations between copyright proprietors of musical compositions and recording companies were largely governed by voluntary licensing arrangements between the parties.

In the early 1960s when the movement for the revision of the 1909 Act was just beginning, the Copyright Office proposed abolishing this compulsory licensing system. The proposal met with strong opposition from the recording companies. While voluntary licensing clearly predominated in the industry, the companies again asserted that elimination of the availability of the compulsory licence would foster monopolies. The strength of this opposition quickly killed the proposal and a compulsory licensing provision emerged which, in broad conceptual terms, was similar to the previous requirement.

The so-called 'trigger' of the compulsory licensing provision under the new law is the first authorized distribution in the United States of a musical composition in phonorecord form. Once this first distribution takes place, any person is entitled to a compulsory licence to make new phonorecords of the composition for distribution to the public for private use.

Under the 1909 Act, performances of musical compositions by coin-operated phonorecord players (commonly known as juke-boxes) were specifically exempt from copyright liability. The precise origin of this exemption is unclear, since it was a last-minute addition to the proposed copyright legislation and was not accompanied by any Congressional debate. At the time this exemption was added, it applied to relatively inconsequential player pianos and similar musical automata. Technological progress, however, allowed the juke-box industry to expand enormously during the 1920s and the loss to copyright proprietors of royalties became substantial.

During the Congressional hearings on the revision Bill in the 1960s, copyright proprietors presented a convincing case of the unfairness of the juke-box exemption. As a result, Congress included in the 1976 Act a provision for the compulsory licensing of juke-boxes.

If a phonorecord player qualifies for a compulsory licence, this is secured by submitting an application to the Copyright Office and paying a fee of $8 per player. The licence must be renewed annually.

In undoubtedly the most complicated provision of the new Copyright Act, a compulsory licensing scheme is established for certain types of transmissions by cable television. The new law generally bases the statutory rate to be paid by cable systems on the amount of carriage of specified types of programming (distant, non-network programmes).

Under the 1909 Act a 'for profit' limitation conditioned the exemptions to the rights of performance of non-dramatic literary works and musical compositions. With the elimination of the 'for profit' limitation in the new law, non-commercial broadcasters urged enactment of a compulsory licensing provision to reduce clearance problems which might arise from total liability. They succeeded in securing the passage of a limited compulsory licensing system: a public broadcaster may perform or display published non-dramatic musical works and published pictorial, graphic and sculptural works in the course of a non-commercial educational broadcast transmission. The compulsory licensing provision, however, avoids government machinery for the collection of royalties and encourages the parties to reach voluntary agreements between themselves.

The new copyright law has considerably altered the approach of the United States to formalities. Under the 1909 Act, copyright protection under Federal law was obtained for published works through publication with notice of copyright, and, for unpublished works, registration with the Copyright Office of a claim to copyright. Under the new law, copyright protection attaches at the moment of fixation. Therefore, from a theoretical standpoint, the new Copyright Act has no formalities which constitute a condition of copyright.

Despite the significant reduction in the importance of formalities under the new law, some provisions remain which impose certain obligations upon copyright proprietors. Essentially, these requirements fall into four areas – the manufacturing clause, the notice requirement, the deposit provision and the registration requirement.

The new law generally requires copies consisting preponderantly of non-dramatic literary material in the English language that is authored by US nationals or domiciliaries to be manufactured in the United States or Canada. Numerous exceptions limit application of the provision, however, and non-compliance will not nullify copyright protection, but only limit the availability of copyright remedies. Even more important, on 1 July 1982, the entire section is scheduled to go out of existence, thereby ending a provision which has been a dubious feature of US law since 1891.

The new law greatly moderates the stringency of the notice requirement that has been a regular feature of US law since 1802. The basic notice requirements of the revised law remain essentially the same as under the old.* Several provisions of the new law mitigate the harsh effects of mistakes and also contain certain safeguards protecting innocent infringers.

Under the new law, copyright deposit is divided into two related concepts. First, there are the mandatory deposit requirements applicable to all works published in the United States with notice of copyright, which is intended to enhance the collections of the Library of Congress. A specific provision of the law establishes, within the Library of Congress, the American Television and Radio Archives. The Archives will be supplied by transfer from other collections of the Library of Congress and by the acquisition of news and other programmes. In addition to the mandatory deposit there are the deposit requirements for securing copyright registration. While compliance with this provision is termed 'permissive', copyright registration is not possible without an appropriate deposit.

Copyright registration in either published or unpublished form is optional under the new law. There are, however, certain advantages to registering a claim with the Copyright Office. Registration, for example, is necessary in order to bring a copyright infringement action in a Federal court.

Under the new law, copyright-ownership initially is vested in the author of the work, and ownership of the copyright or any

---

*For visually perceptible copies, the word 'Copyright', the abbreviation 'Copr.' or the symbol '©', the year of first publication, and the name of the copyright-owner. Likewise, the form of notice for sound recordings under Section 402 generally follows the requirements of the old law: the symbol '℗', the year of first publication of the sound recording and the name of the copyright-owner.

exclusive right thereunder may be transferred in whole or in part. If a work is created by an employee within the scope of his employment, the employer is considered to be the author of the work under the 'work made for hire' doctrine. Where a work consists of a contribution to a collective work, in the absence of an express transfer of title to the owner of the collective work, the author of the contribution maintains the copyright in his work.

In one of the most important changes made by the new law, the internationally accepted standard duration of the lifetime of the author plus fifty years is adopted in place of the fixed term of twenty-eight years, renewable for an additional twenty-eight years. For anonymous works, pseudonymous works and works made for hire, a fixed term is established of seventy-five years from the year of first publication, or one hundred years from the. date of creation, whichever expires first. For works with subsisting Federal copyright protection on 1 January 1978, the basic fifty-six-year term is generally increased to seventy-five years through a provision increasing the renewal term to forty-seven years.

The performer is a creator who seldom receives the direct protection of the copyright law, but often benefits indirectly. The suppression of tape piracy through the extension of a so-called 'limited copyright' to sound recordings marks an important development in indirect performer protection. Under this amendment, the unauthorized reproduction and distribution to the public of sound recordings fixed and published after 15 February 1972 with a valid notice of copyright constitutes an actionable infringement, subject to both civil and criminal sanctions.

The most recent development affecting the rights of the performer is the renewed interest by Congress in creating a performance right in sound recordings. In the study prepared by the Register of Copyrights on the issue, it was reported that only 23 per cent of performers participating in the production of recordings received royalties from the sale of their recordings, and, of those who did, the royalties received represented only a small proportion of their annual earnings. Included within the study was proposed draft legislation which would recognize a performance right in sound recordings under a compulsory licensing system in which half the generated proceeds would go to the performer.

In addition to the recent development of copyright remedies which often work for the benefit of the performer, American jurisprudence occasionally protects the performer under various alternative legal theories. Essentially, the cases outside copyright have arisen in two different areas – the unauthorized use of a performance and the performer's right of publicity.

In cases relating to unauthorized use, an important factor has been whether or not the performer has contractual relations with the user. If a contract exists, the courts have generally applied contract principles to resolve the dispute, and the majority rule appears to limit the rights of a performer to those rights specifically established by the contract.

In cases involving unauthorized use where the performer has no contractual relation with the exploiter of the work, the performer has frequently been protected. The majority of these cases have involved recordings of artists before sound recordings were protectible under Federal law. Utilizing theories of unfair competition and misappropriation, courts have generally been sympathetic to arguments that such unauthorized exploitation of performances violates the property rights of the performer.

Since the turn of the twentieth century, a number of cases have arisen concerning the exploitation of a performer's name and personality for commercial purposes. In the United States these cases aré generally characterized as involving the performer's 'rights of publicity'. While at first there was some hesitancy to recognize such rights, today courts will usually protect the economic rights associated with a performer successfully exploiting his fame. In additon to arguments based on a performer's inherent property right, some cases have successfully established recovery on the concept of invasion of privacy.

In addition to statutory copyright and various common law theories advanced by the cases, two other factors in the United States have a significant impact on the exploitation of intellectual property. The first factor is the large guilds and organizations, prevalent throughout the entertainment field, which advance the interests of the writers, composers and performers they represent. On a day-to-day basis these organizations may have a greater impact on the exploitation of intellectual property than the Federal Copyright Act or case law, since many of the legal relationships of individuals employed in the entertainment field are determined by standard form contracts drawn up by these organizations.

The second significant factor is the impact of the anti-trust laws to prevent price fixing and monopolization in the copyright industries. These laws may be applied against either the users of intellectual property or the large organizations representing the interests of authors and performers.

3 France

Serving as an interesting contrast to the Anglo-American traditions of copyright is the French approach to intellectual property. For many years French copyright rested principally on two enactments dating from the French Revolution which protected the rights of reproduction and the right of public performance. Because of the laconic generality of these statutes, judges were left with wide discretion concerning the applicable principles and, as a result, French copyright law developed on a case-by-case basis. Finally, after many years of study, the French enacted a comprehensive Copyright Bill in 1957 codifying the principles which had been established by the courts down the years.

Under the French concept of copyright, the rights of a creator in his creations are thought of as a dual right. Occupying one branch are the moral rights of an author which attach to the very person of the author and cannot be transferred, disposed of, or waived. In the second branch are the economic rights which are associated with the exploitation of a work. This dualistic concept is, however, marked by the pre-eminence accorded to the moral rights as clearly expressed in the Copyright Act (Articles 1, 6, 19, 32, 71).

The bedrock provision in setting out the moral rights of an author is Article 6 of the 1957 Act which protects the integrity and paternity of an author's product by establishing the author's 'right to divulge his work'. After an author's death this right may be exercised by his designated representatives. An important limitation is provided by Article 20, however, which establishes the right of a court to review the reasonableness of the manner in which the divulgation right is exercised by the author's representatives. The right of divulgation has an important impact on historical research in France, since the heirs of a deceased celebrity may assert this right to protect their ancestor's manuscripts or other intellectual property.

Another significant moral right of the French author is the right to withdraw his work after the work has been published, which corresponds to a similar provision in the German Copyright Act of 1965. Article 32 which establishes this right does provide two conditions, however. The author must indemnify any loss that the transferee suffers as a result of the withdrawal. Also, if the author decides to put the work back in circulation, he must first offer the exploitation rights to the original transferee under the conditions as originally determined.

The economic rights of an author essentially fall into two broad categories – the right of performance (which includes broadcasting rights) and the right of reproduction. While the author may transfer these interests, French law carefully establishes restrictions which are applicable in commercial transations involving intellectual property. Under Article 31 all contracts transferring exploitation rights must be in writing and must be specific as to the rights transferred, including the extent and purpose of the transfer, and limited as to place and duration. However, there are divergent views on the exact significance of the concept of 'destination' (mentioned in Art. 31, para. 3), in particular about the control an author might exercise over the use by the successive purchasers of reproductions of his works (books, records, etc.). In addition, Title III of the French Copyright Act, which includes twenty-one separate provisions, controls much of the substance of performance and publishing contracts.

One of the most significant provisions governing exploitation contracts is the general prohibition against lump-sum contracts. This principle is set forth in Article 35 providing: 'An assignment by the author of his rights in his work must carry with it a proportional share in the proceeds from the sale which shall accrue to the author'. There are, however, several exceptions to this general rule in cases where a proportional share is not practical, or where scientific works, anthologies, encyclopaedias and cheap popular editions are involved.

Another special feature of the French approach – which in a somewhat different presentation also appears in the German legislation – gives the author a right to rescind a wrongful contract. This recession right can be exercised when the rights transferred were more than seven-twelfths undervalued, but it is limited by a provision making it applicable only where the work was transferred for a lump-sum payment.

Of particular concern to the French are the rights of artists in their creations. In 1920 the French passed a statute establishing the 'droit de suite' of artists – the right of continued interest in subsequent sales of a work of art. The purpose of the legislation was to allow artists to share in the enhanced value of their creations by entitling them to a small percentage of the sale price if their work was sold at a public auction (3 per cent on sales of more than 10,000 francs).

Article 42 of the 1957 Act expanded the 'droit de suite' by making the percentage applicable to sales between private persons; i.e. mainly to sales by dealers. However, this extension of the 'droit de suite' requires an administrative ruling which has not been given; thus Article 42 is still applicable only to sales by public auction, because of the opposition of the art dealers.

As to the persons entitled to claim copyright, the French approach varies from the Anglo-Saxon tradition in several respects. Article 1 provides that the existence of an employment contract does not vest in an employer the right to claim copyright. Since the pecuniary rights of copyright are freely transferable, however, an employment contract which specifically transfers the right to exploit a work will be enforceable. In addition, under French case law, a transfer of economic rights in a work is implied in an employment situation if under the circumstances it is clear that the parties intended to vest in the employer a right to reproduce.

When a collaborative work is produced, each creative contributor is treated as a co-author. Where different kinds of authorship are contributed by different individuals, each co-author is additionally entitled to exploit his own contribution separately, provided the exploitation rights in the work as a whole are not prejudiced. In cinematographic works the co-authors are presumed to be the author of the script, the author of the adaptation, the author of the original work in the case of an adaptation, the author of the dialogue, the author of the musical compositions and the director.

Each one of the co-authors of a cinematographic work thus has, independently, economic rights reserved by contract as well as the right to exploit freely his personal contribution in a genre other than cinema on condition that the exploitation of the common work is not prejudiced, and barring a contrary clause in the contract. A limitation on a co-author's rights is established through the rules that a valid contract between the authors and the producer is presumed to include the transfer to the producer of the right to exploit the work, unless a contrary clause has been introduced in the contract.

Under several provisions of French law the right to claim copyright is limited to 'physical persons', thereby preventing corporate entities from asserting many of the protective provisions of the Act. It has been reported, however, that some French recording firms and broadcasting organizations have adopted a practice of designating their employees as co-authors of the material they produce. These designations would appear to be open to dispute in situations where the employee has made no intellectual contribution in the production of the work.

The right to claim copyright by an author is conditioned by the creation of any intellectual work 'regardless of their kind, form of expression, merit or purpose', and without regard to formalities. The only form of authorship in which protection seems questionable is sound-recording material, since this form of expression is not specifically mentioned anywhere in the Act as being protectable. Therefore, for a recording company to assert copyright protection it would appear necessary for it to prove that the act of recording was a creative intellectual process rather than a mere mechanical exercise. The likelihood of prevailing with such an argument is probably small, since record manufacturers attempted to have sound recordings specifically mentioned in the Act as being protectable, and their efforts were soundly rebuffed.

However, there are certain types of protection. If sound-recorded material is taken to refer to the words or music of the phonogram recordings, these are protected through agreements concluded between the manufacturers and the collecting societies. Furthermore, the records themselves are protected through legislation following the French ratification of the 1971 Geneva Convention against unauthorized reproduction of phonograms.

Broadcast material has a special status. It cannot be treated as a 'cinematographic work', 'drama', 'lecture' or 'address'. Following the French public broadcasting monopoly, broadcast programmes are protected by an exclusive neighbouring right over retransmission or reproduction which is vested in the public broadcasting companies.

While there are great similarities between countries' legislation for the protection of authors, the protection of performers is handled in different ways. In contrast to the considerable number of countries that protect performers by special legislation (e.g. West Germany, Italy, Ireland, Czechoslovakia, the UK, the Scandinavian countries), France has not included the protection of performers in a statute. This lack of statutory protection, though, does not mean that performers in France go unprotected. Although there are relatively few cases when French courts have considered the rights of performers, a form of protection analogous to copyright has been extended.

'There has long been a significant, although highly controversial, trend in legal precedent towards agreeing to grant performers very wide powers, restricted to the product of their performance but otherwise comparable to those which authors enjoy over their work' (Gotzen, 1977, p. 32).

In areas relating to the moral rights of a performer, actions must be based on laws concerning personal rights and the protection of privacy, possibly also the law relating to defamation. The most famous judgment in line with this trend was delivered in the Furtwängler case in 1964. The Cour de Cassation (Supreme Court of Appeal) ruled 'that the performer is entitled to prohibit any use of his performance other than that authorised by him; this ground is sufficient to distinguish impairment of the performer's right in the work represented by his performance' (see Gotzen, 1977, p. 33).

'Thus, in terms of this important decision, a performance would constitute a work and, protected as such, would benefit from the principle of the specificity of assignment laid down in the 1957 Act (Articles 31 and 32)' (Cerf-Weil, 1979, p. 13). The Court established an absolute right, in this case over mechanical reproduction, comparable with or analogous to the copyright enjoyed by authors.

The performer's right to make the manufacture, publication and sale of records of his performance subject to his consent was confirmed in further decisions. However, in these and other judgments, the courts refrained from formulating the prerogative granted to performers as authors' rights.

A recent case has been interpreted as changing this trend. In 1977 the Cour de Cassation ruled on the SPEDIDAME case, where the French broadcasting corporation opposed a collecting society concerning the right of authorization and remuneration for secondary uses: here it involved the broadcasting of performances on commercial records. The Court did not, as in the Furtwängler case, designate a performance as a 'work', and thereby renounced the analogy with copyright. 'Only general law and contractual provisions can thus confer upon the artists a right to prohibit certain uses of their performances. In the absence of such resolutions, all control is impossible: the performers are not authors . . .' (Cerf-Weil, 1979, p. 13). For the defence of their rights, the performers have turned to labour and contract law and the development of collective agreements.

4 West Germany

Although similar to the French approach in many respects, the German Copyright Act of 1965 more precisely tackles the modern realities brought about by technological advancements. Like the French, the Germans treat copyright as a dual right – moral rights and exploitation rights. Included among the moral rights of an author are the rights to determine the manner of dissemination, to ensure recognition of authorship, to prohibit distortion of the work, to ensure access to the original or to copies of the work, and to revoke a licence 'by reason of changed conviction' against payment of damages (para. 42). Established as the exploitation rights of an author are the rights of reproduction and distribution, the right of exhibition, and rights associated with the performance or broadcasting of a work.

In 1965 the Germans first recognized the 'droit de suite' of artists, and in 1972 several modifications increasing the return were made. Under para. 26 as it now stands, if an artistic work is resold by an art dealer or auctioneer, the artist receives 5 per cent of the selling price. There is no obligation, however, if the selling price is below 100 German Marks.

Another similarity to the French approach is a provision providing for the revision of unfair contracts. Under para. 36 an author is entitled to demand damages in a licence agreement in which the agreed consideration proves to be 'grossly disproportionate to the income from the use of the work'. Unlike the French Act, however, no specific fractions are set out as guidelines for determining whether the remuneration is unreasonably low.

Under para. 27 of the 1965 Copyright Act, the lending of copies for profit creates an obligation to pay royalties. In 1972 this obligation was extended to public libraries and company libraries which lend materials to employees. The purpose of this provision of German law is to create a writers' fund that is administered solely by collecting societies which represent authors.

As with the French Act, the German Copyright Act attempts to protect the author against large economic entities using their strong bargaining positions to usurp his rights in his work. As a safeguard against this practice, the German Act prohibits the *inter vivos* conveyance of copyright, including moral rights as well as exploitation rights. In order for others to exploit a work, a licence, as opposed to an outright assignment, must be secured from the author. A licence may be exclusive or non-exclusive and may be limited as to place, time or purpose.

In determining who is an 'author', the German Copyright Act closely resembles the French approach. The copyright belongs to the person who is the creator of the work, and if the work results from collaboration with two or more individuals each contributor is treated as a co-author. Copyright is not vested in an employer by the mere existence of an employment relationship, although a licence to exploit the work may be implied if the circumstances warrant. For a cinematographic work, however, the right to claim copyright is awarded to the producer of the film.

To establish generally the subject matter of copyright, para. 2 protects literary, musical and artistic works, pantomimes and choreographic works, photography and cinematography, and illustrations of a scientific or technical nature. Compliance with various formalities is not required under German law, and the duration of protection is as long as seventy years after the author's death. Where the work exhibits minimal new matter or is produced through mechanical skill rather than a creative intellectual process, copyright protection may not be secured. This principle has been used in Germany to refuse protection for reproduction of works of art in certain cases.

A different section of the Copyright Act contains provisions protecting sound recordings and broadcast material. The producer of a sound recording is thereby given the exclusive right to reproduce and distribute his product and to share with the performer equitable remuneration from the broadcasting of sound-recorded material. The broadcasting organization is given the exclusive right to rebroadcast its broadcast, fix its broadcast and publicly show programmes for a fee, thus prohibiting others from charging a fee for public showing. The duration of protection in both cases is twenty-five years.

Although the German approach varies from the French in several regards, one of the most significant differences between the two countries is in their treatment of the issue of 'fair use'. The French have generally avoided delineating the circumstances in which intellectual property may be used without remuneration, apparently preferring to allow the courts to develop the law in this area on a case-by-case basis. The Germans, on the other hand, have enacted eighteen specific provisions on the subject in a section of their Copyright Act entitled 'Limitations on Copyright'. Thus the German law on the difficult issue of fair use appears to be one of the clearest in the world.

Some of the most important provisions relating to fair use in the German Copyright Act involve the issue of news-reporting. Establishing the German policy in this area are provisions relating to public speeches, press articles and broadcast commentaries, visual and sound reporting, and quotations. Essentially, the governing principle established by these provisions appears to be the non-remuneration for incidental uses of intellectual property for news-reporting purposes versus copyright liability for the wholesale reproduction of a borrowed work.

Some of the most controversial provisions in the entire 1965 Copyright Act dealt with the educational and religious uses of intellectual property. Under para. 46 the author's right to claim a royalty would be eliminated if his work was to be incorporated into an anthology for religious, school or instructional use. This provision, however, was declared unconstitutional by the Federal Constitutional Court and so today it does not represent German policy on this issue: instead, the author is to be paid a reasonable fee. On the other hand, the policy advanced by para. 47 concerning the right of teachers to make copies of school broadcasts, subject to certain limitations, was declared constitutional by the same Court.

Another important aspect of fair use is the extent to which an individual can utilize the technological advances of tape recording and photocopying to reproduce intellectual property. According to the German law one may make a single copy of a work for personal use. However, in a rather distinctive provision, the Germans impose a 'copyright obligation' on the manufacturers of tape-recording equipment to be enforced by the collecting societies which represent composers. Thus individuals purchasing tape-recording equipment, in effect, pay an indirect copyright royalty, since the added cost to the manufacturers is undoubtedly passed on in the price of the equipment.

Even where no remuneration is required on account of fair use considerations, generally the moral rights of an author remain unimpaired. Modifications of an author's work are generally prohibited and the authorship of a work must be indicated.

Like the French, the Germans dislike the concept of compulsory licensing because of the limitations it places on the ability of the author to control the exploitation of his work. Unlike the French, however, the Germans have provided for a limited compulsory system for musical works which have been previously recorded. But the compulsory licensing provisions are not applicable if the recording rights are administered by a collecting society, if the work no longer represents the views of the author or if the licence sought is for use in a motion picture.

As an adherent to the Rome Convention, Germany protects various rights of the performer and establishes both civil and criminal remedies for infringement of these rights. Under German law the consent of the performer must be secured to transmit a performance by screen or loudspeaker, to fix the performance in a tangible medium, and to broadcast a performance. In addition, if a performance is publicly communicated by the playing of records or by broadcasting, the performer is entitled to an equitable remuneration. The duration of protection is twenty-five years from the first publication or performance of visual or sound records or, if unpublished, twenty-five years from the date of the first performance.

5 Sweden

Sweden has adhered to all the most important international conventions, including the Berne Union, the UCC and the Rome Convention. Swedish copyright policy is therefore substantially influenced by international thinking about the rights of authors and neighbouring rights and the Copyright Act of 1960 clearly resembles the copyright legislation of many other European countries. However, there are a number of specific features in the Swedish attitude towards copyright policy and its application. Swedish copyright policy and legislation have, moreover, evolved within a common Nordic framework.

As part of the highly developed co-operation between the Nordic countries in the legal field, positive steps have been taken for the harmonization of their copyright legislation. Thus, similar to the international conventions, the copyright legislation of the Nordic countries is based on the principles that the author of a literary or artistic work is alone entitled to decide on the essential forms of its use. These rights are protected through a system of private law provisions and follow the dual concept of moral rights and economic rights. In accordance with similar principles, protection is also granted to neighbouring rights enjoyed by performing artists, producers of phonogram records and other sound recordings, and by broadcasting organizations.

Another feature in Swedish cultural life is the extensive role played by public authorities in supporting and subsidizing cultural activities. Following an extensive public debate, Parliament in 1975 adopted a set of basic policy guidelines and certain practical measures for the support of cultural activities and the co-ordination of cultural policy. The governmental programme which promotes the cultural advancement of Swedish society is channelled through a Cultural Council which works with some fifteen organizations representing authors, translators, artists, photographers, craftsmen, industrial designers, musicians, composers, performers, producers, directors and architects. That these subsidies are extensive is indicated by the total public grants for culture of 2,500 million Swedish crowns (approx. US $625 million) in the fiscal year 1977–8.

This co-operative structure is one characteristic feature of the Swedish treatment of the rights of authors, performers and cultural workers. A substantial influence on the cultural life is exerted by these cultural associations. Thus the Swedish Union of Authors, which represents literary writers, translators, and the authors of children's literature and scientific research, provides members with representation on matters of copyright, draws up standard contracts with other contracting parties and defends freedom of speech. Largely through the efforts of this organization, the bargaining positions between authors and the users of intellectual property appear to be less unequal in Sweden than they are in other countries.

The influence of professional associations is also marked at the Nordic level. Thus, the Nordic Authors' Council is one of numerous organizations working towards closer collaboration between the Nordic countries. The purpose of the Council is to exchange information on copyright and cultural matters and to provide mutual support for changes in legislation which are advantageous to Nordic authors.

The professional associations in Sweden play a predominant role in the administration of rights. Apart from their co-operation with the Cultural Council for the distribution of government subsidies, they participate in the administration of library loan royalties.

The library loan royalty has been a right of Swedish authors since 1954 and represents a form of compensation not available to authors of most other countries. Royalties from library loans are administered by the Swedish Authors' Fund, which is an organization dominated by representatives of authors' associations. While a proportion of the library fund goes to the authors of the works lent by the libraries, a majority of the revenues collected goes into a solidarity fund which assists authors generally by augmenting the incomes of certain writers whose remuneration is deemed to be too low, by providing for long-term grants, and by establishing old age pensions, scholarships and awards. In 1978 the fund distributed some 16 million Swedish crowns.

Also affecting the rights of exploitation of copyrighted works are several provisions in the Act relating to public performance contracts, publishing contracts and film contracts. In addition, the professional associations have negotiated standard form contracts which protect authors' rights more explicitly than the statutory requirements. The activity of the professional associations is even more pronounced in the field of music: the interested organizations can be said to be responsible for the administration of the use of all protected music.

Chapter 2 of the Swedish Copyright Act essentially establishes the Swedish approach to the issue of fair use. One of the most significant of the provisions in this Chapter is Article 11, which allows the reproduction of single copies for private use. In addition, the author's moral right not to have his work altered does not prevail in respect of changes to buildings and objects in common use. Libraries and archives are given a limited right to make photocopies of works for their internal use. News reporting of current events and the recording of statements at public meetings also constitute fair use. Religious and educational institutions are granted exemptions for certain kinds of uses.

Certain restrictions have been included in the legislation in the form of compulsory licences and blanket licences which imply that the author's exclusive right in some respects has been replaced by a right to remuneration. Moreover, solutions to contractual problems have recently been sought which imply the waiving of each author's individual consent and remuneration in favour of collective systems. Thus the state and a great number of organizations in the copyright field have entered into an agreement concerning reprographic reproduction for educational purposes. Teachers may, without the consent of the holders of rights, make reproductions to an extent which considerably exceeds the limits of the Copyright Act. The state pays a fee for the reproductions to a nonprofit association which is established by the copyright organizations, and decides on its allocation.

In the mid-1970s a political debate on the position of copyright in modern society began in the Nordic countries. These discussions led the Nordic Council of Ministers to decide on a general review of copyright legislation and agree on certain guidelines for the revision work, which is carried out by nationally appointed committees that work in close co-operation. Predominant among the reasons advanced for the need to revise existing copyright rules are the implications of the new communications technologies which constantly provide new forms for the distribution and use of protected works. Moreover, societal developments in most countries have resulted in an increased need to use such protected material for information and other purposes in public activities such as education, research and administration. The same is true about the private economic sector. In certain domains, modern technical devices cannot be used to copy and disseminate protected works if permission from the right-holders for each individual use is required. It is pointed out in the directives for the revisions that these developments cause problems for the holders of rights themselves, since they are unable to control when and how their works are used.

Additional directives to the Swedish committee state that the revision of copyright legislation should be based on maintaining the principles of the author's exclusive rights. The reasons given are interesting: this system is seen as better than any other, as it serves the double objective of providing a reasonable compensation to authors and of ensuring a varied, free and independent cultural output. However, it is also noted that other solutions might be required to adapt the legislation to the demands of technical and societal developments, on the basis of a careful assessment of the various interests involved.

In Sweden, the first results of this work concern new rules for photocopying and for the legal deposit of works. The amendments to the existing laws on photocopying imply the introduction of extended collective agreement licences to photocopy in educational institutions. Thus, in certain circumstances the provisions contained in a collective contract on photocopying are also to be applicable to authors who are not members of the contracting organization. Since it is also considered essential to create a machinery for acquiring and safeguarding the rights necessary for such photocopying, a further innovation concerns a new Act on arbitration in certain copyright disputes.

The other legislative changes are intended to provide coherent and comprehensive requirements on legal deposit. In 1978 the Swedish Parliament adopted an Act on Deposit of Works in Writing and of Recordings of Sounds and Images. The Deposit Act thus concerns not only printed matter but also sound and audiovisual products, including broadcasting programmes, films, phonograms and videograms. A new public institution, the Archive for Sound and Image, has been created.

The most controversial parts of the Acts were the rules on films, which were opposed by the film producers and particularly by foreign film companies whose products are imported into Sweden. The Act prescribes that if a 16mm or 35mm film has been examined and accepted for public performance by the National Board of Film Censorship, a copy shall be deposited with the Archive within one month. The deposited copy shall be returned, after a reasonable time, when the Archive has made a copy for the exclusive purpose of preservation in the Archive. Strong safeguards are provided against prejudicing the interests of authors and other holders of rights and in this respect the legislation is more restrictive than the original proposals made by a special government committee set up to study this matter. Thus copies of deposited material can be made only for purposes of preservation and research (and, under certain conditions, for 'defence and similar purposes'; this rule does not, however, apply to feature films).

Modern technology has provided a further reason for close cooperation between the Nordic countries over copyright. The plans for a joint Nordic satellite system intended for the direct broadcasting of the television programmes in each country to audiences in the other Nordic countries have raised further issues concerning the harmonization of the relevant legislation, including copyright laws. Also under study are such practical aspects as the form of 'all-Nordic' contracts for broadcasting purposes. Politically, the project is seen as a means to strengthen Nordic cultural cooperation, but it has been opposed by a number of interests, among them authors and performers. A decision is not expected until 1981.

6 USSR

At present the copyright legislation in the USSR appears to be going through a transitional period resulting from the Soviet adherence to the Universal Copyright Convention which was effective 27 May 1973. Before this date Soviet policy was primarily dictated by domestic considerations. With foreign authors receiving the benefit of national treatment in the Soviet Union, in exchange for national treatment regarding Soviet authors, a greater dialogue concerning Soviet copyright principles is likely to ensue both inside and outside the Soviet Union.

During the early years of the Soviet state, there was a tendency to treat copyright relations as labour relations. Some rules which originated from this attitude are still retained, but at present copyright rules fall under civil law, not labour law.

The Copyright Act of 1925, which represented the first comprehensive legislation, established the basic approach of the USSR in copyright policy. This law was replaced by a new Act in 1928 and was substantially revised in 1961, when it became part of the Fundamental Civil Legislation of the Union of Soviet Socialist Republics and the Union Republics. In 1973 the legislation was further amended in order to implement the changes made necessary by the Soviet Union's adherence to the UCC.

The copyright legislation of the USSR is enacted both at national level and by the republics of the Union. The national legislation provides the general guidelines for the copyright laws of the various republics which contain the very important copyright royalty schedules.

The specific attitudes of the USSR towards copyright and the protection of authors go beyond the principle that the state simply protects the rights in intellectual products as it does in other property. The state also undertakes to provide reasonable economic conditions for the intellectual worker through such measures as pension schemes, incapacity allowances and allowances for periods between the creation of work. As a counterpart the state sets rules for the use of works that will promote cultural development, mainly by making them widely available.

Like many other countries, the Soviet Union divides rights under copyright into two categories – personal rights and property rights. The content of these rights is thus determined within the framework of both a moral rights tradition and a socialist legal philosophy.

The personal rights of a Soviet author are roughly equivalent to the moral rights recognized by most other nations. Essentially, personal rights comprise three basic rights:

(1) the right to be acknowledged as the author of the works;
(2) the right to publish, reproduce and disseminate the work by all lawful means;
(3) the right to have the work protected against improper alterations or adaptations by others.

Concerning the author's right to be recognized as the creator of the work, Soviet law appears to be similar to the copyright legislation of other countries which advance a moral rights doctrine. Under the 1961 legislation a Soviet author has a right to receive credit for creating the work and this right applies even if no royalty accompanies the use because of considerations of fair use. In addition, the author may choose to circulate his work pseudonymously or anonymously, although the right of anonymity does not appear to exist if concealment of the author's name is deemed to be prejudicial to the interests of society.

Of the three 'personal' rights of Soviet authors, undoubtedly the meaning of the author's right to publish his work is the most unlike Western concepts of copyright. In the USSR, this right encompasses the author's right to determine when his work will be publicly disseminated and the form in which the publication or performance will take place. This right, however, cannot be exercised without the assistance of an official or semi-official organization, such as a publishing house, a theatre or a film production company. In addition, once publication or public performance has occurred, certain kinds of uses are permitted without the author's consent. Therefore the essence of the Soviet author's right of publication is the right to control the first public dissemination of the work.

The third of the 'personal' rights, the right of inviolability of the work, appears to be a strongly held conviction of Soviet jurists. Several cases have arisen in the USSR regarding this issue, and the protection afforded to the author appears to equal the protection extended in most European countries. Under the copyright legislation of the Russian republics it is further provided that upon an author's death the right to authorize changes passes to the person designated in the author's will to carry out such a function, or, lacking such testamentary provisions, his heirs.

As to the concept of 'property rights' of an author, Soviet legislation differs substantially from the approach of market-oriented countries. Following the socialist doctrine, an author's right is not regarded as the equivalent of private property. This right should therefore not primarily be a means to economic gain but a means to popular education and cultural dissemination, with the objective of giving the works as wide a distribution as possible. Consequently there are considerable limitations to the author's rights in favour of public interests. The legislation enumerates two types of cases: those when the work can be used without the author's consent but against payment, and those uses when neither consent nor payment is required.

Once a work is published in the USSR, it may be used, without the consent of the author but upon payment of royalties, for public performance and for film or sound recording with the object of public reproduction or dissemination. However, no royalty is paid if the work is intended for use in radio, television or cinema. Similarly, published literary material may be used by composers of musical works with texts; artistic works and photographs may be utilized as a basis for industrial products.

These rules thus provide for a kind of compulsory licensing. Other provisions can be compared with a system of fair use in that they permit a broad range of activities for which neither the consent of the author nor the payment of copyright royalties is necessary. Greater attention to issues of limitations may be given in the future, following the adherence of the USSR to the UCC. Whether any changes in present practice will result is, however, uncertain.

The 1961 Soviet Copyright Act, as amended in 1973, enumerates seven instances in which the fair use doctrine may at present be invoked:

(1) the utilization of a published work for the creation of a distinct new independent work (other than the conversion of a story into a dramatic work or scenario, and *vice versa*, and the conversion of a dramatic work into a scenario, and *vice versa*);

(2) the reproduction of scientific, literary and artistic works within the limits specified by the legislation of the Federal republics, in scientific and critical compilations, in scholarly publications and in popular political and educational works;

(3) the communication of information in the mass media (periodicals, cinema, broadcasting and television) concerning published literary, scientific and artistic works;

(4) the reproduction, by means of cinema, broadcasting and television, of speeches delivered in public and of debates and of published literary, scientific and artistic works. This possibility of freely utilizing works – which does not include the right to translate or modify them – is obviously very important; it is grounded on the reason that a reproduction in these media increases the interest in the work and thus also its dissemination;

(5) the reproduction in newspapers of speeches or lectures delivered in public and also of published literary, scientific and artistic works, either in the original or in translation;

(6) the reproduction in any manner, other than the reproduction of copies produced by a mechanical process, of works of fine art located in places accessible to the public, with the exception of exhibitions and museums;

(7) the reproduction on a nonprofit-making basis of printed works for scientific, educational and cultural purposes.

Soviet legislation differs from the practices of non-socialist nations in that exploitation is not possible except through the government-supervised cultural corporations such as publishing houses, entertainment enterprises or motion picture studios. Once a work has been accepted for publication or performance by such an enterprise, the terms of the contractual relationship will be influenced by standard form contracts which have been developed by various public organizations. Although the provisions of these standard form contracts are not mandatory, the copyright laws of the various republics provide that any provision of a publication or performing contract which is less favourable to the author than those provided in law is invalid.

Two types of copyright contracts are provided for in Soviet law. The transfer contracts are those which allow the use of a work in the form in which it was created by its author, including contracts for the publication of a work in the original language, the public performance of a work, the production of a film on the basis of a script, etc. For such uses model contracts have been established and are subject to statutory rules. Through a licensing agreement the author grants the right to use the work in a different form; these contracts concern publication and public performances in translated form, the adaptation of a narrative work into a dramatic work, etc. There is no detailed legal regulation for this kind of contract (see Fleishits and Makovsky, 1976).

Soviet copyright legislation is characterized by the detailed regulations of the compensation to be paid to authors, the procedure for payments and the definition of key terms in copyright contracts. Mandatory royalty rates are enacted by the various republics with upper and lower limits for the negotiation of remuneration. However, it is reported that disputes over compensation frequently arise because many schedules are ambiguous.

As to the subject matter of copyright, Soviet law recognizes a broad range of material which may be brought under the umbrella of copyright protection. Under the 1961 Act, copyright may generally be extended to every scientific, literary or artistic work irrespective of its form, purpose, value or method of reproduction, whether published or unpublished. The copyright legislation of the various republics clarifies this general language by listing categories of material in which copyright may subsist. Included among the enumerated classes are both works to which copyright has traditionally been extended (such as written material, works of art, music, choreography, photographs, dramas, and oral works) and works of recent origin resulting out of technological advancement (such as motion pictures, radio and television broadcasts and sound recordings).

Soviet law requires compliance with no formalities, with one exception. In the 1928 Act a claimant in photographic material was required to place his name, or the publisher's name with an address, in the corner of the photograph, together with the year of publication. Furthermore, the publisher was also obliged to deposit copies in certain designated libraries of the USSR. In a case to clarify these requirements it was held that non-compliance with these formalities nullified copyright protection. In the 1961 Copyright Act, which superseded the 1928 Act, these special requirements concerning photographs were deleted. However, subsequent legislation in the various republics has re-enacted the notice requirement, thereby continuing the formalities relating to photographic material.

Like the copyright legislation of virtually all nations, Soviet law generally provides that the author is the owner of copyright. The legislation also provides a full list of cases when a legal entity is recognized as the copyright-owner. Among these are (1) organizations that publish scientific collections, encyclopaedias, dictionaries, magazines and other periodical literature; (2) copyright in a motion picture or a television film belongs to the organization which made the film, and copyright in radio and television programmes to the producing broadcasting organization. Earlier Soviet law also specifically recognized that rights in photographs belonged to the firm which commissioned them and that copyrighted news material belonged to TASS.

About works created in the line of duty, Soviet practices seem to be unclear. Soviet courts interpreting the Copyright Act of 1928 generally refused to uphold the copyright of civil servants in works created within the scope of employment. Article 100 of the 1961 Act seemed to change this policy by extending copyright to 'authors of a work created by virtue of a contract for service within a scientific or other organization'. It appears likely, however, that the copyright in such a case is limited to the 'personal' rights of an author, since he has already received compensation for the work through his contract of employment.

Finally, in certain instances, the state itself becomes a copyright claimant through nationalization. The precedent for this procedure began with the decree of 29 December 1917, which nationalized the works of many deceased authors. Under present Soviet law decisions as to compulsory purchase by the state are made by the Council of Ministers of the various republics. While the compulsory purchase provisions were initially promulgated to eliminate the remnants of the private enterprise system, it is reported that today they are used primarily to terminate royalty payments to heirs of popular Soviet authors.

One feature of Soviet copyright law which changed after the adherence of the Soviet Union to the UCC was the duration of copyright protection. The previous duration, the author's lifetime plus fifteen years, was amended upwards to the author's lifetime plus twenty-five years in order to comply with the minimum term of duration established by the Convention.

Copyright legislation in the USSR does not contain any rules on neighbouring rights; the reason, according to a Soviet expert, is that 'differences in social and economic conditions often render unnecessary in the USSR regulations that are quite natural in other countries. These differences also account for the use of a different set of principles to handle problems as compared with those applied in other countries' (Voronkova, 1978, p. 71). Thus Soviet law provides for the protection of broadcasting organizations through copyright legislation. Like the broadcasting organizations, all commercial producers of phonograms are united in one organization (Melodia). This eliminates the need to establish special rules for the protection of phonogram producers from misuse by other parties. Performers' rights are protected by labour law which is 'sufficiently effective in dealing with problems that in other countries impel performers to seek legal protection for their rights' (Voronkova, 1978, p. 72).

Remedies against violations of the copyright laws essentially fall into three categories – criminal prosecutions, actions by authors under civil law and remedial action by government agencies. Out of these categories, criminal prosecution for wilful violations of the copyright law is the least utilized, because the law fails to define precisely the area of criminal responsibility.

Remedies available to the author under civil law include protection for both 'personal' rights and 'property' rights. In the case of moral rights the author's remedy is limited to curing the defect in the publication or performance. In cases involving property rights, the damages are generally limited to payment of the applicable rate of the royalty schedule.

The author may also seek to secure his rights through administrative action by filing a complaint with the government body responsible for supervising the publishing house or theatre with which the author has a disagreement. If the author's grievance is not satisfied, he may still pursue the case through the courts.

With the adherence of the Soviet Union to the UCC, a mechanism had to be developed to facilitate commercial transactions in intellectual property. The Soviet solution to this problem was the creation of the Copyright Agency of the USSR (VAAP). VAAP was created from the existing associations of authors, composers, artists, journalists and performers (including the Academy of Sciences of the USSR) and various public bodies that utilize protected works. Since VAAP was given the responsibility for both collecting licensing fees for foreign publications of works originating in the USSR and paying royalties to foreign copyright proprietors for the use of their works in the USSR, the government has the advantage of complete central control over the revenues engendered from foreign transactions.

While generally the establishment of international copyright relations by the USSR met with enthusiasm around the world, there were a few features of the implementing legislation which have caused comment. In the decree establishing the intention to adhere to the UCC, a provision was included which allowed 'legal successors in title', as well as authors and heirs, to secure copyright. In addition, it was stipulated that the procedure for transferring rights to Soviet authors for publication abroad would be established by subsequent legislation. These provisions troubled some Western analysts because potentially they could be used to transfer involuntarily to a state agency rights which should naturally accrue to an author.

When the Presidium of the Supreme Soviet created the Copyright Agency approximately six months later, a provision was included which caused further consternation. The licensing for foreign publication of all Soviet works, whether published or unpublished, was required to go through the offices of VAAP.

Whether any problems will develop over foreign publication of 'unauthorized' Soviet works is still unknown. Obviously any attempt by the USSR to give its domestic copyright restrictions an extra-territorial effect would meet with considerable controversy around the world. The official VAAP position is that the Soviet Union could not take such action.

In the long run it seems unquestionable that the establishment of international copyright relations by the USSR will benefit both Soviet citizens and peoples of foreign nations. By establishing a procedure for the orderly exchange of intellectual property, a basis for greater understanding can be developed.

7 Tunisia

Although Tunisia is a small nation, its voice among the developing countries is important because of its long experience in international copyright. As a net importer of intellectual property, Tunisia shares with other developing countries the need to acquire material, particularly for educational purposes, without causing a further erosion in its balance of trade. Tunisia is also concerned about protecting its native authors, artists and musicians from inequitable exploitation at the hands of commercial enterprises. 'What is vital for us is that authors can enjoy a right in their work. The legal nature of this right is of little importance for the authors of the developing countries. What is essential for them is to be able to participate, in the same way as the exploiters of works, in the fruits of their labour' (Amri, 1977, p. 51). In addition to these traditional concerns of a developing country, Tunisia has had long experience of international copyright issues and the attitudes of industrialized countries: its position is that of an original member of the Berne Union dating back to 1887.

The Tunisian Copyright Act of 1966 therefore represents a unique synthesis of various strands in African thinking on intellectual property coupled with some principles which are of a specifically Tunisian character. Since Tunisia was a protectorate of France from 1881 to 1956, the primary European influence is French. The draft African Model Copyright Law drawn up under the joint auspices of WIPO and Unesco has served as a significant reference in the drafting of the Tunisian law.

The subject matter of Tunisian copyright is established by Article 1, which generally provides protection for 'all original literary, scientific and artistic works', and lists thirteen specific categories of copyrightable material. Two of the categories set forth refer to the protection of broadcast material. Clause 10 protecting 'cinematographic works . . . and works producing visual effects analogous to those of cinematography' appears to apply to televisual works fixed in tangible form, while clause 3 covering 'broadcasting (sound or visual)' applies in all other cases. Not listed among the thirteen categories are sound-recordings.

One of the most interesting features of the 1966 Copyright Act is the Tunisian approach to folklore. Identified as one of the categories of copyrightable material are 'works inspired by folklore', which is defined by Article 6 as 'any work composed with the aid of elements borrowed from the cultural traditional patrimony of the Tunisian Republic'. A copyright in such works may not be assigned or exclusively licensed unless the transaction is approved by the Department of Cultural Affairs.

Since the dividing line between folklore itself and 'works inspired by folklore' is difficult to draw, Tunisia further regulates the exploitation of folklore in general. Except for national public bodies, a licence must be secured from the Department of Cultural Affairs in order to record works of Tunisian folklore for the purpose of commercial exploitation.

The purpose of these restrictions is to regulate teams which frequently tour Africa to record performances by local musicians and artists and secure exclusive world rights in the exploitation of the records for miniscule sums. Since these restrictions apply only on Tunisian soil, however, the extent to which native musicians and artists are protected at an international level appears to be uncertain.

The rights secured by copyright cover both the economic and the moral aspects. Among the economic rights are rights of reproduction, public performance, broadcasting, cable transmission, translation and adaptation. The moral rights recognized in Tunisia are paternity rights and rights against alteration.

Concerning the 'work for hire' doctrine, Tunisia differs from the draft African Model Act by vesting the copyright in the employee rather than in the employer. Tunisia decided to make this change in order to encourage public officials to create works of importance for the development of the country. Copyright protection in cinematographic material is extended to the producer, provided he has established a contractual relationship with the authors of the utilized works. In the chapter entitled 'Limitations on Copyright', the Tunisian law establishes several uses which require no payment of a copyright royalty. One such use is the nonprofit performance or broadcast of a work for private or educational purposes. In addition, individuals may make single-copy reproductions for private and personal use and schools may reproduce broadcasts, sound-recordings and audio-visual material. Finally, a limited use of quotations and reports of current events is permissible for commentary and news-reporting purposes.

In addition to free uses in certain cases, licensing arrangements are established in two instances. Under the auspices of the Department of Cultural Affairs, 'public libraries, non-commercial documentation centres, scientific institutions and educational establishments' may reproduce literary, scientific or artistic works provided they pay equitable remuneration. If an agreement cannot be reached between any organization representing the author and the public organizations seeking use of the work, a commission is set up to resolve the dispute.

The second instance involves provisions for the compulsory licensing of public performances, broadcasting and cable transmissions of works lawfully accessible to the public. If an author is not affiliated to the Society of Authors and Composers of Tunisia, Article 16 of the Tunisian Copyright Act allows the work to be used, provided fair compensation is paid as established by an adjudicating commission. A commentator, reporting on the administration of the Tunisian Copyright Act five years after its enactment, indicated that no compulsory licences had yet been issued under the provisions of Article 16. This would appear to indicate that the users and the organizations representing authors have been successful in negotiating voluntary licensing arrangements.

8 India

The position of India in relation to intellectual property rights appears at the same time unique and typical of the problems faced by many developing societies.

India not only is one of the world's most populous countries but also possesses one of the longest and most varied cultural traditions in the world. The six major religions, the sixteen official languages – each with its own system of writing and its own literature – attest to this diversity. The range of cultural expression is wider than in the more homogeneous industrialized countries. Traditional arts and crafts, including folk drama, classical dance and music, live alongside an often successful use of modern forms of expression. India has become the largest film producer in the world with a burgeoning record industry and a vigorous movement of modern painting and sculpture. Despite the still high level of illiteracy, some 12,000 newspapers and periodicals are published in fifty-six languages, and the book-publishing industry is one of the most important in Asia.

There is thus a great variety of expression from the most traditional to the most modern. This mixture and juxtaposition of the traditional and the modern would by itself pose a number of specific copyright problems. At the same time, the development needs of the country require access to and wide dissemination of intellectual works, particularly scientific and technical. As a result, India's attitude towards intellectual property rights has to take into account the need to promote and encourage indigenous creation and expression in both the traditional and the modern sector, and also to provide for an active public role in the widespread dissemination of intellectual property. Indian copyright policy might therefore be seen as founded on two basic principles: encouragement of authorship through protective copyright, and provision of safeguards against undue barriers to the exploitation of works.

The earliest statutory law in India concerning copyright was the Indian Copyright Act of 1847 which was passed by the Governor-General in order to remove doubts about the applicability of British copyright law. In 1911 the codification of British copyright laws in the Act of 1911 was made applicable to all His Majesty's Dominions, including India. Under this Act a legislature of any British possession could modify or alter the provisions of the 1911 Act through the necessary legislation. Pursuant to this authority the Governor-General of India enacted the Indian Copyright Act of 1914, which made some modifications to the provisions of the 1911 Act. The statute remained in effect until an independent India enacted the Copyright Act of 1957, which remains today as the Indian law on the subject of intellectual property.

An analysis of the 1957 Act reveals the Indian utilization of a wide variety of copyright principles in order to formulate a law uniquely suited to its needs. The Indians have a Copyright Office which performs some similar functions to the US Copyright Office, regulates performing right societies in a similar fashion to the United Kingdom, and establishes under its copyright law some of the 'moral rights' recognized in most continental European countries. Distinguishing Indian law from European and Anglo-American legislation are several provisions that, under certain circumstances, allow the government to play an active role in encouraging the exploitation of needed intellectual property.

Copyright may be secured in 'original literary, dramatic, musical and artistic works, cinematographic films, and records' without regard to formalities. The duration of copyright for original literary, dramatic, musical and artistic works is the lifetime of the author plus fifty years. A lesser term of a flat fifty years applies to photographs, films, records and government publications.

The rights enumerated in the Act generally correspond to those found in other national laws and include the rights of reproduction, publishing, translation and adaptation, public performance, film-making, recording and broadcasting. The law also grants protection for certain neighbouring rights; phonograms and broadcasts are protected more or less to the extent envisaged under the Rome Convention. There are, however, no specific provisions to protect the interest of performers as such apart from what is available to them under the law of contract. The reasons for protecting Indian performers have recently been given an unusual slant in the statement by a judge that 'this disentitlement of the musician or group of musical artists to copyright is un-Indian because the major attraction which lends monetary value to a musical performance is not the music maker so much as the musician. Perhaps, both deserve to be recognized by the copyright law' (see Rao, 1978, p. 13).

Recognizing certain of the so-called 'moral rights' is Section 57 of the 1957 Act which prohibits the distortion of an author's work or engaging in activities prejudicial to an author's reputation. Once an author's work is published, however, he has no right to withdraw the work from public circulation and, in fact, compulsory licensing provisions are established in order to ensure a continued public access.

On the subject of the transfer of copyright, Indian law is generally similar to English traditions. While copyright initially is vested in the author, it is freely transferable either by complete or partial assignment or through a licence arrangement. In the case of a work created within the scope of an author's employment, the employer becomes the initial copyright-owner. Likewise, in the case of government publications it is the government which is recognized as the copyright-owner.

Section 52, one of the longest provisions of the Indian Copyright Act, establishes India's policy regarding the fair use of copyrighted works. Coming within the scope of 'fair use' of literary, dramatic, musical or artistic material is use for research or private study, criticism and review, and the reporting of current events. Furthermore, collections which are primarily of non-copyrighted material may include 'short passages from literary and dramatic works', provided the publication is intended for educational institutions. Literary, dramatic, musical or artistic works may also be reproduced by teachers or students in the course of instruction. Certain nonprofit performances of literary, dramatic or musical works also constitute fair use.

So that the system may be administered efficiently, India maintains a Copyright Office somewhat similar to the functioning of the Copyright Office in the United States. Unlike the United States, however, the registration of claims to copyright is voluntary and serves as *prima facie* evidence of copyright-ownership and the facts stated in the entry of registration.

Overseeing the activities of the Copyright Office is the Copyright Board, whose members are appointed by the government and on which the Registrar of Copyrights serves as secretary. Errors in entries of registration are rectified by this Board and appeals against the decision of the Registrar of Copyrights may be brought before it.

In addition to serving as final authority over the functioning of the Copyright Office, the Copyright Board regulates the tariff fees charged by the performing right societies and also grants compulsory licences in two particular situations. The first case involves Indian published works which are withheld from the public because the copyright-owners refuse to republish the work, perform the work in public or communicate the work to the public by broadcasting. The second case involves the translation of an Indian work or a foreign work from a country that is a member of the UN. India has adhered to the Berne, Universal and Geneva Phonogram Conventions, but not to the Rome Convention. Among the questions currently 'under consideration' figure the protection of folklore and popular works and of performers.

9 Japan

Before the Meiji era when the foundations for modern Japan were established (1868-1912), there was no protection of authors in keeping with present ideas, but only regulations for the control of publications. Adopted early in the Meiji era, the Publication Ordinance of 1869 provided both for the control of publications and for the protection of certain works. The Copyright Ordinance, the Dramatic and Musical Composition Ordinance and the Photographic Copyright Ordinance, all adopted in 1887, advanced further in the direction of protecting authors beyond the provisions of the earlier Ordinance and its revisions; materially they can be regarded as the first copyright law in Japan.

However, in view of its modernization programme and the importance given to relations with foreign countries, Japan wished to accede to the Berne Convention and the Paris Convention for the protection of industrial property rights. This required an overall national copyright law. Legislative work therefore continued with reference to European laws, in particular the German legislation. In 1899 Japan adopted a Copyright Act which allowed her to accede to the Berne Convention. Thus this legislation depended on Japanese international relations rather than on domestic requirements.

The Copyright Act of 1899 thus marks the establishment of modern copyright legislation in Japan. Even though this law was based on Western models, some provisions specific to Japan were included as the result of several revisions, such as the protection of performances and phonograms through copyright. Besides, Japan's decision to absorb Western civilization and to develop as a modern nation had led to the inclusion of some unique provisions to cover this situation. Examples of this regime for development were the ten-year period for the right of translation and the limitation on copyright of broadcasts and public performance of works through recordings.

However, before the Second World War, the level of protection could not always be described as high; it corresponded to the level of the 1928 version of the Berne Convention. After the war, Japan for a considerable time was not in a position to revise the legislation in order to accede to the more recent versions of the Berne Convention.

Therefore it proved necessary to revise the 1899 Act entirely with the further objective of providing new protection, based on the neighbouring rights concept, for performances and phonograms which had been protected by the copyright provisions, as well as for broadcasting. A special committee was set up in 1962 which presented a revision plan in 1966. After lengthy negotiations, the new Copyright Act was approved by the Diet in 1970.

In general terms, the 1970 Act corresponds to the modern copyright legislation adopted in other countries, while at the same time it includes a number of provisions that seem to be uniquely Japanese.

The 1970 Act has been described as resting on four fundamental principles: '(1) improved protection of authors; (2) consolidation of neighbouring rights; (3) consideration for a just and fair exploitation of cultural products; (4) assurance of contribution to the development of culture' (Nomura, 1971, p. 43).

The purpose of the law is to provide for the rights of authors as well as for neighbouring rights which are enumerated in keeping with the Rome Convention, 'having regard to a just and fair exploitation of these cultural products, and thereby to contribute to the development of culture' (Art. 1). Helpfully, the law provides in its second Article an extensive list of definitions, which also reveal the modern character of the law: it includes not only definitions of broadcasting, sound and visual recording but also of 'diffusion by wire', and communication by means of telecommunication installations not falling within the terms 'broadcasting' or 'diffusion by wire'.

The Japanese Act provides an interesting balance between the continental European and the Anglo-American systems by providing for a dual system of rights, moral rights defined as the rights of paternity, integrity and also a right of making the work public (Articles 18–20); economic rights as usually defined which, in the law, are explicitly referred to as 'copyright'.

The list of economic rights is not only illustrative but exhaustive, and comprises the right of reproduction, performance, broadcasting and wire diffusion, recitation, exhibition, cinematographic presentation and distribution, translation and adaptation.

The rights of authors subsist in a work which is defined as 'a production in which thoughts or sentiments are expressed in a creative way and which falls within the literary, scientific, artistic or musical domain' (Art. 2(1)). Although a requirement for material support is laid down for cinematographic works and works analogous to them, the law does not provide such a requirement for other works. Explicitly excluded from protection are 'news of the day and miscellaneous facts having the character of mere items of information' (Art. 10 (2)), as well as laws and regulations, judgments and decisions by law courts and administrative organs.

The term 'author' is defined to mean 'a person who creates a work'. The authorship of a work created by an employee on the initiative of a legal person or other employer and made public under the name of such a legal person is to be attributed to that legal person unless otherwise stipulated in a contract or work regulation. Copyright in cinematographic works belongs to the maker of the work, provided that the authors who have contributed to the creation of the film have undertaken to participate in its production. However, authors of novels, scenarios, music or other pre-existing works adapted or reproduced in cinematographic works are not included in this provision.

Even though Japan has not adhered to the Rome Convention, neighbouring rights are modelled on its rules. Protection is thus extended to performers, producers of phonograms and broadcasting organizations. Performers and producers of phonograms are granted the right to secondary use fees when broadcasting organizations and wire distributors principally engaged in offering music have broadcast commercial phonograms or distributed them by wire.

A series of provisions in the Japanese Act corresponds to fair use with regard to limitations on copyright sanctioning the free utilization of works under certain conditions. Although these provisions generally are of the same kind as those provided in the laws of other countries, some provisions unique to the Japanese law were also included. Thus there are special provisions applying to the reproduction of works included in examination questions and the recording of works for the blind. The provisions pertaining to the utilization of works in broadcasting programmes for schools (requiring payment of reasonable compensation) and reproduction of works in schools and other educational institutions are similar to those in other countries. In all these cases, though, the works must already have been made public. Similar provisions of limitations apply, with necessary modifications, to neighbouring rights.

It is interesting to note that, in the old Act, the reproduction for private use was permitted by hand only, excluding the use of mechanical or chemical devices. The new Act permits reproduction for personal or family use by means of modern equipment on condition that the user makes the reproduction. A study of these problems has been initiated by the Copyright Council, particularly with regard to the economic influence on holders of rights of the reproduction of works, performances, phonograms and broadcasts by modern scientific and technological means.

The Japanese Act recognizes a compulsory licence system which applies in some specified cases: where the copyright-owner is unknown, where a broadcasting organization has failed to reach an agreement or was unable to enter into negotiations for broadcasting rights, and the recording on commercial phonograms of works that had already been recorded with the copyright-owner's permission on records on commercial sale in Japan for three years. This provision was introduced in order to facilitate the free movement of musical works and avoid a monopoly by record companies.

The operation of the compulsory licensing system is entrusted to a government authority, the Agency for Cultural Affairs, which in a number of cases consults with the Copyright Council which functions as an advisory body to the Commissioners of the Agency. The Agency is empowered to issue compulsory licences and to determine the compensation to be paid to authors. The Act includes detailed rules of procedure and conditions for the issue of licences. The Agency also has power to designate an association of performers or producers of phonograms to collect the fees for secondary uses of commercial phonograms. At present, the Japan

Council of Performers' Organizations is designated as the association for performers, and the Japan Phonograph Record Association (which includes the musical tape industry) for producers of phonograms.

Another task of the Agency represents a unique feature in Japanese copyright legislation when compared with that of other countries. In a dispute over rights granted by the Copyright Law, the claimant can bring a suit to court. Since litigation is generally not favoured in Japan, the law provides for a special mediation procedure. When a dispute arises, the parties concerned may apply for mediation to the Commissioner of the Agency for Cultural Affairs who appoints up to three mediators from among persons of learning and experience in the field of copyright or neighbouring rights, and submits the matter to them. After their decision, the mediators report to the Commissioner of the Agency (Articles 105–11). A further unique feature of Japanese copyright legislation is the special Law on Intermediary Business Concerning Copyrights of 1939. This regulates enterprises acting as experts and collecting societies on behalf of holders of rights. Authorization to act as an agent is granted by the Commissioner of the Agency for Cultural Affairs.

The organizations now licensed to act as such agents are JASRAC (Japanese Society for Rights of Authors, Composers and Publishers), which consists of poets, composers and publishing houses, the Japan Literary Works Copyright Protection League, which controls the rights for such literary works as novels and essays, and the Writers' Guild of Japan, which controls the rights of literary works such as plays written mainly for broadcasting on radio or television. So far, no unions of performers like those in the West have been established in Japan, but some such organizations are gradually being developed. The Japan Council of Performers' Organizations, which comprises fifty-three performers' organizations, has been making energetic efforts to protect the rights of performers.

The 1970 Act can be considered as a law which keeps a fair balance between the protection of authors and various social demands, and provides comprehensive regulation over a wide area. Following this Act, Japan acceded to the latest conventions as follows: the 1971 versions of the Berne Convention and the Universal Copyright Convention in 1975 and 1977, and the Geneva Phonogram Convention in 1978.

Since the time when work on the revision of the Copyright Act was officially begun (1962), interest in copyright has noticeably been on the increase. The idea of copyright has become widespread even among the general public. In this regard, the copyright seminars which the Agency for Cultural Affairs holds throughout Japan every year have played an important role.

The parties concerned have also discussed problems related to the enforcement of the new Copyright Act; interim provisions are included which permit the continued validity of some of the former ones in some specified areas. No special difficulty has developed concerning the enforcement of the Act. However, as in Western countries, new problems which require to be studied in the fields of copyright and neighbouring rights have arisen with the advance of science and technology. The sub-committees which were set up by the Copyright Council of the Agency for Cultural Affairs have ended their studies on computers, video-recordings and reprographic reproduction, and have published their reports. At the instigation of concerned societies and organizations, further studies are under way on the problems of recording sound and visual programmes for private use. These organizations claim that the economic interests of authors, companies, record producers and performers are greatly impaired by the increasing use of tape- and video-recording machines for private purposes. One of the possible solutions considered is the system of surcharges on equipment, such as that adopted by the Federal Republic of Germany.

10 People's Republic of China

The People's Republic of China is the only large and important country that does not have a comprehensive copyright law. This fact alone should give pause for thought. Even more so since China possesses one of the most distinct and continuous literary and artistic traditions in the world without any system of rules that could be compared to Western copyright concepts. Neither classical nor modern China seems to have felt the need for Western-type copyright protection.

The comparison with Europe is revealing. The emergence of copyright concepts in Europe is tied to a specific level of social and technological organization symbolized by the invention of printing and the development of book publishing in the fifteenth century. In both these areas China was in advance of Europe. Methods of printing texts had been developed as early as the second century and movable type was invented in the middle of the eleventh century. The highly sophisticated organization of social and cultural life had by then had a longer tradition than anything comparable in Europe, and it would require an extensive analysis of Chinese culture and philosophy to explain the differences in underlying principles and social organization. In this context, some pointers will have to suffice.

The importance of learning was emphasized even more than in Europe, but in a different manner. The qualities tested in the famous state examinations were not specialized, professional knowledge but artistic style and mastery of the classical literature. 'In Chinese traditional society, the intelligentsia have been a class without technical knowledge. They monopolized authority based on the wisdom of the past, spent time on literature, and tried to express themselves through art' (Fei Hsiao-Lung, quoted in Levenson, 1964, p. 21a). During various periods of Chinese history academies and schools were established, yet the contempt for professionalism and commercialization persisted: 'In matters of calligraphy and printing, one is not to discuss price.' This statement by a painter in the eleventh century is echoed 500 years later in the rule that the painter 'is not acquisitive in the world, nor does he distract his heart with considerations of admiration or detraction' (quotations from Mi Fu and Tsuo I-kuei in Levenson, 1964, pp. 29, 30).

While it seems impossible to find references to concepts recalling notions of copyright, there existed rules about access to books. Since book-learning was essential for the examinations, access to a good library was a privilege highly valued in China. How highly valued is revealed by rules concerning the use of libraries belonging to the 'tsu', the patrilineal clan which had important social and judicial functions. One set of such rules from the Ming dynasty stipulated that the keys to the library were to be distributed to the male members of the family, and that unless all the representative male members were present, no single person was allowed to open the library. Removal of any book from the building was prohibited and if anybody was found to have sold books he would be banished from the family and never allowed to participate in the ancestral worship (Sprenkel, 1966, p. 84).

Cultural attitudes and social organization did thus not require a policy expressed through copyright. As a legal concept, copyright seems even less attuned to the Chinese concept of law with its reluctance to rely upon rigid codification and abhorrence of litigation. The traditional Chinese conception of law is so different from the Western concept that it has often been described as a rejection of the idea of law. Basic to Chinese philosophy and social conduct is the idea that order in society is achieved by action which is in accord with the order of nature. Natural order and social order react constantly upon one another. The reflection of this attitude in what the West would call legal discourse is through the concept of 'li', which has been translated as ceremonies, rituals or rules of social conduct, or more generally that which conforms to social order and universal harmony. In this sense, 'li' is in opposition to law, the strict rule ('fa'). 'In this conception, there is no place for law in the Latin sense of the term. Strictly speaking, there are not even individual rights sanctioned and guaranteed by the law. There are only duties, mutual prestations, governed by notions of order, responsibility, hierarchy, harmony . . .' (Escarra, 1936, p. 17). The result is 'a subtle regime of interdependence and solidarity which could never be based upon unconditional prescriptions: upon law . . . In the idea of rule there is no more than the idea of model. The Chinese notion of order excludes the notion of law in all its aspects' (Granet, quoted in Escarra, 1936, p. 70).

The primary purpose of 'law' is not to establish who is right or wrong but to eliminate a threat to or violation of the natural order. Since the natural order includes the observed particularities of each situation and of each human being, the exactitude of law becomes a negative factor and not a benefit. 'Precedents are like traces of writing in ink: they indicate only a pattern and outline and that is all. If you insist on quoting one as a standard to be followed, this is like making a mark on a moving ship to show where to recover a sword which has been dropped off its side into the river . . . Human nature is infinitely varied and there never is a case which is exactly the same as one that has been decided before' (Wang Hui-tsu, in Sprenkel, 1966, p. 147). In this system, trials are condemned since they are a sign of troubled relationships. Before resorting to trial every possible means of reaching agreement must be exhausted. The possibilities are numerous, since many social groups – family, neighbours, clans, villages, guilds, associations – are ready to intervene and act as arbitrators or mediators.

Accounts from present-day China often emphasize a continued reliance on mediation, the involvement of social groups, the relative absence of written rules and what appears almost as a repugnance to apply them when they do exist (see, for example, Pepinsky, 1975). The Western concept of statutory defined and legally enforceable exclusive rights vested in the individual has little place in this system.

If, then, both traditional and modern Chinese attitudes to law present features which militate against copyright, what can be said about the current organization of cultural life and of information flows? Chinese policy and practice do not seem to be favourable to Western copyright concepts. The objectives of communication in modern China concern national integration, modernization, the creation of a new society and a new man. They require a specific organization of cultural life characterized by the integration of communications and politics. According to a recent study, the twin principles of centralization and functional specialization are the main features of the cultural organization (see Liu, 1971).

The book publishing system contained two centralized structures: the People's Publishing Houses which paralleled the territorial organization of the Party and the government (as did the New China Bookstore which had a monopoly on book distribution) with national headquarters in Peking and regional divisions corresponding to province, municipality and county. In addition to these centralized systems were publishing houses designated to produce specialized books, such as the Workers' Publishing House, Youth Publishing House and Science Publishing House. The publishing policy pursued in the mid-1950s was explained by an article in the *People's Daily*: 'The demands for scientific and cultural books by the state and the people are varied. Publishers must meet this demand. In order to develop scholarship and culture and uplift the ideological and cultural standards of the people, all types of books that are basically not in conflict with the main principles of Marxism–Leninism and are of value to us should be published' (quoted in Liu, 1971, p. 150). Cultural policies are integrated with political policies. In 1971 there was a call for a major diversification in the publishing industry with emphasis on five types of reading matter: (1) works by Marx, Engels, Lenin, Stalin and Mao; (2) popular readers in politics and philosophy; (3) popular art and literary works based on revolutionary model plays; (4) popular readers in science, technology, medicine and public health; and (5) popular books, periodicals and comics intended for youth (Liu, 1971, p. ix).

What could be the place of copyright in this context?

During the early 1950s, it appeared as if the People's Republic was in the process of drafting copyright legislation and developing a policy similar to that of the USSR. The Government Administration Council (GAC), then the highest executive organ of the country, issued a policy statement on 11 August 1950 indicating that measures and regulations on copyright questions were to be drafted by the Cultural and Education Committee of the GAC. Following on the heels of this statement, the Five Resolutions of the First National Publications Conference of 1950 established that authors did not have to sell their rights of authorship and required both public and private publication enterprises to respect their rights. Furthermore, Resolution 2 of this Conference specifically prohibited unauthorized printing, plagiarizing and altering of manuscripts.

These initial statements seemed to imply a move in favour of copyright, but a comprehensive statute was never enacted. The immediate reasons for what appears to be a rejection of basic copyright principles are uncertain because of the lack of official commentary, but seem to be in accord with both traditional attitudes and modern ideology.

Since China lacks any copyright legislation, a determination of the degree of protection afforded to Chinese authors must be based on an analysis of standard form contracts such as the Contract for Publication of Works by the People's Publishing Houses and Measures Governing the Payment Given by the People's Publishing Houses for Manuscripts. These documents were included in a 1957 compilation of civil law materials published by the Chinese People's University and may be regarded as typical of the forms used for routine transactions. The two instruments are designed to be complementary, and matters not covered by one of the documents are generally dealt with by the other.

The document entitled 'Measures Governing Payment' sets out varying amounts of compensation for three types of literature:

(1) Chinese translations of classical works of Marxism–Leninism, (2) popular and hortatory literature printed in great quantities, and literature for study, and (3) original works in the social sciences and Chinese translations of such original works. Payments are based upon the length of the manuscript and the number of copies printed. In practice, this approach seems very similar to the royalty schedules of the Soviet Union, in that the rate of compensation is determined by governmental policy rather than negotiation by the author.

Under the provisions of the Contract for Publication of Works it appears that, in practice, the Chinese follow principles relating to copyright rules on infringement and moral rights. In this instrument, the publisher receives an exclusive right to publish the work throughout China during the length of the contract and the author covenants not to compete through authorizing publication by another publisher. The author is further made responsible for any infringement of another person's right of authorship and is liable to the publisher for any losses incurred as a result of such infringement. Thus it appears generally that principles of copyright infringement are recognized in Chinese law, although no official statement appears to be available explaining the precise concepts behind these principles.

Another provision of the Contract for Publication of Works establishes that the publisher may require the author to revise his manuscript, provided a proper explanation is furnished. If the author refuses, the publisher has the option of rejecting the manuscript and any compensation already paid is to be returned. Since this provision would imply that a manuscript cannot be altered without the author's permission, a right similar to the moral rights doctrine relating to the integrity of an author's work appears to be practised.

Among the factors that might indicate a Chinese rejection of traditional thinking regarding remunerative awards for creative individuals is the Chinese experience with patent legislation. Initially, the Chinese enacted a patent statute similar to that of the Soviet Union, but protection for the individual was gradually lessened. Today, it appears that recognition serves as the main incentive for inventors. As a matter of principle, laws protecting the exclusive economic rights of authors seem to run counter to the theoretical basis of socialist society.

Despite these important factors militating against the establishment of comprehensive copyright legislation, there appear to be several considerations favouring such legislation which may receive greater Chinese appreciation in the future. For one, the lack of a copyright statute does not eliminate all considerations of rights in intellectual property. Rather, it may merely transfer the authority for determining some of the relevant issues to the government. In the past, Chinese leaders have criticized the Soviet Union for what they perceive as an excessive use of government bureaucracy in formulating domestic policies. As the Chinese generally dislike large government institutions, it appears possible that they might reassess the need for copyright legislation in order to maintain the size of government within manageable proportions.

Another factor which, at least in Western opinion, would favour the enactment of legislation would be the efficiency that only a definitive, comprehensive statute can provide. Moreover, in order to achieve greater technological advancement, it appears necessary for China to consume a steadily increasing amount of intellectual property, both internally and externally produced. Therefore any inefficiency inherent in the present system will greatly increase as China transforms its economy.

Cultural agreements between the People's Republic of China and other nations have occasionally stipulated that the copyright of the citizens of the other party shall be protected. The enforcement by the Chinese government of agreements to protect certain works of foreign nationals within its own territory could be possible, since enterprises disseminating intellectual property are government supervised.

The most recent developments in China might also contribute to a change in attitude. As early as 1956, it had been pointed out at the 8th Party Congress of the Communist Party that 'we still lack several urgently-needed, fairly complete basic statutes such as a criminal code, a civil code, rules of court procedure and so forth' (quoted in *Broadsheet*, vol. 16, no. 10, October 1979, p. 2). As part of a new process to correct this situation, seven draft laws were presented to and approved by the National People's Congress in June 1979. The laws cover local People's Congresses and local government, elections to national and local People's Congresses, criminal law and procedures, People's Courts and Procurators and joint ventures between Chinese and foreign investment. Ling Yun, the Vice-Minister of Public Security, explained that the Criminal Law and the Law on Criminal Procedure were not copied from any other country, neither were they extensions of the Law in old China: instead they are based on New China's Constitution, and the experience, both positive and negative, gained in public security and judicial work over the last thirty years (op. cit., p. 3).

Similarly, recent reports indicate the emergence of a new policy in the copyright field.

This policy appears to be based not only on domestic requirements but equally on considerations of foreign relations and the need to regulate the reproduction of foreign works. It seems that China will adopt a phased approach: first, the adoption of domestic legislation; second, bilateral agreements with other countries and, finally, adherence to one of the international conventions.

Chapter V · Challenges to copyright: new technologies and media

1 Gadgets or trends

The regulation of communications and information activities currently presents an image of rapid change and great confusion. The basic legal framework antedates the communications revolution. Concepts and rules evolved for traditional modes of expression and communication are being stretched to the limits of their capacity to cover new situations.

All the branches of law applicable to communications experience these difficulties, although to different degrees. To some extent, certain traditional concepts in telecommunications law and intellectual property rights have shown a remarkable resilience and adaptability. However, the pressure exerted by new services and modes of communication is such that they can barely be contained within the existing conceptual framework. It is not only the speed but also the nature of current developments in communications technology which strains the legal fabric.

To many observers, the advent of electronic communications represents a revolution: the fourth communications revolution. The first of these revolutions is represented by the development of speech, followed by the invention of writing and of printing. Since the introduction of the printing press, no major changes in communications technology occurred until the nineteenth century and the development of photography and motion pictures. Even more important, though, was the invention of the telegraph, and telephone and wireless transmission. These new techniques represent the beginning of what has been called the 'subsidiary electro-electronic revolution within the industrial revolution' that only now is making its effect fully felt (see Asimov, 1970).

The evaluation of the characteristics and impact of the electronic communications revolution has proved to be singularly difficult.

Beyond cryptic formulations of the medium being both message and massage, attempts at a coherent approach are rare. Generally, the work of engineers and technicians that has produced the present spectrum of information devices has related to only one particular service or branch, to one particular mode of communication, without any overall view.

The fauna of communication services once had a commendable but deceptive simplicity. The small number of services could easily be grouped into a few neat categories. Place of pride was given to the print media. Next came the telephone and the telegraph, which belonged to the world of telecommunications. Cinema was different – a public spectacle. Radio and television were subsumed under the new notion of broadcasting. Telex, mobile radio communications and other newcomers did not attract the public interest they deserved, since they seemed tied to the corporate world.

Thus the most obvious feature of the present communications scene has been the proliferation of unconnected gadgets which both decorate and clutter our environment: telephones, radio sets, record-players, telex printers, television receivers, microfiche readers, video-recorders, photocopiers, data terminals and pocket calculators. Generally, each piece of equipment has been used for one service only. Each communication service was associated with a special transmission or distribution system and developed within a specific institutional framework with its own mode of financing, set of policies and legal rules. Each species was seen as inherently distinct in terms of the technology used, the services provided and the regulation required.

Current changes in technology are producing new patterns, with traditional services being combined into unexpected hybrid shapes and uses, in defiance of the established categories. The marriage of the telephone and television begets the videophone. The postal letter is supplemented with telefacsimile or messages recorded on cassettes. The cinema goes to the home and the videotape to the cinema. Traditionally, radio was intended for mass audiences and the telephone for two correspondents; both are now being used for and by groups of various sizes. Artists work at electronic consoles. The written or printed word loses its physical support and is transformed into an insubstantial flicker on a visual display unit. The combination of the telephone, television and computer systems provides for unprecedented services which break the barrier between print and electronics.

Policy-makers and lawyers have been given very little guidance by technologists and social researchers on how to deal with this new situation. The by now voluminous body of literature and research on new communication technologies, systems and services often contains no more than a catalogue of innovations and expectations – or fears. Most available studies concern a particular technology and its uses, be they satellites, cable television or computers. Some concentrate on larger systems such as the telephone system, or broadcasting. Others concern the institutional or legal problems in a given area and country. However, national and international arguments about the allocation of radio frequencies show how far we are from agreement on clear criteria for evaluating the relative social importance of different communications services: navigation, broadcasting, radio astronomy or national security.

No more successfully than other branches of communications law has copyright been able to escape the technological trap. Rules are still being developed for a particular device or technology in a situation where services and uses are in constant evolution. What is required is an attempt to discern underlying, major trends and the implications of current developments as a basis for evaluation and rule-making.

It is an accepted fact that one of the characteristic features of the new communications technology is a vast increase in the capacity to generate, transmit and receive information. However, there are other trends which may be more significant: flexibility and opportunity of choice, convergence and complementarity and the inequality of access.

The flexibility offered by new technologies is a fairly obvious feature. The satellite is more flexible than a terrestrial system, which always has to follow a given path on earth. Over-the-air television is primarily a one-way service, whereas cable television can easily provide various kinds of two-way functions. Another aspect of this flexibility has attracted less attention: the availability of many options where previously there was only one – or none.

We now have at our disposal a number of fundamentally different ways of distributing recorded music:
—through records or cassettes and individual players;
—through broadcasting and similar forms of distribution;

—through access to audio archives which, in turn, can be organized in two different ways: through physical access at specific locations, or through access by electronic means.

Similarly, for television distribution, we can now choose between traditional terrestrial broadcasting, cable systems, satellites or the mail for recorded programmes. Originally, 'news' was distributed orally, followed by writing and print, then by film, radio and television, with each medium presenting the news according to its own characteristics and constraints. These patterns are now changing: 'printed' and graphically presented information is regularly distributed electronically and the printed physical form may be reconstituted at reception.

This diversity also functions in a different way. Traditionally, the television set has been used for one purpose only, the reception of over-the-air television broadcasting. At present, new uses are being added at great speed: reception of cable or satellite transmissions, playback of videograms, electronic games, new two-way services in combination with telephone or broadband networks, display of computerized data, surveillance and control of production processes or traffic patterns. The television set should more accurately be described as a multipurpose visual display unit, but its definition and legal status is essentially tied to the one original function.

Another aspect of the new flexibility is the possibility of combining different, so far separate, methods and systems. Cable systems can be combined with terrestrial broadcasting, and either one or both of these with satellite systems. The combination of technical systems corresponds to an integration of services: television and facsimile combine in telefacsimile; the data bases used for electronic photocomposing can also be used for information retrieval. The combination of television and telephone is at the origin of the videophone, and these, together with computerized data systems, result in teletext and videotext services. In fact, certain videotext services already represent a combination of telecommunications, computer, broadcasting and print information systems.

This trend towards overall integrated configurations meets another trend in an opposite or complementary direction: a trend towards decentralization and individualization in concept and use. Small is beautiful. This trend is obvious in the demands for localized broadcasting and in the activities of the video-groups who have taken the electronic media out of the mass media sphere and transformed them into an individual or group medium of expression, similar to what had already happened in the cinema. Individual choice is the main argument for the video-cassette and videodisc: choice of timing and choice of content. Remote access to computerized data banks could serve the same purpose of allowing the individual user to control his search for information. In this perspective, the ultimate goal of a comprehensive, integrated electronic communications system is to serve as a global infrastructure which would give all users instantaneous access, permitting them to choose the time, form and modality of their communication.

All these opportunities exist; many are already in operation. But for whom? Basically, only for the privileged, whether within or between countries. The most dangerous trend in current developments is the inequality, the imbalance, of access. Information is power. We are in the process of creating a new class distinction between the 'information-rich' and the rest. Within as well as between societies, the information elite is located in the institutions that can command or afford access to hardware and software, and among the well-educated individuals who know how to handle both facilities and information. The statistics on any communications factor, whether it be literacy, cinema seats, radio transmitters or trained communicators, show the imbalance between the information-saturated and the information-poor.

In general, the law applicable to communications has not yet been able to catch up with the new circumstances. Current legislative work, nationally and internationally, is mostly gadget-oriented, focused on specific technologies and services. The legal concepts, whether in copyright or in other legal branches, are mainly backward looking, at best centred on the situation of the 1960s or possibly of the 1970s, but not on that of the 1980s and beyond. With the lawyers continuing to run behind the technologists, the regulatory approaches to new services are still piecemeal. And very little attention has been paid to one effect of successful technological change, the 'multiplication of interest groups organized around new technologies. The increase in number of interest groups causes an increased incidence of inter-group conflict. This often results in additional rules as well as more complex rules regulating group interactions' (Department of Commerce, 1977, p. 5).

Since current legislative work in the copyright field follows the technology-based approach, this chapter will discuss some current issues in this light; in the following chapter the discussion will centre on possible new approaches.

2 An electronic triad: satellites, cable and video

The three most visible technologies introduced over the last two decades were met by waves of enthusiasm. Satellites were supposed to provide the infrastructure for the global village and furnish education and culture to all villagers, particularly to those in the developing countries. Cable systems would provide the opportunity to choose between the offerings on a large number of channels. And while lightweight video could open new avenues for community action and self-expression, video-players would free the viewer from television schedules and usher in an era of 'non-broadcast television'.

In the eyes of the enthusiasts and the promoters, these new technologies opened the door to an electronic utopia. The reactions of copyright-owners made them appear as an unholy trinity. The policy-makers and legislators found themselves faced with legal problems that had to be handled in widely differing contexts.

Satellites

As mentioned earlier in connection with the preparations for the Brussels Convention, copyright issues related to the use of communications satellites represented only one aspect of the work on international law in this field. On one side were the politico-juridical issues which were discussed in the United Nations with reference to direct broadcast satellites and the further development of space law; the key problem concerned the balance to be struck between the right of each country to decide on its own communications system and the free flow of information. On the other side were the technical regulations for all kinds of satellite systems which are the preserve of the ITU. Given this situation, the approach adopted in the Brussels Convention appears logical: to locate protection against the poaching of satellite transmissions in public law rather than in private law and to move the object of protection from intellectual property to the technical signals.

Apart from the problem of poaching, point-to-point satellites which function as relays between earth stations do not cause any new uses of protected works which differ in kind from those occurring in terrestrial transmissions. This technology, then, should not give rise to any problems to which solutions have not already been found in existing conventions. However, the international copyright experts found a new field for learned analysis, since they disagreed on the interpretation of existing definitions of a 'broadcast'.

> When does a broadcast take place? It could take place at a number of stages in the total process. It could take place when the programme is initially recorded for later broadcast. It could take place when the domestic station transmits the programme for microwave or wire to the transmitting ground station. It could also take place when the ground station transmits the programme to the receiving ground station. It could finally take place when the receiving ground station transmits the signals to the home receivers (Siebert, 1971, p. 22).

Further elements, such as the role of the satellite itself, could be added to this list. In fact, copyright arguments have been pushed far enough to lay themselves open to the criticism 'that it would be absurd to speak of a public performance in outer space, since this concept necessarily presupposes a public which as far as is known does not exist in space' (Lokrantz, 1969, p. 307).

Apart from the difficulties experienced in applying traditional copyright concepts to new technologies, the debate on copyright problems in relation to television transmissions via point-to-point satellite systems proved to be largely academic. Most transmissions do not contain material protected by copyright, such as public events, news and sport.

Copyright-owners have subsequently expressed considerable anxiety over the implications of broadcast satellite systems which allow reception by individual receiving installations. However, even these direct broadcast satellites do not represent a new medium requiring new rules and rights. They represent a new technical method that may do better what terrestrial broadcasting already does. Satellite broadcasting is different from terrestrial broadcasting not in kind, but in scope. Or, in the words of a Unesco/WIPO Working Group, which noted 'that the expansion of the direct reception zone did not change the basic principles applicable, and that the distributing body, whatever it was, would be required to obtain the necessary authorization from the beneficiaries concerned. On this point, the situation is similar to that where the distribution involves not one but several countries' (Unesco/WIPO, 1977, p. 7).

The concerns expressed by copyright-owners are well exemplified in the current debate on the plans for a joint Nordic satellite system for the distribution of each national television programme to the other Nordic countries. Both authors' and performers' associations have expressed their strong opposition. Although some of their arguments are founded on copyright considerations most fall outside the copyright domain and refer to employment opportunities, labour law and above all cultural policies. They are instructive in the sense of making clear that legal-technical copyright issues can be solved only in a larger social context.

There remains one problem. Even with further technical advances for the precise pointing of the satellite beams, it will never be possible to shape the beam in such a manner that it precisely follows the contours of a given country. There will always be a certain amount of unavoidable spill-over. In kind it is no different from what has been accepted in terrestrial broadcasting; it is a question of scope. Such spill-over has been accepted in the Radio Regulations of the International Telecommunication Union (see Art. N28/7 of the Radio Regulations, also the Final Acts of the World Administrative Radio Conference – Broadcasting Satellites, 1977). The same approach has been adopted in the UN discussions on the legal principles for direct broadcast satellites. Insistence on extended protection by copyright-owners would collide with two sets of accepted international public law principles; i.e. those evolved in the context of space law and those of telecommunications law.

In this case, the hierarchy of issues seems relatively straightforward: the agreements so far reached on such politically sensitive issues as satellite signal spill-over would not be at risk on account of claims founded on an extension of private rights. The political, legal and economic stakes in these agreements are too high.

Cable

It seems altogether typical of the current confusion of terminology that the expression 'non-broadcast television' has been used about two completely different phenomena: cable television and video-cassettes. Cable television is not a very good expression, either, since it is used to designate cable systems that may carry besides television programmes a host of other services which in no way can be described as 'television'. It just so happens that, historically, cable systems developed from central antenna systems to provide better reception in remote areas of broadcast television and also that we chose to call the receiving equipment a television set.

From a technical point of view it is fairly easy to define cable systems according to criteria of carrying capacity, technical parameters and configuration. The legislators appear to have had a more difficult time. In some countries cable systems are subsumed under a wide broadcasting concept, in others they have been given a special status and regulation. In the majority of countries where the law is silent, cable transmissions automatically fall under telecommunications law. Consequently, national regulations with regard to cable differ widely.

At the international level, discussions in the concerned organizations continue to use the expression 'television by cable' basically as shorthand for cable distribution of television programmes. However, under this expression are also included transmissions originated by the cable operator or, in another version, 'the cable distributor's own programmes'. And these 'own programmes' are supposed to comprise not only programmes produced by the cable operator but also the use of pre-existing films or other audio-visual materials as well as the retransmission of broadcast programmes in certain circumstances. The point of these contortions is that the distribution of 'own programmes' would be subject to the exclusive rights of the copyright-holders and thus to special negotiation and royalty payments. This point does raise a number of problems.

From the copyright point of view, a key issue is the concept of 'communication to the public' as one of the uses of works which demand authorization and negotiated conditions. But when is cable distribution 'communication to the public' separate from broadcasting? Collective antenna installations have to be excluded so that when a group of households installs a common equipment for reception of television broadcasts there would be 'mere reception, not subject to any exclusive rights, rather than communication to the public, and the use of mere reception apparatus rather than an act of public distribution' (Unesco/WIPO, 1977, p. 3). So far, so good.

It gets even more complicated if a cable operator distributes television signals within the normal reception zone of the broadcast; i.e. within the area where it can be received with normal aerials off-the-air. Not surprisingly, experts relying on a strict interpretation of the relevant article in the Berne Convention (Art. 11b) maintain that the sheer fact of a third party intervening in the distribution process subjects the transmission to copyright obligations: in their view there would be a new 'communication to the public'. This would result in the same programme intended for an identical public being treated differently if it were distributed only over-the-air or partly by cable.

At this point, copyright demands might well clash with public regulations, as when rules ban individual antennae for environmental reasons or when any cable operator is required by law to carry available national broadcast programmes. It would be patently absurd to include such cases within a double system of exclusive rights.

To a large extent, these problems depend on the legal construction of copyright. The method of attaching the exercise of rights to specific technologies will lead to difficulties. In the case of broadcasting, the originating organization would often not have control over the method of distribution, since the transmitting network is established by and belongs to other entities, public or private. A broadcast intended for a specific public (regional, national or international) should not change legal status with the choice of technical distribution method, which could be normal terrestrial wireless broadcasting, cable, satellite or various combinations. Tomorrow there will be other methods: optical fibres, tightbeam very high frequency waves, laser beams.

Problems of a more practical nature arise when television programmes are taken off-the-air and transported to areas where they otherwise could not be received. Through this practice, Canadian viewers receive programmes from the United States, and there is a widespread transborder flow of programmes via cable systems in Europe. Thus the programme reaches, without the authorization of the originating organization, audiences for which it was not intended and for which fees or payments were not negotiated. The solution here appears to be relatively simple: it is up to the originating organization to assert its rights and to prohibit such distribution. Reality is otherwise complex. In Europe, the transport of foreign television signals is often undertaken by public authorities: the telecommunication administrations which refuse to concern themselves with questions of content and private rights. In many countries it would be politically impossible to stop this long-established practice.

Furthermore the protection granted with regard to cable distribution varies with the nature of the rights. It seems agreed that the authors' rights are adequately protected through the copyright conventions. The situation of the neighbouring rights protected through the Rome Convention is different. Unlike the copyright conventions, the Rome Convention does not protect owners of exclusive rights when programmes are distributed by cable. It has therefore been proposed that an additional protocol to the Convention might be considered. Since such a protocol would be tantamount to a revision of the Convention, it is felt to be premature. Not only is the number of contracting states small, but there are as yet only a few countries that have adopted special regulations for cable distribution which could serve as a basis for international agreement.

Video
There is much to be said for terminological confusion – particularly by those who work beyond established categories. 'Video' covers an extraordinary variety of new technologies, uses and users, ranging from 'videofreaks' to corporate heavyweights like Philips, Sony and RCA. The video enthusiasts are involved in self- and group-expression, in community action and the arts; their symbol is the Portapak. The firms are in business; their market is non-broadcast television on cassettes and discs for training, education, corporate management and general consumption. The two groups are far apart with regard to copyright. There has not been one word about copyright from the first group, who are looking not for protection but for support and access. The activities of the second group have put the entire international copyright machinery in motion: studies, meetings, working groups worrying

at the legal problems of the video-cassette and videodisc. So, what are the problems? To start with, there is the problem of determining the legal status of these new devices. But before that can be done, it is necessary to define what we are talking about. Or, in the more official language of a Unesco/WIPO Working Group which 'devoted its efforts to agreeing on terms to designate, on the one hand, the material support in as much as it comprised sequences of sounds and images and, on the other hand, the intellectual content of the support (software) and where that content might, depending on the case, consist of pre-existing work or a work specially made for such fixation and either of those two categories of works might or might not be protected under copyright' (Unesco/WIPO, 1977, p. 3). No wonder that 'attention was drawn to the need, from a strictly legal point of view, to avoid terms used in everyday speech to denote different situations by means of the same word and thus run the risk of creating confusion' (ibid.).

The Group 'expressed its preference' for the term 'videogram' to mean both the tape or disc and the content ('the material support for any sequence of images and sounds and the actual fixation of the sequence'). 'Videocopy' would refer to the reproduction of a pre-existing work and 'videographic work' to a work specially made for fixing on a videogram.

These distinctions made it possible at least to state that the videocopy did not present any new legal problems: the fact of fixing a pre-existing work on a videogram in no way alters its legal status or nature. The second case proved problematic, since opinions differed as to what kind of legal animal a videographic work is supposed to be. Can it be assimilated into a cinematographic work in the traditional copyright sense, or are there different kinds, some constituting cinematographic works and others not; or are they of a special kind altogether? So far, conclusions seem vague in the sense that the international conventions do not impose any one solution and that it is for national legislation to decide the legal status of these works.

The difficulties traditional copyright encounters when faced with such new communication devices as videograms are clearly revealed by the Unesco/WIPO Working Group. It considered that the 'most awkward problem with videograms arose from their very nature: they were relatively simple, highly movable carriers' – which supposedly are the advantages for people wanting to buy them in the first place. The real problem perceived is that these carriers are 'placed at the disposal of the public without there being any practical possibility of controlling the use made of them, whether private or public, commercial, lawful or unlawful' (ibid., p. 4).

Some of the major difficulties are based on the private, semi-public and public use of videograms (see Klaver, 1975). On this point again, certain implications of traditional copyright notions applied to new media tend to look absurd. If citizens in a given country are allowed to sell and buy equipment that can be used for recording purposes, how is one to deal with the contention, and in certain countries the fact, that even recording for private purposes is illegal in that it violates the exclusive rights of copyright-owners? In that case, most of the advertising for this equipment is an incitement to criminal behaviour.

On the subject of private recordings in the home, the holders of rights contend that although such recordings may be made in good faith, the owners of rights suffer a loss in each case that should be mitigated even if it cannot be avoided. It is now admitted that it would be impossible to prevent large numbers of 'uncontrolled' recordings while still respecting individual privacy. A recent meeting of the Unesco/WIPO/ILO Working Committees concerned recommended for both audio-visual and sound recordings, a single, standard compensatory royalty on the sale price of recording equipment and of blank cassettes also. Such a system would correspond with the rules of the German Copyright Act, with one important difference: in Germany the levy is paid only on the recording equipment and not on the cassettes, since it would be impossible to establish in advance how the buyers would use the cassettes.

However, it has been pointed out 'that such payment would be in the nature not of a tax or other monetary imposition but rather of an indemnification for being deprived of the opportunity to exercise exclusive rights' (Unesco/WIPO, 1977, p. 6). Such reasoning seems dubious. Francesca Klaver has put the problem in more sensible terms:

If, with the minimum of drawbacks, the maximum use is to be allowed of intellectual works in their present forms (films, videocassettes, discs, tape recordings, television, etc.) . . . the absolute right of the copyright owner is bound to suffer restrictions; however, care should be taken not to lose sight of the moral and economic interests of the author or his successors in title (1975, p. 18).

Others are less patient and more alarmed:

> The panic reaction to this situation, whether it be the German copyright tax on the sale of [tape] recorders or the suggestion that the sale of such dangerous machines should even be banned . . . is based on the extreme proposition that the copyright monopoly is absolute and all-pervasive, and extends even to the private domestic sphere . . . I would suggest that, as a matter of droit commun, of common law, the rules contained in a copyright law do not apply to the private sphere at all (Hunnings, 1979, pp. 177–8).

3 Reproduction: print and copy

Reproduction of intellectual property is a key element in the entire copyright system. The specific cultural and economic organization expressed in copyright is conditioned by the ability to reproduce works – and to control reproduction. New methods of reproduction starting with the printing press have made possible a greater dissemination of works and thus greater economic benefits for the author and publisher. The new relationships between owners and users of works which were required with the introduction of cinema, broadcasting and the record-players were regulated through the extension of copyright rules. In view of the capital expense of the equipment and the industrial production forms, these relationships generally involved large public or commercial enterprises. While the issues over the nature and extent of protection were frequently controversial, prior legal and administrative experience in regulating the commercial relationships of large private and government enterprises fostered statutory rules.

Various forms of new technology pose problems of a different order: the user/reproducer of intellectual property is often an individual rather than a large corporation. Thus, to control the use of new equipment involves regulating the activities of the population as a whole. These issues are naturally more difficult to deal with than the regulation of corporate or institutional behaviour.

The full impact of the widespread use of video-cassettes is yet to be felt. However, the use of other new methods – the photocopier and microfilm – has been a problem for copyright-owners and legislators for some twenty years.

Like the typewriter, the photocopier is one of those apparently unassuming innovations that have a vast and reverberating impact. It has transformed working methods in public and private administration and in libraries, documentation centres and educational institutions. It has also given the individual new opportunities of access and of participation in communications processes.

Photocopying raises in an unusually clear manner the fundamental issue of reconciling the users' interests with the protection of authors. The rights of authors and their assignees, in particular the publishers, must be balanced against the advantages photocopying offers to individual users, and to public and private institutions.

Photocopying obviously falls under the author's rights of reproduction which are recognized in the legislation of many countries and in international conventions. However, many countries seem to experience problems of interpretation and application of the current rules with regard to photocopying. At the international level, major issues concern the effects of the differences in national solutions and therefore the possible need for new rules. In particular, attitudes and requirements differ between industrialized and developing societies. Of the developed nations it appears that those organized along socialist principles have the least problems over photocopying. According to a statement by a representative of VAAP,

> practically, the problem of reproducing locally printed works did not exist in the Union of Soviet Socialist Republics since the works were published in big editions and the prices of printed works were low. In addition to that, the interest of authors and publishers were not affected because royalties were paid in accordance with the rates determined by the

government. Reprographic reproduction was made . . . as a rule either in those cases when it was impossible to obtain a copy of the work by the usual means or when a customer was interested only in separate articles from a journal or in parts of a book. The recipients of such copies were libraries and other organizations but not individual persons (Unesco, 1975, p. 15).

The developing countries find themselves faced with a series of different problems. Generally speaking, they are clearly opposed to the establishment of any international standards which would tend to raise the price of intellectual property. They experience problems over the acquisition, conservation and circulation of documents.

In particular, the costs of locating and acquiring printed matter and periodicals are very high, and in many cases conservation presents serious problems because of the climate . . . as increasing numbers have to be served, important works soon go out of print and become unobtainable . . . photocopies, microfilms and microfiches, by making available to research workers writings or information not in the possession of university libraries render the greatest service and undoubtedly meet an urgent need (Unesco, 1972, Annex, p. 7).

In the West, several factors have transformed the issues of photocopying into a multifaceted problem. A major fear is that large-scale photocopying might jeopardize the economic viability of publishing enterprises, particularly in the scientific and technical sector. If these publishing activities are made uneconomical through unchecked photocopying, there might be an undesirable reduction in the number of published works, or governments might have to intervene through subsidies or the transfer of publishing activities from the private to the public sector. On the other hand, constraints on access to intellectual property would strike people in these countries as violating fundamental rights. Major institutions using and providing photocopying services belong to the nonprofit public service sector such as libraries and schools. Finally, there are difficulties in designing efficient systems of remuneration, as it is not easy to record the use of photocopies and the distribution of royalties.

In the search for solutions, a first step is to identify the various users of reprography and the rules applicable to each category.

The general principle that reproduction for personal use should be free is widely recognized. Not unexpectedly, even this apparently simple case presents unresolved difficulties: must the user make the copy himself, for example, and is a distinction to be made between a person making a copy for his 'own' use and a researcher making a private copy?

More important are the issues of photocopying by another category of users: nonprofit libraries, documentation centres and public scientific research institutions. In many countries it is an established practice that libraries may provide a single copy, not for profit, of material they have purchased. In the view of the library profession such copies should be available for library use, for other libraries and for individuals requesting copies. Reference is often made to the provisions of UK legislation (Copyright Act 1956 and Copyright (Libraries) Regulations 1957). The libraries covered by regulations may supply, on certain conditions (for purposes of research or private study) to anybody who so requests, a single reproduction of a single article from any periodical or a reasonable proportion of any other copyright work. Authors and publishers have expressed apprehension about requests for copies by third parties: any use beyond fair use of copyrighted works was harmful and it was irrelevant whether the use was for nonprofit purposes. It is understandable that librarians react against finding themselves caught in the middle of a discussion on a problem which in reality concerns users and copyright-owners.

In contrast to these problems, there seems to be less disagreement in the case of copying by commercially operated libraries and similar institutions: they should strictly adhere to statutory copyright requirements.

Photocopying for educational purposes in schools and other institutions has been a focus of controversy in many countries. A major issue is what is and what is not 'fair use' in relation to classroom teaching. The kinds of problems discussed in this respect are well reflected in the US Congressional Report on the Bill for the revision of the Copyright Act.

The report declared that fair dealing would extend to reproduction for classroom teaching and then outlined a number of factors to be considered in determining whether, under particular circumstances, activities would constitute fair use or infringement. Among these factors were the following: whether the educational institution operated for profit; whether students were charged for reproductions; whether the teacher acted spontaneously in responding to classroom needs or was acting under direction or as part of a general operating plan for the school; the number of copies made in relation to the number of students in the class and the size of the portion copied; whether reproductions were made for circulation beyond the classroom or were recalled; whether excerpts were compiled by the teacher into informal anthologies; and whether or not the work copied was in print (Unesco, 1975, p. 14).

A variety of solutions to the problems raised by photocopying appear to be available. Probably the most usual arrangements today are collective contractual agreements between associations representing copyright proprietors and similar organizations comprising users. The major problem with this approach is the difficulty in maintaining records and distributing the accruing royalties. It may be possible to use computer technology to simplify this problem. The experience of the Copyright Clearance Center in the USA will provide factual data on this approach.

Several European countries have experimented with contractual arrangements, although it is too early to tell whether such schemes will be viable. In West Germany an agreement has been negotiated between the Federation of German Industries and a collecting society representing publishers of scientific works and organizations of scientific workers. Remuneration collected through this agreement is divided equally between the publishers and organizations of scientific authors. In addition, a different type of agreement has been concluded between the West German government and a collecting society representing journalists which covers the internal use of copyrighted news reporting.

In Sweden a collecting society called BONUS, comprising authors and publishers, has successfully established a system of remuneration with a group of enterprises based on a per copy page rate of payment. This same group has also concluded an agreement regarding photocopying in Swedish schools, although it has been reported that opposition from teachers remains high.

One criticism of current collective arrangements is that the remuneration collected is not distributed to the individual authors. Record-keeping problems are deemed too complex to make such a widespread distribution practical. Instead, the money collected is used to benefit the community of authors in general through the establishment of pension funds and scholarship grants. As a result, to a certain extent, the most popular authors subsidize those authors lacking a large following.

Another option is variable pricing, whereby publishers charge higher subscription prices to users who propose to make photocopies. Unfortunately for the publishers, however, merely raising prices is often a self-defeating proposition. In order to cut costs, users can reduce subscriptions and replace the eliminated copies with photocopies, leaving the publisher no better off than he was before the price increase.

A variety of statutory methods have also been considered whereby the licensing of copyrighted material is made compulsory. Although compulsory licensing systems are often imposed on the mechanical reproduction of music, only Sweden has adopted such a course in the photocopying area. While such a system would guarantee public access to intellectual property, problems would still remain over the distribution of the accruing royalties.

The last option which has been advanced is the possibility of establishing a fund through a surcharge on photocopying equipment to be distributed to collecting societies representing copyright proprietors. The foremost nation to consider such an approach is West Germany, where a levy is placed on tape recorders. While such a scheme undoubtedly has simplicity on its side, its opponents argue that a levy is an unfair burden on an individual who seldom uses the photocopying services at his disposal to reproduce copyrighted material.

In summary, it seems clear that the issue of photocopying of copyrighted works is not a problem which will be quickly resolved. It appears that only through the establishment of an efficient system of remuneration, in instances involving substantial photocopying, can both the creator and the user of intellectual property be protected. Since a host of issues will have to be met and resolved, before the formation of such a system, the ultimate solution to the problem of photocopying works is probably years away.

A further question has been raised with regard to photocopying and other new technologies: if technology has caused new copyright problems, can technology not be relied upon to solve these same problems? This would in effect require the development of technical methods to make copying difficult or impossible. But how would publishers and the public react to the following proposals for the 'un-photocopiable journal': to make photocopies more expensive by spreading articles over more pages; to make the page-size larger or smaller than the normal photocopier working area; to use thick paper or to try colour combinations which will produce an unreadable result (Weston, 1977, p. 657)? A better approach would be to ask the lawyers and the parties concerned to go back to work on acceptable legal rules.

4 Computers

'The computer can justly be called one of the major scientific innovations of all times: it will soon, if it has not already done so, change all our lives' (Bloom, 1974, p. 1). Few would quarrel with this statement on the importance of the computer revolution; there is less agreement on its long-term impact. In relation to copyright, one aspect requires particular attention. In fact the computer must be seen not just as a machine that can perform a number of set tasks but as part of a whole information-processing activity. Through the advent of minicomputers and microprocessors, the technology is coming within the reach of the individual. At the other end of the scale the computer has been subsumed under more comprehensive concepts such as information networking and, in particular, informatics. Informatics comprises not only the computer and automated data bases but also the telecommunications links between them and the attendant range of technical, social and political issues.

So far, the concerns of the copyright community seem to have centred on the computer itself. Essentially, the copyright issues that have been raised fall into three broad categories: the protection of computer software (i.e. the computer programmes); the computer uses of intellectual property; and the role of computers in the creation of works.

One of the pressing problems in modern copyright is whether

computer programmes can or should be protected as intellectual property.

Instructions for a computer are written by a human being in special programming language that the computer can process. Should this computer program be considered the writing of an author? The computer reads the program as electronic impulses from magnetic tapes. Is this writing, which is invisible to the human eye, copyrightable? (Radack, 1979, p. 15).

The investment of time and money in computer software is great. It has been estimated that during the 1970s the worldwide cost of creating and maintaining software systems has gown to 15 billion US dollars a year. Software is by far the most expensive element in the total cost of operating computer systems. As a result, the developers of computer software are anxious to protect the product of their time and financial investment. At the same time, modern society has an obvious interest in ensuring ready access to the use of this new technology, particularly with regard to the needs of developing countries.

The law has been at pains to meet the need for protection of computer software. A main difficulty arises from the nature of computer programmes, since traditional distinctions between various stages in the creation cannot be maintained: these programmes are both writings, descriptions and processes. Individual nations have, during the past decade, explored the possibilities of protecting software by attempting to adapt its problems into already existing legal concepts, such as patent protection, trade secrets and copyright. Since most of these efforts have been on a case-by-case basis, rather than attempts to establish a framework of statutory principles designed specifically for software protection, the emerging law on the subject has often been inconsistent and ambiguous.

It has been maintained that patent protection would be desirable from the software manufacturer's point of view, since it would cover the technical idea behind the industrial product or process. It would afford remedies against the unauthorized manufacture and use of the protected product and the unauthorized use of the patented process. However, countries have to date been reluctant to recognize patent protection for computer software. The reasons are various and somewhat contradictory. Only the exceptional computer programme would meet the requirement of 'novelty' standards for granting patents, whereas all written works are eligible for copyright. 'Patents may be used to protect "processes" which may lead to a virtual monopolization of ideas in a way not permitted by copyright' (Meyer, 1977, p. 17). Also the independent development of the same programme would infringe a patent but not a copyright.

In the past the computer industry has relied heavily upon trade secret protection and contract law for the protection of computer programmes against piracy. However, trade secret protection is based upon restrictions on the flow of information. It has been seen as anachronistic in even the current state of computer development, since it assumes that a single firm uses a work secretly and restricts its use by 'outsiders'. In addition, protection through trade secret and contract law seems unpredictable. The scope and conditions of such protection vary from case to case and from country to country. It is also difficult to prevent disclosure of information from former employees.

The third existing legal system to which software producers are increasingly turning for protection is copyright. There is, though, a great divergence of opinion about whether copyright is the best form of legal protection for software.

Several reasons are advanced for the view that copyright is more appropriate than other legal mechanisms for computer pro- grammes: 'programs are writings and do not need another form of protection; other mechanisms impair access to and use of in- formation to a greater extent than does copyright; and many proposals for "new forms" of protection are virtually in- distinguishable from copyright' (Meyer, 1977, p. 116). However, in the view of many software producers, copyright is unsuitable, since it may not protect against the use of a programme by contrast with the actual copying of a programme.

The only recent legislative measure to extend copyright protection to computer software is in the 1976 US Copyright Act. Although they are not explicitly mentioned, computer programmes are within the subject matter of copyright. The definition of 'literary works' refers to works expressed in 'words, numbers or other verbal or numerical symbols or indicia' (Sec. 101). Also, copies are defined as 'material objects . . . in which a work is fixed by any method now known or later developed, and from which the work can be perceived, reproduced or otherwise communicated, either directly or with the aid of a machine or device' (ibid.).

An interesting counter-argument has been advanced by the American novelist John Hersey:

> Programs are dramatically different from other copyrighted works of authorship . . . All programs share a common goal – to control electrical impulses in a machine, i.e. to do work . . . All other works for which copyright has traditionally been available are designed to assist their creator to communicate with others. Computer programs are designed to control machines. The mechanical and commercial nature of computer programs will pollute other legitimate artistic work if programs are awarded copyrights (quoted in Meyer, 1977, p. 21).

Hersey, who is a member of the National Commission on the New Technological Uses of Copyrighted Works (CONTU), proposes that something other than copyright should be used for protecting the text of computer programmes in the form of a hybrid of patent and copyright.

At present, the situation of the availability of legal protection for software and that of the genre of protection can best be characterized as fluid. Many of the advanced technological nations are currently studying the problem, and possibly proposals will be forthcoming that take into account the unique features of the computer software industry.

Similar to the studies of individual nations have been the efforts of the World Intellectual Property Organization. During the 1970s WIPO solicited advice from programme producers and the developing countries concerning the best form of national protection and the most desirable form of international arrangements for protecting computer software. In 1974 and 1975 meetings of an Advisory Group of Non-Governmental Experts on the Protection of Computer Programmes considered industrial practices and existing laws with regard to software, as well as existing systems for the registration and dissemination of programmes. They discussed a proposal for establishing an international register of programmes administered by WIPO.

With regard to legal protection, one proposal was for a special type of legal protection for programmes without prejudice to the continuation of existing practices in the various states. This special protection should be available for both original programmes and related materials, it should be tailored to the particular technology involved and it should be commensurate with the degree of creativity evidenced in the programmes.

As computer technology has developed, the use of protected material in information storage and retrieval systems has become more widespread. As stated by the Whitford Committee in the UK, 'the development of sophisticated computerised information storage and retrieval systems may revolutionise information dissemination as we know it today, even to the extent of replacing printed works altogether' (Sec. 506).

This development has raised the issue of if and when copyright liability for computer use of such material arises. In reports to WIPO and Unesco, Professor Ulmer of Germany has pointed out the distinction between the index, the abstract and the full-text methods: 'The rights of authors and publishers are notably infringed in the case of unauthorized storage and retrieval of the full text of protectèd works . . . In the case of the abstract method, a distinction is to be drawn: if the abstract is composed by the author of the full text himself, the copyright in the abstract belongs to him . . . In the case of abstracts composed by other persons, the question arises whether they are to be regarded as adaptations of the original work', which would depend on the extension of the abstract. Finally, 'in the case of the index method, the storage and retrieval of documentary data . . . is generally not an infringement of the copyright in the works concerning which the data is provided' (Ulmer, 1977, p. 2).

As might have been expected, disputes have arisen concerning the starting-point of control: should copyright-owners have control over the input of their works into a computer system or over the output from the computer? Copyright proprietors generally argue for 'input' protection while the software producers and educational institutions advance 'output' as the logical line of demarcation between liability and non-liability.

In arguing against establishing 'input' as the first incident of liability, the software industry and the educational institutions present a variety of contentions. They point out that designating input as a copyright infringement would hamper the development of information storage and retrieval systems as tools in scholarly and commercial research. They maintain further that the sole act of input is not commercially important. In their view, to require payment at this stage would be like requiring a restaurant customer to pay before seeing the menu. The copyrighted material that constitutes the 'input' might never be used in any way that could harm the copyright-owner economically, or the material might be used only in ways which are legally permissible under the doctrine of fair use. Since the real danger, it is argued, is the later dissemination of the copyrighted material in derogation of the owner's rights, the proper time for control and payment is when such dissemination occurs – at the time of 'output' rather than at 'input'.

Countering these contentions are several arguments that are advanced in particular by authors and publishers. They insist that 'input' without authorization would be a violation of their rights. They point out the difficulty of accounting control over 'output', whether in tangible form or visual display, once the protected material has been placed in a data bank. As computer technology develops and interconnections between data banks grow into information networks, a work stored in a computer may become available to a vast number of users, finally even to the entire population of a country. Those who support 'input' control feel that the copyright-owner should have the right to license others to reproduce his work in the necessary form for computer storage and to charge for read-out by the computer, whether in physical form or visual display. The supporters of the 'input' as infringement of copyright point out that it would be inequitable even if it were feasible to limit copyright control to the 'output' of a particular computer system. The technology to control and monitor the use of all copyrighted documents within a computer system does now exist.

On this point, CONTU in the USA is terse: 'Current computer technology is such that the placement of a work into a computer necessarily involves the preparation of a machine-readable copy as defined in the new law' (Meyer, 1977, p. 10). The British Whitford Report also deals with the input-output issue. A key point in the discussion is whether the input into the computer represents reproduction in a material form. Beyond this point, the Report states a principle: 'In any event, we think that storage of copyright material in a computer should be clearly restricted' (para. 508).

These problems are also under discussion at the international level, in the context of the Berne Convention and the UCC. The present sense seems to be that these developments are still in flux and that the time is not yet ripe for the formulation of recommendations for an international legal settlement.

In commentaries on the impact of computer technology on the law of copyright, the issues that have received most attention involve the protection of computer software and computer uses of intellectual property. Less consideration has been given to copyright in works that have been produced with the assistance of computers.

One of the reasons for this conspicuous omission appears to be the inherent complexity of the subject. Computer technology can be used to assist in the creation of a broad range of intellectual products such as musical compositions, works of visual art, architectural designs, poetry, translations, directories and sound recordings. Within each of these categories there is a wide range of potential applications.

In a recent study, the composer Jean-Claude Risset has analysed the different uses of the computer in relation to artistic creation, particularly in music. He distinguishes between automatic musical composition which is characterized by the complete automation of the composition process once the programme has been laid down; computer-assisted musical composition when the composer uses the programmed computer as a tool; composition by the manipulation of musical data; synthesis and processing of sounds by computer and matrix workshop which denote unfinished, incompletely finalized works that remain to be finished and individualized by someone else, perhaps a performer but more probably a patron, user or consumer (Risset, 1979).

These cases pose different problems with regard to the central issue of copyright in computer works: the requirement that copyright material must contain original authorship. The mere fact that a computer has been used to assist in the creative effort does not necessarily raise doubts over the fulfilment of this requirement. When computers are used as tools and the ultimate selection of the various artistic combinations remains with the author, a work would clearly contain the required human authorship. The main difficulty arises in cases where the computer is programmed to make all the decisions. Most authorities on copyright would probably be cautious about the possibility of bringing such a work within the ambit of copyright because of the lack of human authorship.

However, there are counter-arguments. Other authorities dispute the proposition that the computerization of artistic expressions renders the work devoid of human authorship. Since the programme driving the decision processes of the computer contains human expression, it is argued that products produced by computers are in fact ultimately made by humans.

Another problem mentioned in connection with the full protection for computer-originated works is the further concentration of ownership of intellectual property in an industry already dominated by economically powerful enterprises. Until recently, only sizeable institutions, private or public, had extensive access to sophisticated computer hardware. In most instances, these institutions rather than the individual programmer were the beneficiaries of any protection which was extended to machine-authored works. Militating against the trend, however, is the explosive growth in mini- and micro-computer technology which, increasingly, is placing these powerful machines within reach of an ever growing number of people.

Risset puts the entire range of issues in an interesting historical perspective. In his view there is no doubt that data processing can revolutionize the conditions in which works are created. However, despite appearances, the legal problems do not so far appear to have been greatly changed by the use of computers.

> The current intrusion of the computer is reminiscent of the technological revolution brought about by the invention of printing: the technological ease of multiple reproduction and distribution of copies introduced at that time obscured the idea of intellectual property, and it was only gradually that the idea of copyright re-emerged, whereas actually the technological novelty made no difference to the situation. It may be that the same is true today: the profusion and complexity of data-processing techniques convey an often misleading impression of entirely new situations . . . It is essential to safeguard the ethical and financial interests of authors, but care must also be taken not to impede the development and use of data-processing tools by unduly restrictive or complex legislation (1979, pp. 13–14).

Chapter VI · The outer limits of copyright

1 The uneasy case for copyright

As the previous chapters have shown, there has been a steady trend towards the expansion of intellectual property rights. Nationally and internationally, rights and protection have been extended to cover new categories of 'authors', 'publishers' and 'works', to include new methods for the generation, reproduction and dissemination of information, and to provide for ever longer periods of protection. At the same time, there is a concerted drive to extend territorial coverage by persuading non-adhering countries to ratify international conventions and generally to prompt high levels of protection in national legislation.

This trend seems to have become an accepted fact, even though there has been resistance against one aspect or another of international agreements or national legislation. The battles fought have mainly concerned the relationships, within copyright, between the directly involved groups and institutions which have joined in various alliances depending on the issues involved. However, there are also reactions of another kind.

> More generally, it is arguable that copyright terms have now passed the reasonable limits of protection. Profit, as a possible return for risk-taking, is essential if entrepreneurs are to continue to flourish in the arts as in industry and commerce. However, there is no evidence that the present limits are any incentive to the production of works of art. If only because these limits tend to be extended as of right, and to embrace more and more only marginally creative activities, they deserve re-examination in the light both of economic analysis and of the public's right to enjoy art more widely, more cheaply and with more advantage to themselves (Thomas, 1967, p. 46).

Thus one major dimension seems to have been neglected in the evolution of copyright: the interests and requirements of the general public and society at large. Copyright is supposed to serve a number of social functions, but the emphasis has been on the defence of the – legitimate – interests of certain groups in society. Copyright is portrayed as the natural or only method to deal with a cluster of complex issues and to function as the guarantor of the rights of intellectual creators and workers. Copyright has been discussed mainly as a narrow professional matter among the various interest groups concerned and in terms of the balance to be struck between the directly implicated parties. In recent years, though, the effects of new technology and changing socio-cultural attitudes have transformed copyright into a matter of wider social concern. It is no longer possible to avoid fundamental issues: does copyright as currently conceived and practised fulfil the social functions it was designed to serve? In other words, what is the case for copyright?

Of the traditional reasons in favour of copyright, some might be accepted or acceptable in all currently applied systems, whereas some of them would be applicable principally in countries with a market economy. Consequently, critical analyses arising from within these market economy systems themselves provide the most revealing insights.

A critical discussion of copyright presents a particular set of difficulties. Most of the expert writing in this field is in defence of copyright, but 'bias, and fear of bias, make an author's judgment on copyright a little unreliable' (Plant, 1934, p. 168). This defensive attitude also has the unfortunate result that a critical analysis of copyright concepts and practices is taken as an attack on those who are protected by copyright. In this respect, the differences between the Anglo-American and the continental European copyright philosophies have had an interesting effect. Since the continental approach starts with the concept of the rights of the author based on notions of natural law and human rights, it becomes more difficult to discuss copyright than within the Anglo-American tradition which starts from more pragmatic and less 'sacred' principles. Even specialists from outside the copyright field have shown interest in this subject matter; in particular economists seem to have a predilection for committing the heresy of putting the 'uneasy case for copyright'.

This unease is not a recent phenomenon. When the House of Commons in England discussed a new Copyright Bill in 1841, the only alternatives seen were copyright and patronage: 'the least objectionable way of remunerating them [the authors] is by means of copyright . . . The system of copyright has great advantages and great disadvantages . . . For the sake of the good we must submit to the evil; but the evil ought not to last one day longer than is necessary for the purpose of securing the good'. And, as a final point: 'The principle of copyright is this. It is a tax on readers for the purpose of giving a bounty to writers. The tax is an exceedingly bad one; it is a tax on one of the most innocent and most salutary of human pleasures; and never let us forget that a tax on innocent pleasures is a premium on vicious pleasures' (Hansard, vol. 56, 5 February 1841, quoted in Plant, 1934, pp. 170-1). A more extreme stand was taken by Sir Louis Mallet in his minority report to the Royal Commission on Copyright some thirty-five years later. He in fact stated the case against copyright:

> property exists in order to provide against the evils of natural scarcity. A limitation of supply by artificial causes, creates scarcity in order to create property . . . It is within this latter class that copyright in published works must be included. Copies of such works may be multiplied indefinitely, subject to the cost of paper and of printing which alone, but for copyright, would limit the supply and any demand, however great, would be attended not only by no conceivable injury to society, but on the contrary, in the case of useful works, by the greatest possible advantage . . . The case of a book is precisely analogous to that of a house, of a carriage, or of a piece of cloth, for the design of which a claim to perpetual copyright has never, I believe, been seriously entertained. [However] in a matter which affects so large and valuable a property, and so many vested interests as have been created under copyright laws, it would be both unjust and inexpedient to proceed towards such a change as has been fore-shadowed, except in the most gradual and tentative manner (Plant, 1934, pp. 193-4).

Breyer, in his provocative essay on 'The uneasy case for copyright', comes to the conclusion that none of the traditional reasons in support of copyright is particularly valid.

Starting with the non-economic goals served by copyright law, the moral rights aspects of copyright do not in his view provide an adequate or sufficient justification for a copyright system. Alternative legal arrangements to protect the non-pecuniary interests of the author can readily be devised; for example through a comprehensive system of tort protection. This approach also ties in with another observation which focuses on certain aspects of the Anglo-American copyright system: since copyright initially was designed mainly to protect the publisher and only later was supplemented with concepts defined in terms of rights granted to the author, there has arisen a confusion between the protection of the publisher and the protection of the author, with the former being able to hide, as it were, behind the author, despite their often conflicting interests.

In dealing with the economic arguments for copyright, Breyer's conclusion is that one must know the facts about a particular industry - book publishing, broadcasting, film production - before one can accurately analyse the conditions for and benefits associated with copyright protection. As an example, he uses the concrete situation in book production, with regard primarily to textbooks and general 'trade books'. The conclusion of this economic analysis is that the case for copyright in books considered as a whole is weak.

'First, it shows that the argument most frequently advanced to support copyright protection is shallow: To demonstrate that an initial publisher's costs are high, while reproduction costs are low, is not sufficient to establish the need for copyright protection'. Second, this analysis points out that copyright is very much of a mixed blessing: 'It can lead to prices higher than necessary to secure production; it can impose large transaction costs; it can even help a firm or group of firms to limit competition throughout an industry' (Breyer, 1970, p. 351). Third, the desirability of copyright protection will vary from one type of 'writing' to another, and thus from one kind of intellectual production to another. This analysis then leads to the conclusion that 'it is difficult to do other than take an ambivalent position on the question of whether current copyright protection - considered as a whole - is justified . . . The position suggests that the case for copyright in books rests not upon proven need, but rather upon uncertainty as to what would happen if protection were removed' (ibid., p. 322).

A similar point has been made, starting from the statement that 'the promise of copyright protection has nothing to do with the creative impulse. It can never have been remotely responsible for a masterpiece, even if it does affect the output of writers, artists and composers whose work is intended specifically for the mass market' (Thomas, 1967, pp. 21–2). An economic analysis should therefore begin by asking whether the extra price involved in copyright is necessary to secure the flow of output. The problem thus concerns the position of the artist in the economy. 'Does the ever-lengthening term of copyright protection enter his calculations very much, or indeed at all? Is it an inducement to give up one means of livelihood and instead take up writing, painting, composing or design?' (ibid., p. 21). Or the same thought put another way: 'for three, if not four, centuries, the advocates of property in the right to copy have argued as though book production were the conditioned response of authors, publishers and printers to the impulse of copyright legislation' (Plant, 1934, p. 167).

Such questions are obviously extremely difficult to answer. At this stage, the only conceptual tools we have at our disposal for investigating this kind of problem may be the approaches developed in the very recent analyses of the 'information economy' discussed in the following section. For the time being, such issues can only be noted: they are of a kind which also require an answer on the basis of the social efficacy of copyright. If few seem prepared to go this far in stressing the unease of the case for copyright, it is important that these questions be raised – if for nothing else than to elicit a careful analysis of the problems involved as a basis for the search for the most adequate solutions.

Very interesting is an analysis originating from within the copyright community itself. At a recent congress held in Paris, Michael Freegard, General Manager of the British Performing Right Society, spoke of the future of the author's copyright which he intended also to cover most neighbouring rights. He starts by professing his faith in copyright: 'my experience has led me to become increasingly aware, and more convinced, of the fundamental desirability, for the sake of society as a whole, of the protection and encouragement of authors' (1977, p. 2). None the less, he believes it is legitimate and even obligatory to put the question: 'is there, in the long term, a future for the author's right at all?' The reason for putting this heretical question is that in

Freegard's opinion it would be unrealistic to suppose that copyright would go unchallenged 'in the ferment of change that affects every aspect of contemporary life'.

Freegard lists the challenges to copyright under three broad headings: technological, economic and social. The technological factors obviously relate to the evolution of new means for the reproduction and transmission of works. While these advances should not be seen as presenting dangers but opportunities, the point is made that the new media all share one central characteristic: they involve the use of protected works on a scale and in a manner which precludes the possibility of individual control.

In the economic sphere Freegard mentions among the most important developments influencing copyright the extension of state intervention and the trend towards the establishment of trading blocks (COMECON, EEC, etc.). In so far as the administration of authors' rights is carried out on a collective basis, a conflict has arisen in certain countries between the copyright laws and the laws regulating monopolistic trade practices. Since it is expected that collective copyright licensing practices will increase, so will the incidence of governmental intervention. The effects of policies evolved by trading blocks in the copyright field have so far been visible within the EEC. The EEC Commission has directed its attention to the relationships between authors and their societies, to national subsidies to the film industry and the rights of performers. On some of these matters it might well be that treaty obligations under the Berne Convention will collide with interpretations of the Treaty of Rome.

Such collisions between opposing principles represent a major challenge to copyright. Copyright law might conflict with public law, as has happened in the case of employees in media institutions subject to public regulation: the moral rights of permanently employed producers in a public service organization with regard to the integrity of their works have been opposed to the application of public law regulation concerning balance and objectivity in programme content. There is an unresolved conflict between the principle of the free flow of information and the exclusive rights assigned to authors and performers. The often-heard argument that copyright promotes free flow hides the problem but does not resolve it. A similar conflict arises on the one hand with official policies favouring cultural exchanges and on the other with attitudes expressed by holders of rights, in particular performers who might resist the dissemination of their performances as being detrimental to employment opportunities.

The demands for greater access to cultural and intellectual works create conflicts with copyright at national and international levels. Domestically, issues of access arise with new educational and cultural policies. More flexible and open educational patterns in the perspective of permanent or lifelong education presuppose a widespread and flexible use of educational and cultural products. Similarly, policies of democratizing and decentralizing cultural activities may collide with the principle of exclusive rights assigned to authors and other categories of creative talent. Interestingly enough, this conflict may become particularly pronounced in those countries where the demands for support of authors and other cultural workers have been met by the provision of major subsidies for the arts and other cultural activities. A case in point is Sweden, where traditional copyright practices have been placed against the concept of a 'common cultural right'.

A similar conflict between protection and access is one of the major issues developing countries have to solve in their national legislation. To these countries, the dilemma is also presented in another form: the protection and encouragement of national culture versus the need to have access to protected works as a tool of development in education, science and technology.

2 The rights of authors

Even traditional doctrine would admit that there are partly compatible, partly conflicting, interests between authors, publishers and public needs, between the equally legitimate demands of protection for works and of access to works, between policies for the encouragement of creative work and policies for the wider dissemination of cultural products in society. Where should copyright end, and the public domain start? Which rights should be protected and which can be protected? How far can current copyright policy and legislation solve these dilemmas?

In one perspective, the focus is on the elements which make up the triangle of relationships between the author, the publisher and the public at large. One set of issues may be expressed in terms of the rights of authors, the role of publishers, their interrelationships and their interaction with society.

In discussing the rights of authors, a first distinction should be made between the principle of copyright and the exercise of this right. From its beginning, copyright was conditioned by print technology; i.e. the production of copies. Each step in the production process is easily discernible: the writing of a manuscript, the setting, the printing, the binding, the distribution. It is relatively simple to identify these separate functions, and to find objects in this process to which a right can be attached. The expression 'copyright' reflects this process: it is literally a right to copy a work. The addition of public performance does not in general terms present difficulties. The basic assumption is that an individual independent author negotiates, on the best terms he can get, the transfer of a set of easily identifiable rights to a publisher, a concert organizer or a theatre-owner for the specific exploitation of his work. The protection of the author's rights is fundamentally taken to mean that the use – i.e. the copying or performance of a work – is lawful only with the authorization of its author, or of the person or enterprise to whom the author has transferred his rights. This situation provides the starting point for and background to the traditional reasons for giving the author such an exclusive right. The protection given to the author is assumed to put him, economically and socially, in a position of being able to negotiate such conditions for the sale of his rights that he will be able to create new works and thereby contribute to the cultural and scientific heritage of his society. Conversely, the development of this heritage requires the stimulation of creativity and learning by giving authors certain economic and social guarantees through copyright.

Thus, in general terms, the rights of authors under the law of copyright should be determined by a delicate balance between two socially necessary but partly antithetical interests. On the one hand, sufficient protection should be accorded to the author to encourage the production of works vital to the cultural and scientific needs of society; on the other hand, the protection should not be so extensive as to frustrate the societal needs for reasonable access to such works.

Many aspects of these traditional concepts have been challenged as being inadequate or outmoded. Thus, an oft-mentioned example refers to the results of regulating the economic conditions of the author through market forces reflected in royalties: they are often inequitable in that a few authors get much (too much, according to some), while others do not get enough. Most societies have therefore found it necessary to resort to additional methods for the encouragement of creativity: through public commissions or government subsidies and through new forms of patronage by business enterprises and foundations. The question remains, though, as to what extent satisfactory solutions can be provided by either the market-place, patronage or government action. To some, the market-place gives the author a guarantee of freedom, while government subsidy is likely to engender bondage. To others, the market forces represent an unacceptable form of dependence and commercialization which might be avoided if, say, government subsidies were channelled to the authors through their own associations or societies. And even though widely practised, patronage appears to elicit ambivalent reactions.

Such questions have the advantages of going beyond the legal confines and of putting copyright in a larger social and cultural context. The fundamental problem concerns the ability of copyright to fulfil adequately all its social functions in present circumstances.

In addressing this matter one must begin with the concept of 'author', the creator of a 'work'. In the early print media it was easy to identify and locate the author. The same is true in the case of a traditional play, musical composition or painting. The special cases represented by, say, collective works could without undue stress be incorporated into the traditional system based on the concept of an individual, easily identifiable, author with a clear relationship to a similarly identifiable work.

Changing circumstances, both technical and social, now provide for 'authorships' and 'works' of a radically different kind from those foreseen in classical copyright legislation.

The impact of new communications technology on the concept of the 'author' is obvious. New methods for the creation or production of cultural products have resulted in new categories of 'authors' and 'works' that can only with difficulty be assimilated into the traditional concepts. Some examples may help to show the pressure on the outer limits of traditional copyright concepts.

A first difficulty arises in connection with the definition of the communications systems and modes to which the various rights refer. International conventions and national laws deal differently with, say, broadcasting and cable distribution, and concepts such as 'publication', 'public display' and 'performance' change their meaning in relation to different media.

In the present situation the terminology in the communications field is anything but clear. To compound the confusion, the definitions adopted in public law may vary from country to country. As was mentioned previously in the case of broadcasting, the definition adopted by the International Telecommunication Union refers only to wireless transmissions, whereas a number of national laws include wire and cable distribution in the concept of broadcasting. The difficulties of defining, in the broadcasting production and transmission process, the point or points where the rights of copyright-owners should be attached are considerable and have led to debates of scholastic intricacy. Video-cassettes and videodiscs have given rise to a similar set of problems: should they from a legal point of view be integrated with cinematographic works, or do they represent a category by itself which requires special rules? The teletext and video services, some of which are distributed as a subsidiary television service, have caused acrimonious debates over whether they should be defined – and regulated – as broadcasting, press, publishing or telecommunications. The public law definitions obviously influence copyright legislation and practice.

The copyright field suffers greatly from this confusion because its own definitions start from traditional assumptions; furthermore, the definitions tend to become more abstruse and complicated as time passes and new communication modes are introduced which cause a distortion of these traditional categories.

One characteristic of modern communications technology is a trend in the direction of decentralized, individualized use of communication modes which, so far, have been mainly available in capital-intensive and often heavily institutionalized environments. Symphony concerts, opera performances, film production and broadcasting, newspaper publishing, are all typical examples of these environments. Current and different uses of greatly simplified and inexpensive equipment can be exemplified by the alternative press, underground cinema, 'guerrilla television' or video-group activities. They represent the emergence of new forms for the creation/production of messages and involve new types of authors/producers who cannot be integrated into traditional categories and have a totally different attitude towards 'rights'. They do not want protection, they want to get their message across; they are thus not interested in rights of protection but rights of access to facilities, whether economic, technical or institutional for the dissemination of their 'works'. In that respect, they resemble scientists who want to disseminate the results of their research, even if they have to pay. Often the production and communication of such works took place in an environment which was local, community-oriented or intended for inter-group communication. Such expressions as 'group communications' and 'mini-media' were in fact rather apt. However, with new forms of 'access' within institutionalized media structures and the trend towards more localized mass media activities, such 'works' have also started to enter the larger, formally organized communications systems.

Another extreme is represented by new forms of electronic production and of 'computer-originated' works. In the first case, it is the 'electronic producer', the producer/director and/or the person who operates the equipment who composes the final work. The contribution of an 'author' or a 'performer' may be identified in a manner similar to that in a cinematographic film; however, these contributions lose their identity when they become elements of an electronic ensemble which does not even have to exist in traditional physical forms.

As indicated in chapter V, the issues of authorship of and protection of works created with the assistance or intervention of a computer still present great uncertainties.

All previous technological developments, from movable type through television and reprography, have been methods for the recording and transmitting the audible and visible manifestations of human creativity. An author inscribes the words of his choice, whether with a quill pen, a typewriter or a photocomposition machine. A musician plays a chord, or even random notes, according to his proclivities. A painter may spatter colours upon a canvas with no real conception of the final result but that result is dependent upon his choice concerning the manner in which the colours are applied. In each of these examples the resulting work may be copyrighted.

When, however, a computer is used during the creation of a work, the nexus between man and work is less clear (Meyer, 1977, p. 24).

These considerations by CONTU in the USA led to an analysis of various ways of dealing with such works for copyright purposes, none of which is found to be satisfactory. At one extreme is the position that computer-originated works are not eligible for copyright protection because they are not the result of human creativity. At the other extreme is the argument that a computer can never exercise independent judgment so that any work produced as a result of its use depends on human creativity and therefore is a work of authorship. An intermediate argument maintains that a work eligible for copyright has been created if it is the result of significant human intervention. This position demonstrates the weakness of them all: how is it possible to distinguish between these different cases?

There are more subtle effects of new media on our attitudes towards art and artistic creation. The art critic John Berger, in an analysis of the effects of the camera on our perception of visual arts, states that 'the uniqueness of an original painting now lies in its being the original of a reproduction . . . its first meaning is no longer found in what it says but in what it is . . .' (Berger, 1972, p. 21). He goes on to make the point that in the age of reproduction the meaning of paintings is no longer attached to them, but becomes transmittable and thus a sort of information which can be put to many uses.

The art of the past no longer exists as it once did. Its authority is lost. In its place there is a language of images. What matters now is who uses this language and for what purposes. This touches upon questions of copyright for reproduction, the ownership of art presses and publishers, the total policy of public art galleries and museums. As usually presented these are narrow professional matters . . . what really is at stake is much larger (ibid., p. 33).

The age of reproduction has thus had the effect of destroying uniqueness. Not only objects but also performances can be reproduced and are thus no longer unique. This might be one of the reasons for the recent interest in the stages leading to the work more than in the finished product, in the process of creation more than in the created work. Again, the 'work' becomes more elusive. The same trend is even more obvious in the creation of uniqueness through 'happenings' or environmental art. A 'happening' is by definition not a reproducible performance but a unique event with no author except the participants. Equally, environmental art is not an object but an experience which, like a sunset, cannot be owned.

In many of these cases the elusiveness of the 'work' corresponds to the difficulty of identifying an 'author'. Often it is no longer possible to separate the various steps in the production of a work to which the various rights are attached. The 'production' of a work may no longer be an act separate from its 'performance' or its distribution. The function of authorship is combined with other functions.

The different identifiable stages and associated functions in the original chain of creation, multiplication and distribution have diversified and combined in a series of new patterns. The time scale of the different steps has collapsed so that previously separate operations occur simultaneously. The distinctiveness of the separate functions disappears in certain new modes of communication.

There is thus a need to go beyond the classical concepts of 'works', 'product' (in tangible physical form) and also of 'performance' (in the sense of the presentation of a pre-existing work). The focus has to shift from objects to processes of communication and flows of information. To a large extent the concept of property becomes inadequate. One cannot 'own' processes or flows of communications.

Social developments have also affected the position of the creator. Increasingly the application of copyright no longer takes place between individual authors and individual publishers, but in negotiations at national and international levels between strongly organized interest groups: unions of 'creators', associations of producers or media conglomerates.

There is, therefore, a need to consider more closely the role of different categories of intellectual workers in the creative process, particularly with regard to production forms conditioned by new technology. The definition of the role of the author and associated rights on the basis of traditional principles of copyright, while adapting these concepts to modern conditions, is difficult enough.

However, even more in need of fundamental reconsideration is the exercise of authors' rights.

According to the traditional concept, it is obligatory to secure the permission of the author or the copyright-owner before using his work. To many analysts this system is completely out of date, except in some particular obvious situations characterized by the circumstances of exploitation of the work; for example books, or performances of works in the theatre. This procedure is seen as outdated because of the impact of the revolutionary changes in communications technology: motion pictures, radio, television, cable television, computers, reprography and satellite communication, all of which may be coupled in a single communications spectrum. The authors are no longer able to control and, *a fortiori*, to permit the utilization of their works. Therefore, their 'exclusive' rights which were defined in terms of a certain level of technology cannot be exercised according to the traditional patterns. The old licensing methods for granting rights are ponderous and inefficient; furthermore, technology has made possible new uses for which the exclusive rights of the author are neither clearly defined nor established.

There is thus a need to formulate criteria for defining the methods applied to the exercise of copyright: a recurrent demand is that such methods should be simple and that they should be enforceable without the kind of control or policing that would be unacceptable in a wider social context.

In principle, there seems to be a general and apparently unavoidable trend towards replacing the exclusive right of the author with a system of compulsory or, better expressed, legal licensing whereby the author's rights are subject to a statutory defined licence at a reasonable royalty. There are, however, different views about the effects of such legal licensing systems, specifically in terms of whether they would weaken or strengthen the bargaining position of the author.

Another method which some people think would alleviate the need for legal licensing is the generalized use of collecting societies. These societies are seen to be in a stronger position to exercise the rights of authors, particularly in terms of controlling the use of their works and collecting on their behalf the royalties due to them. However, this method also presents a number of inconveniences. In order to function satisfactorily it requires that all creators should belong to a collecting society. To many this seems an unacceptable imposition. Also, how do the royalties effectively flow through the collecting society to the individual author/creator? What is in this respect an equitable mechanism, procedural or technological?

The use of collecting societies is therefore in most countries a contractual and not a statutory matter. In terms of copyright legislation, one is left with the proposal that authors' rights may be subject to use according to a legal licence, against a reasonable royalty, at least under certain specified conditions such as:

—where it is not possible effectively to regulate the uses of a work;
—where, because of the nature of the medium, it is unduly cumbersome to obtain a licence from the author;
—where there are overriding social reasons, which, however, would require definition.

Both systems – the use of legal licensing and the use of collecting societies – are often seen to suffer from the same basic drawback: it would be difficult to get the royalty payments through to the intended ultimate beneficiary: the author, creator or performer. Furthermore, there often tend to be definite nationalistic overtones to some of these systems which favour national holders of rights over foreigners.

So far we have been mainly concerned with one of the elements in the triangle of relationships between the author, the publisher and the public: the author, his position and remuneration, the exercise of his rights and his relationship to the other participants in the production/distribution process.

In this connection, it should again be stressed that copyright is only one of the means for protecting the economic interests of the author. There are other means, such as public subsidies, prizes, funds of all kinds, taxes on hardware, salaries and patronage. But not enough attention has been paid to an economic analysis of how revenue and added value relate to the use of protected works, how they are distributed and flow through the communications system, or to the economic consequences of various methods of remunerating intellectual creation.

3 The role of publishers

From a historical and current perspective it is impossible to separate the role and rights of the author from the role of those institutions and individuals that serve as intermediaries between the author and the public. Traditionally, this intermediary has been defined as the 'publisher'; however, as in the case of the author, the concept of publisher requires reconsideration.

The diversity of these intermediaries and their different objectives and functions already makes it difficult to use a unitary concept of 'publisher' – who may be a government authority, non-commercial public body or commercial enterprise. It is useful to start by considering the functions of these intermediaries, which in the present situation include not only the traditional 'software' side, but also to some extent the 'hardware'. Three of these functions appear to be particularly important:

—the 'publisher' in the traditional sense published the work or organized its performance; now the concept of publisher also includes various 'producers' in areas such as cinema, broadcasting, cable television, video-cassettes and probably the 'information providers' in videotext services, etc., as well;

—in certain of these new communication forms such as video-cassettes and videodiscs, the transfer mechanism represented by the 'publisher' needs to be defined in terms of a process that comprises production/manufacturing/multiplication;

—a further function exercised by various categories of 'publishers/producers' is distribution, which to varying degrees may be combined with the two other functions or carried out independently.

The urgency of this question is enhanced by the emergence of further categories of 'publishers/producers'. At one extreme, it has been suggested that computers in certain respects may function as 'electronic publishers'; at the other end of the spectrum, certain new technologies permit anyone to become his or her own combined 'author-publisher'.

These considerations relate to previous observations on current trends in communication developments. The importance of the 'publisher' has grown with the increased use of capital-intensive high-technology forms of communication which tend to increase the cost of software in the publication network but reduce the personnel cost.

Another trend with important implications needs to be mentioned: the decreasing absolute costs inherent in the new information technologies. The constantly falling costs for input, storage, retrieval and dissemination of information will have an even greater impact, particularly on the information transfer between industrialized and developing countries.

While recognizing the complexity and fluidity of the present situation, certain major aspects of the function and situation of the 'publisher/producer/distributor' may be defined.

The publisher depends on (a) a supply of inputs, which conditions his relationship to the author, and (b) a demand for outputs, which concerns his relationship with the public and society at large.

Within any country there is a collection of publishers which may be defined in terms of the types of messages distributed and the medium of distribution; size and market dominance; source or revenue; type of ownership and legal status, particularly in relation to the state. Every country is characterized by a particular blend of various publishing units defined according to the above criteria.

The publisher will have one or more of the following objectives: to fulfil socially, culturally and politically defined and accepted needs and to optimize revenue or economic efficiency. In terms of organizational goals it could be expected that the publisher, as any other organization, would tend to become larger, to develop a good image and to compete with other 'publishing' organizations.

Some of the main functions fulfilled by the publisher are to provide a supply of information, instruction, education and culture; to provide access to resources for self and group expression; to organize processes and flows of information in society. The publisher also plays a key role in the patterning of the flow of information from the author and other sources to the public and society and in regulating the flow of money from society to the creators. In other words, the publisher functions as a two-way medium of information: an intellectual flow out, an economic flow back.

Issues concerning the rights of authors and the role of publishers must be set in the context of the relationship between these two groups. The terms of this relationship have been changing gradually and have been differently conceived in various copyright systems of the world. One of the most important differences is between those countries which recognize an inalienable moral right of the author as creator to enable him to protect the integrity of his work and those, mainly in the Anglo-American tradition, where the shift in copyright from being almost exclusively a publisher's right to the incorporation of elements of an author's rights has tended to obscure the relationship between author and publisher.

This relationship raises the problem of monopoly, since copyright is based on the concept of a monopoly, albeit with limitations. It has been pointed out that even though the exclusive rights of authors have been put in the foreground, the real source of the monopoly danger is not the author, but the publisher. This danger has been seen by a number of people in the increasing trends of concentration in the communication/entertainment industry. Communications conglomerates which encompass all the traditional processes for promoting and distributing intellectual property are increasingly common. An example is the combined ownership of book publishing houses, newspaper/magazine publishing, film studios, cable systems, radio and television stations. In this view, the problem has been obscured because the availability of copyright to the publisher is screened behind the idea of copyright as an author's right. This, in turn, has obscured the difference between the interests of the publisher and the interests of the author.

As a case in point may be mentioned the relationship between composers and music publishers. According to some analyses, a conflict of interests arises naturally and obviously in a situation where one sells rights to another. The exercise of musical copyright has led to situations which have been strongly condemned by informed musicians. Controversial 'editings' by publishers have been disclosed by musicians, particularly of scores by Mozart, Schubert and Verdi. Some music publishers have followed the practice of withholding works from sale so as to secure high returns from copies made available on a hire-basis only. Thus, since the 'sales of sheet music, parts and scores are no longer the greater part of their business, music publishers in general may be said to have abandoned their traditional publishing function and to operate virtually as agents' (Thomas, 1967, p. 38). These and other practices once caused the administrator of the Orchestre de la Suisse Romande to exclaim that the international community 'can have no more useful and urgent task than to free music, its composers and performers, and the concert societies, from the sordid protection of the publishers' (from Unesco, 1963 Report, quoted in Thomas, 1967, p. 41).

The relationship becomes even more complicated when the nature of creation and publication, the role of the author and the publisher change so that both compatible and opposing interests are combined and stratified in new ways. One of the most vexing issues concerns the relationship between 'author' and 'publisher' in an employment situation. Using broadcasting as an example, the basic question is: Which uses of a programme produced by permanent employees are covered by legislation and contracts? Here both copyright law and labour law could be applicable and they might conflict on certain points.

Of particular relevance in this context are copyright rules that in the case of cinema and television films provide for a presumption that the film producer or broadcasting organization has the right to exploit the work. However, national laws regulate in sometimes opposing ways the ownership of copyright in the works of employees. French law declares that an employment contract implies no exception to the exclusive right that the author enjoys by the mere fact of creation. Thus an agreement is needed for the transfer of copyright to the employer. The attitude in countries in the Anglo-American tradition is different: where a work is made in the course of the author's employment under a contract of service, the employers are entitled to any copyright in the work except in the case of any contrary stipulation in the contract. Other countries steer a middle course. The premise is that copyright is assigned to the employer to the extent necessary for his customary activities.

One point of major disagreement between employer and employees in broadcasting concerns what is to be understood by 'normal' or 'customary' activities. The broadcasting organizations claim extensive rights of programming use, for domestic broadcasting as well as for broadcasting abroad, for education, documentation, library and museum use. In contrast, the employees' associations or unions often adopt a very restrictive attitude, claiming that the broadcasting organization would have the right to use a programme only for one transmission within the country or during one year, while the employees would have the right to refuse any other uses without special supplementary payments on top of their salaries.

Here, the point has been made that it would be absurd to treat broadcasting organizations as completely static entities. As with other media institutions, their activities are influenced by technological progress which makes it possible – and desirable – to distribute their programmes in new ways. When for reasons of cultural policy broadcasting organizations are requested to assume new functions, any possible conflict with the claims of employees based on copyright and/or labour law must be solved.

4 Fair use – and unfair

To a large extent the application of copyright has centred on regulating the relationship between the 'author' and the 'publisher'. Copyright has a further function: to regulate the uses to which a work is put, thus its flow and dissemination; or in other words the relationships between on the one hand the 'author' and the 'publisher' and, on the other, the individuals and institutions who together make up the public and society at large.

The basis of this relationship is that the author and publisher use the rights assigned to them under copyright law to decide the conditions on which work may be used. Copyright has legally been constructed in the form of exclusive, more or less absolute rights granted to the author and his assignees. In order to provide for a socially workable system, the way out of the dilemma posed by an abstract and absolute legal construction is the awkward procedure of defining necessary 'limitations', 'exceptions', 'exemptions' or 'fair use' principles.

The concept of limitations is a relatively straightforward proposition, at least in terms of the most important example: the limits set on the period of protection. The other concepts are more difficult and create more problems. Exceptions and fair use concern fundamental issues in the field of intellectual property. They are used for the purpose of striking a balance between the interests of authors and publishers protected through their exclusive rights to authorize or prohibit uses of a work and the interests of the public and the requirements of public policy. From an even more pragmatic point of view, they are also employed to avoid obvious absurdities which a too rigid or absolute application of copyright would entail.

The expression 'fair use' seems to be used in two ways: in a more general sense it encompasses all exceptions to copyright in the public interest; more narrowly it determines the limits of use without the consent of the author. In what follows, the expression will be used in the more general sense.

The issue of fair use has been described as the most troublesome in the whole of copyright. It has always been controversial. In principle, there is not even agreement as to whether fair use should be regarded as a 'privileged' infringement of copyright or whether fair use simply does not infringe copyright at all. Despite the doctrinal disputes, fair use by someone other than the copyrightholder appears to have been recognized from an early date, at least by the courts. Today, fair use limitations are included in the relevant international conventions and in national legislation, even though the detailed rules vary considerably. Thus the UCC includes a very general rule to the effect that states may, by domestic legislation, make exceptions that do not conflict with the spirit and provisions of the Convention (Art. IVb). The Berne Convention, on the other hand, includes a series of detailed and complex rules under different headings referring to different kinds of works and different types of exceptions. The Rome Convention and the Geneva Phonogram Convention also include provisions for exceptions couched in relatively general terms.

While the national legislation of most countries seems to comprise some fair use provisions, the West German Copyright Act is generally regarded as being both advanced and unusually clear on this topic. This Act includes in one Section (III) some eighteen articles dealing with fair use. These provisions include exceptions to the exclusive rights of authors for specific purposes such as judicial proceedings, religious and educational use, reporting on current events, personal private use, demonstrations by commercial enterprises of sound and video equipment for prospective buyers. Exceptions in the case of particular kinds of works concern public speeches, newspaper articles and broadcast commentaries. Further rules regulate the right of citation, public reproduction of works in certain circumstances, or pictures in exhibition catalogues or works in public places, and the reproduction of commissioned artistic works.

The legislation in some other countries which have introduced in their copyright acts special sections dealing with 'limitations on copyright' resembles the German Act. Thus the Swedish Copyright Act of 1960 and the Japanese Copyright Act of 1970 include a series of limitations similar to those in the German Act, with minor additions such as special rules for the reproduction of works for use by the blind. However, national approaches vary considerably. In some countries such as Belgium and France the regulation is strict and narrowly circumscribes the free zone exempt from authorization. Countries in the Anglo-American tradition generally take a more liberal approach, and even include uses that are permitted without the author having a right of payment. Other countries provide for a relatively generous attitude, compensated in certain cases by providing the author with a right of equitable payment. In countries with a socialist economic system, exceptions and fair use dealings are often expressed in terms of permitted uses with or without remuneration.

The diversity of current national legal provisions can best be shown by a concrete example such as the issue of rights in broadcasts used for educational purposes. The relevant international conventions, with one exception (Brussels Convention), authorize states to legislate at their discretion for the exercise of intellectual property rights in the educational field, provided that the permitted use does not overstep the extent justified by the purpose and is compatible with general fair use concepts. However, even in a region as relatively homogeneous from a copyright point of view as Western Europe, national laws differ considerably. Some countries such as Austria, Belgium, France, Italy and the Netherlands do not in general terms provide for an exception from protection for audio-visual materials used in schools. Other countries have included special provisions for this purpose. The German provisions are well known and confer a right to produce copies of single works included in school broadcasts by schools, institutions for teacher training and advanced training as well as youth educational centres. Similar provisions have been included in the laws of such countries as Luxembourg, Malta, the United Kingdom and the Nordic countries. Attempts are now being made to work towards a harmonization of national laws through the Council of Europe and the EEC.

In view of their specific requirements, most copyright laws of developing countries include special fair use provisions intended for development purposes. The Tunis Model Copyright Law for use by developing countries includes first of all a section of exceptions similar to the provisions in such laws as those of West Germany and Sweden. In addition there are certain provisions specific to developing countries in terms of possibilities to translate and reproduce protected works according to the provisions of the 1971 revisions of the Berne and Universal Conventions.

A basic question is thus whether fair use is well suited to resolve the problems of reconciling the partly compatible, partly conflicting, interests of the author and publisher and the general public and society. Some analysts have stated that while the interests of the author and the publisher have received much attention, little consideration has been given to the interests of the individual user and thus to society. In principle, only the 'nebulous and uncertain doctrine of fair use' refers to the individual user's rights (Patterson, 1968b, p. 227).

The 'fair use' doctrine has created even more uncertainties in the modern communications environment. High-speed photocopying machines, new devices for the recording and copying of sound and audio-visual materials have given the individual new opportunities of participation in the communications process. According to traditional copyright concepts, one response to this new situation would result in such absurdities as the prohibition of even the private use of videotape recorders for the recording and viewing of broadcast television programmes. At least in those societies where the manufacture and sale of such equipment cannot simply be forbidden, the kind of control and policing required would be unacceptable in a wider social perspective.

The point has therefore been made that it is no longer possible to make a clear-cut and rigid distinction between the 'exclusive' zones covered by copyright and the 'free' zone, representing the legally defined series of exceptions and fair use dealings. There is also an increasing intermediate zone where the use of a work is permitted in certain circumstances without the authorization of the author but against payment. According to many of those immediately concerned, there is a new danger for copyright: the increasing trend towards reducing the author's exclusive right to a simple right to receive payment.

Where protected works are reproduced for private use, the legislator is faced with a dilemma. If he sticks to a very strict interpretation of the right of reproduction, the result is a situation of massive infringement of copyright with no possibility of copyright beneficiaries preventing it. If, on the other hand, the legislator accepts provisions in favour of the users of protected works, the number of illegal reproductions will certainly be fewer, but the author or publisher runs the risk of suffering legally accepted inroads into the normal exploitation of his work. An example that has been mentioned is the real risk to scientific journals because of the more generalized use of photocopying machines which results in a decrease in their paid subscriptions.

The traditional solution would be to confer an exclusive right on the author and leave it to the interested parties to negotiate suitable arrangements. However, the massive use of reproducing equipment would imply the conclusion of collective agreements between associations of users and associations of authors. Another solution would be for governments to liberalize fundamentally the rules concerning these generalized uses – since, in any case, they cannot be prevented – and to grant a right of remuneration to the author and other holders of rights. A third solution would be to exempt from authorization and payment certain users of protected works. As could be expected, this type of solution is favoured by such user groups as schools and libraries and opposed by the holders of rights.

In this situation, it seems generally agreed that the West German Act provides an ingenious and practicable solution. Sound and audio-visual recording for private use is permitted, but supplemented by a payment. However, it was realized that an individual right of remuneration conferred upon the holders of rights would imply an inadmissible control of privacy. The law therefore adopts an indirect solution in the sense that the manufacturers and importers of recording equipment pay a certain sum for each apparatus sold. These sums are distributed to the holders of rights through a collecting society.

The provision represents the first example of an indirect regulation of copyright payments in a national law.

> This German regulation constitutes a compromise between the concept that activities of use in the private sphere should basically be free and the concept that such activities cannot be free when the private making of reproductions endangers the economic exploitation of the work since private reproduction would totally or almost toally replace an industrially fabricated reproduction (Dietz, 1976, p. 133).

Whether or not one agrees with the assumptions of this statement, the fact remains that the new techniques of reproduction and recording have made possible a generalized use of protected works; the concession of an exclusive individual right is no longer an adequate solution either for practical reasons or for reasons of principle.

All the derogations expressed in terms of exceptions or fair use operate automatically once the prescribed conditions have been met. The national legislation of some countries provides for an additional system: public authorities have been given powers to replace the author or take measures which have been seen as an expropriation of copyright. In the first case a designated authority (Copyright Board, Council of Ministers, etc.) may authorize the publication or republication of a work which is of particular public interest. For example, in Mexico a work may be republished once it has been found impossible, over a period of one year, to obtain copies in the capital and in three main towns. In other cases a work may pass into the public domain after the lapse of a certain time (Canada) or if copies are not available after a specified time (Spain). Another method used is the assignment of copyright to the state, which either republishes the work itself or hands it over to a third party.

'Fair use' can be said to act as a buffer between copyright protection and public requirements. But how far can fair use absorb the shocks of conflict between copyright policy and public policy in education and culture?

The extent to which fair use presents fundamental problems can be seen from a controversial and interesting comment made by a former Swedish Minister of Education. In recent times, the Swedish Parliament re-introduced an ancient Nordic legal rule concerning the right of everyone to 'trespass' on privately owned land for reasons of recreation, etc. (allemansrätt, or common public right). By analogy with this right, the Minister proposed a similar common public right in the field of intellectual property. This statement was caused by the difficulties experienced in balancing the new principles of cultural and educational policy adopted by Parliament and copyright as traditionally perceived. The reactions of interested parties, particularly authors and publishers of various kinds, were, as could be expected, violent in tone. It was even found necessary for the government to clarify in the directives for the revision of the copyright legislation that

Sweden had no intention of abandoning either its international treaty obligations or its adherence to the basic principles of an author's individual rights.

Technological innovation certainly causes new problems of fair use, but the problems arising from practices that are definitely unfair are anything but new. Piracy is as old as copyright, and history has a way of repeating itself. The piracy of books was an immediate reason for the move towards the first international agreement in the copyright field, exactly as the piracy of records and sound tapes caused governments rapidly to conclude the Geneva Phonogram Convention. Piracy has also led to more direct and stronger reactions. 'It is recorded that at the end of the nineteenth century, the London music publishers, led by Chappell & Co., employed retired police sergeants and other tough characters to raid premises of pirates, and cases are reported of pitched battles with buckle-belts and even pokers' (Thomas, 1967, p. 11). Today, Hong Kong has found it necessary to use special police against pirates.

As the manufacture of information and entertainment through books, films, music and television has become big business, so has piracy. According to one estimate, the pirate book industry turnover was more than one million pounds in 1967. Commercially more important is the music business. The unauthorized duplication of sound recordings began almost as soon as the record industry came into existence. It did not present a serious problem until tape became a popular medium and new techniques made copying easy. Recent estimates allege that of the annual 2.3 billion pound record music business, at least four hundred million pounds represent the turnover of pirates world wide – about 15 per cent of all sales. The rate varies considerably, from less than 1 per cent in certain countries to about 80 per cent in others (Poole, 1978; ILO/Unesco/WIPO, 1979).

Concerned organizations like the IFPI (International Federation of Producers of Phonograms and Videograms) are making 'strenuous efforts' to combat this piracy. At one level, the industry is seeking to promote acceptance of substantive rights and remedies by urging governments to ratify the Rome and Geneva Conventions or to introduce corresponding rights into national legislation. At another level, the emphasis is on the development of effective enforcement procedures which in the opinion of the IFPI should include provisions permitting injunctive relief; seizure and destruction of infringing material and equipment used in the manufacture of copies; penalties in the form of heavy fines; and penal sanctions, including imprisonment.

The most famous example of the fight against piracy comes from Hong Kong 'where copyright infringement was a widespread and flourishing business. Most of this illegal activity was confined to sound recordings although some involved literary and artistic works and cinematograph films. It was generally believed that, for every legitimate cassette tape recording sold, there were thirty pirated copies' (Lo, 1979, p. 138). In 1973 Hong Kong began its big drive against the pirating of records and tapes. The government established a special Copyright Investigation Unit of the Customs and Excise Services, originally consisting of seven officers and later increased to over forty, 'who were instructed to carry arms on all raids' (Neary, 1978, p. 102). During the period 1974–8 over four hundred people were arrested, fines totalling more than one million Hong Kong dollars were imposed and over half a million illegal copies of tapes, records, books, street guides and films were confiscated (Lo, 1979, p. 138).

However, human ingenuity will leave neither business nor the legislator any rest. Bootlegging, which is the unauthorized recording of an artist's performance live at a concert or from broadcasting studio outtakes, is reported to be increasing. But the major battle concerns video. The video-cassette is already the main instrument of the 'pix pirates' (*Variety*, 9 May 1979). The main target is films which are recorded off the air when transmitted by broadcasters, off closed-circuit performances in hotels or off prints in laboratories. The copies sell at vast profits: copies of the film *Saturday Night Fever* which were seized in Ulster in 1978 reportedly cost £700 each.

The industry is obviously fighting piracy by all means at hand. The American trade magazine *Variety* not unexpectedly talks of the uncovering of international piracy rings of 'enormous proportions' during two years of investigation and of gangs involved in motion picture piracy having links with drug-running and illegal arms trading.

However, another opinion maintains that the situation is more complicated. According to some experts, unless the industry itself makes legitimate programmes available, it will have only itself to blame when piracy takes over. Apart from a few programmes on various specialist subjects, hardly anything is available that can be shown on video-machines – except what is recorded from television. All the parties involved, from film producers to performers' unions, are opposed to home tape video-recordings by individuals. The industry wants to put out only its own 'canned' programmes. 'In the USA, where home video is two years ahead [of other countries] this head-in-the-sand attitude has led to a vast, almost underground, video culture, typified by magazines like the *Videophiles Newsletter* published by the Small Potato Publishing Co., in whose current issue are advertised tapes of at least 200 BBC and ITV programmes' (Poole, 1978).

As to what can or should be done about these new forms of piracy, the situation is one of confusion. As indicated earlier, it would be impossible to prohibit home recording for individual use – unless there is some form of policing machinery which would represent a new means of invasion of privacy. The only remedy open seems to be the adoption of the German solution of a special levy on the video-machines to be distributed to the holders of rights of programmes that people might record. When real piracy occurs in the form of copying for sale, court and police actions are being taken in a number of countries. However, one might ask whether this is the right way to proceed, whether the legislature and hence the police would then always be running behind new technology and new uses of technology, trying to provide protection by means that are often unenforceable.

In one sense, the history of copyright is the history of regulating and controlling the flow of information and of cultural works. The history of piracy, in this context, is part of the history of anti-control and deregulation. At this stage, copyright will have to cope with pressures from two sides. When the expression 'piracy' is used about private uses of copyright works, we face the unresolved problem of defining 'the proper place of the consumer in the creation/diffusion/copyright/performing right syndrome and ultimately . . . the proper place of the private sphere, of the right to privacy' (Hunnings, 1979, p. 78). When 'piracy' refers to the transport of television programmes outside the normal reception zone and their transmission on cable systems, we face the equally unresolved problem of the proper balance between the rights involved and explicit or implicit public policies.

Chapter VII · Policies for the information age

1 Copyright: international relations and interdependence

Throughout the field of intellectual property the international dimension is a dominant factor as reflected in the high level of international co-operation and organization. Its importance is increasing with the spread of modern communications services and this trend can be expected to continue at least in the medium-term future. National policy and legislation concerning copyright are conditioned by both international communications developments and the international legal framework. The criss-crossing pattern of relationships established by government authorities and professional groupings is growing denser and more complex. In this situation how do copyright relations fit into overall patterns of international relations? And what do studies of international relations have to say about copyright relations? Not much has so far been said about either aspect. From the copyright side, no attempt seems to have been made to draw upon the insights provided by new approaches to international relations. Conversely, copyright does not figure in writings on international relations. There is, though, much to be gained by an analysis of copyright relations in the context of international relations generally.

As could be expected, copyright is not a priority issue in traditional international relations analysis, which has almost exclusively focused on the activities of states in terms of power balance, military security and other elements of high international politics. In recent times, international affairs theory had to widen its approach in order to cope with both the changing international system and emerging new ideas. Economic policy issues are now regarded as inseparable from politics. Problems of the environment, of resources, population and energy have been placed high on the international agenda. During the last few years, the transfer of science and technology, communications and information have emerged as new and controversial international issue areas.

Together, all these issue areas represent new dimensions in international relations theory and model-building. In this perspective, copyright has a given place and should attract attention beyond the circle of specialists and lobbyists.

Although no one model or theory of international relations has as yet gained general acceptance, several new approaches and concepts provide useful tools for the analysis of international copyright relations. In what follows, we shall first indicate their potential validity when applied to copyright.

The evolution in international relations concepts to fit current reality is clearly reflected in the reactions against the traditional, 'realist' approach which has dominated much of post-war attitudes. According to this view, the nation-state is virtually the only kind of subject or actor appearing on the international scene. The approach is based on a state-centric view which has been combined with theories about roles and actors in social life. The result is the 'state-as-the-only-actor approach' (Wolfers, 1959). According to this model, the most important characteristic of states is their sovereignty, which is seen as both absolute and indivisible. The ultimate product has aptly been described as the billiard-ball model of a multi-state system in which each state represents a closed, impermeable and sovereign unit which is roughly equal to all other units. Since the sovereign states recognize no higher authority, they find themselves internationally in a 'state of nature', living in conditions of mutual competition and conflict. A further implication of this model is an almost total separation of politics within nations and politics between states: within countries a legal order, between states the law of the jungle.

This 'realist' model has been challenged on all essential points. It has been declared defective, since divorced from reality, and dangerous when used by statesmen as a self-fulfilling prophecy. It has not been able to account for major aspects of current international life and would be hopelessly inadequate if applied to international relations in such areas as communications and copyright. The challenges have come from a variety of new approaches and concepts, some of which will be described.

To start with, the image of the state and the notion of sovereignty implied in the billiard-ball model are proved to be outdated, in so far as they ever gave a true picture of reality. Sovereignty is no longer accepted as absolute and indivisible but as a relative concept that is used to encompass a great variety of national 'actors' from super-powers to mini-states. In contrast to the so-called realist model, recent thinking on international relations emphasizes not the legal equality of states but their actual heterogeneity and the attendant inequality. In such a system, interdependence implies varying patterns of dominance and dependence. In the copyright field it is the combined effect of the interdependence and the differences between states that has resulted in the complicated system of international arrangements with their varying degrees and kinds of protection and varied constituences. Those factors also account for the crisis in copyright relations between industrialized and developing countries to which solutions were sought in the Stockholm Protocol and the 1971 joint revisions of the Berne Convention and the UCC.

A closely related feature in currently proposed models of international relations concerns the blurring of the strict distinction between international and domestic politics and policy-making. This linkage or interdependence of national policy and international politics is characteristic of the entire communications field. These linkages totally dominate international relations and regimes in the complex issue areas designated by such headings as freedom of information, the free flow of information and the new international information order. The same holds true in the copyright field. National legislative developments are to a large extent dependent on the international legal framework and on pressure from both national and international professional and trade groups. Negotiations at government level concern common standards and the harmonization of national policies; agreement depends on the appreciation of how both national objectives and multinational professional interests can be accommodated within an emerging or sought-after consensus. In this as in other areas, multinational companies try at the same time to use and to escape national policies and regulations. The various national professional groups have combined at the international level not only to defend common interests but also to strengthen the pursuit of their national interests. These complex patterns of relationships and interdependence both express and condition the linkages between national and international policies.

The linkage between domestic and international policy-making is in turn closely related to another typical feature of the new paradigms in international relations theory: the diversity of 'actors' operating at the international level. As regards the traditional notion that states are the only actors in the international arena, reality in the copyright field preceded theory in international relations by decades. Theory now admits the fact that states are confronted with a variety of 'actors' ranging from multinational companies to extranational terrorist groups which are not territorially bound but have established sets of relationships both within and across state boundaries.

In the copyright field nongovernmental organizations and interest groups play a role almost as important as that of governments. It is significant that intergovernmental organizations such as Unesco and WIPO have made provisions for associating a host of nongovernmental organizations with their work. Governments often seem reluctant to act without the agreement of these national and international interest groupings which represent the different holders of rights, be they authors, performing artists, publishers, record companies, film producers, broadcasters or others. To a large extent the battles about the Rome and Brussels Conventions were fought not primarily between governments but between the various interest groups concerned.

Another interesting development in international relations and law is tied to the concept of 'international commons' or, otherwise expressed, the 'common heritage of mankind'. From a legal point of view, these concepts are formalized in terms of the internationalization of certain areas through rules prohibiting national appropriation. They have been introduced in the evolving legal codes for outer space and for oceans and the seabed; they represent an attempt to balance a diversity of national interests and the common interests of all countries or rather of the international community as such.

In the communications field, national interests have conflicted with the need for agreed rules to govern the use of 'international commons' in connection with the plans for the allocation of radio frequencies and geostationary orbits for communication satellites.

At first glance, this concept would seem highly relevant to

copyright, since copyright is often tied to such commonly used notions as 'knowledge being a common international resource' or 'the development of the cultural heritage of mankind'. However, the application of these concepts to copyright gives rise to a series of dichotomies. There is a contradiction between the notion of an international commons which in principle should be freely available to all and the notion of exclusive rights protected in national law and by international conventions. Even though 'freely' does not necessarily mean unconditionally, the balance to be struck between the various interests and requirements involved requires a rigorous, objective analysis before the concept of 'international commons' can be applied in the copyright field.

In this connection, another related contradiction warrants attention. There is still unresolved conflict between the equally legitimate concepts of free flow of information and protection. On the one hand is the entire set of principles expressed as 'freedom of information', 'the free flow of information', with the more recent addition of a wider individual access to and participation in cultural life; on the other hand, the set of principles developed in the field of intellectual property. Interestingly enough the countries that most staunchly defend the free flow principles are those that promote the most extensive protection of copyright. At the international level, the same two sets of principles figure in the Universal Declaration of Human Rights: Article 29 prescribes both the right of participation in cultural life and the right of creators to control the use of their works.

The same dichotomy can be observed in another context. Governments may enthusiastically adopt principles and conclude agreements for cultural exchanges which then are opposed by some concerned national groups. While authors and composers may well support wider cultural exchanges, performers have often for a variety of reasons taken a more restrictive if not negative attitude. In some industrialized countries, unions of intellectual workers in the cultural and communications fields have adopted downright nationalistic attitudes based on numerous complaints about widespread unemployment which supposedly would be alleviated through fewer cultural exchanges.

Following a more pragmatic approach, the lofty principles symbolized in the Universal Declaration of Human Rights often seem to mask commercial and industrial realities which basically concern the distribution of wealth within and between societies. In an international perspective, it is curious to watch economically poor countries adhering to international copyright conventions while none of the 'oil-rich' Middle Eastern states has done so. In general terms one cannot but agree with the statement that 'in the long term, the future of copyright in the least well-off countries (at any rate as regards their continued adherence to international conventions) will depend upon a solution being found to the wider global problems of trade and wealth distribution' (Freegard, 1977, p. 47).

Moving beyond such specific concepts, there are also a number of more fully developed approaches or paradigms of international relations which can assist in the analysis of international copyright relations.

An interesting approach has been adopted by Susan Strange to the analysis of the international political economy. Starting from a critique of liberal economic theories in their concentration on the efficacy of the international system in allocating resources, she stresses the importance of perceptions of inequality in the operation of the system.

> In any political economy, whether family, national or trans-national, there is what I would describe as a triple trade-off between efficiency, equity and order. The potential and acceptable balance between the three is affected by a fourth factor, the input of political direction or authority over the system. The triple trade-off can, I believe, be applied to the main infrastructural aspects of the international political economy – above all to its security system and to its monetary system, its transport, communications and its knowledge systems . . . (Strange, 1976, p. 342).

Preliminary analyses in the light of this proposed triple trade-off have been done on international shipping and oil issues but, as far as is known, not on information issues, even though Strange explicitly mentions the communications and knowledge structure as possible fields of application. Even a cursory look at the copyright field in terms of this approach indicates its usefulness. The search for efficiency is obvious in the attempts to find common minimum standards and in the demands for simple and clear international rules which conditioned for example the formulation of the Geneva

Phonogram and Brussels Satellite Conventions. The formulation of agreed Model Laws can also be considered in the light of efficiency.

Considerations of equity seem to underlie much of the present complex structure of international agreements and structures. In this respect, efficiency has been traded off against equity in the search of a balance between the different interests involved: balance between the claims of different holders of rights, balance between copyright claims and social requirements and between countries at different stages of development.

The quest for order conditions the entire international structure in this field, which in one perspective is intended to harmonize national laws. More specifically, reasons of order required the joint revision of the Berne and Universal Conventions, the co-ordination between Unesco and WIPO. Order would also be a major reason underlying the sought-for ideal of one all-embracing international agreement. However, order is traded off against efficiency when required, as when agreements on new international conventions partly overlap existing ones (as in the case of the Rome and the Geneva Phonogram Conventions). The application of this particular model could thus provide a revealing and fruitful contribution to the study of international copyright relations.

In most new paradigms of international relations the notion of interdependence occupies a central position. It has in fact become one of those fashionable catchwords that are used to cover the most diverse phenomena – and even to obscure a clearer grasp of reality. Among the many concepts of interdependence that are now being proposed is one that is of particular interest in this context. It has been given the name of 'complex interdependence', with three main characteristics:

(1) Societies are connected by multiple channels. These channels include not only the formal arrangements between foreign offices but also other ties between governmental and non-governmental actors, as well as transnational organizations (multinational companies, etc.).

(2) The agenda of interstate relationships consists of multiple issues that are not arranged in a clear, consistent hierarchy. Issues are considered by several government departments and at various levels: different issues therefore generate different coalitions, both within and across governments,

and involve different degrees of co-operation and conflict.
(3) Military force as an instrument of policy is not used by governments toward other governments within the region or the issues where complex interdependence prevails (Keohane and Nye, 1977).

Copyright relations conform to all three characteristics. They depend on and use multiple channels connecting governmental authorities as well as the nongovernmental national and international interest groupings. Governments do not go to war over copyright issues – which satisfies the third criterion. The second criterion is in many respects the most interesting and revealing. In general terms, copyright issues are not placed in a clear hierarchical position relative to other issues, except in the sense that they would not be given a high priority in ordinary interstate issue agendas. However, this statement must be qualified. In a number of countries the concerned government departments show a consistency of interest in copyright which makes for a continuous institutional commitment. Even within the copyright field the hierarchy is not clear cut. Whatever they may say to the contrary, it is difficult to expect governments to give a high priority to harmonization of, say, moral rights rules. In contrast, when economic interests are threatened – as in piracy of phonograms – a particular issue can be given enough importance for a new international convention to be concluded at express speed.

The last example concerns an approach which concentrates on international responses to technological developments (Ruggie, 1975). As a first step four analytical dimensions are used:
—the increased politicization of issues;
—the type of policy interdependence exhibited by such politicized issues;
—the location of policy interdependence;
—the distribution of interdependence among the national societies concerned.

The politicization of issues is understood to mean that an increasing number of issues and activities are placed within the area of conscious social choice and thus subject to public, as opposed to private, decision-making. There are many reasons for this movement. Among the more obvious may be mentioned the linkages between national and international policies, the need to adjust competing domestic interests and the implications of new technology and the resulting changes in patterns of relationships and communications. This trend has become very obvious in the communications field, particularly in respect of the media. In this sense it affects copyright which also in itself is becoming increasingly politicized (as the concept is used in this model).

The type of policy interdependence refers to the manner in which policy-making in one country affects and is affected by the same process in other societies. The location or 'locus' of interdependence indicates how directly the domestic policy pursuits of a state are linked to the situation of interdependence. These two dimensions are closely interrelated, particularly in the copyright field. If, for example, one country decided to expand copyright protection by including new rights or new groups of right-holders in its national legislation, concerned groups in other countries would press for the same advantages, and together they would lobby for recognition of this expansion of rights internationally. Unilateral action by one state would therefore directly influence policy-making in other states.

What in this approach is called the distribution of interdependence appears closely related to what in a previously discussed model is described as the lack of hierarchy among multiple issues.

A further aspect of great interest in this context concerns the level of institutionalization in international relations. In Ruggie's approach, three levels are distinguished: the purely 'cognitive' communities, international regimes and international organizations.

The concept of 'cognitive' or 'epistemic' communities is based on what Ruggie, borrowing from Michel Foucault, calls the 'epistemes' through which political relationships are perceived. By 'episteme', Foucault means a dominant way of looking at reality, a set of shared symbols and references, mutual expectations and predictability of intention. Epistemic communities may thus derive from the role of representing national public authorities at the international level or may be based on bureaucratic position, technical training, scientific outlook or shared disciplinary paradigms.

In the communications field such 'epistemic' or cognitive communities are abundant, and involve both governments and other 'actors'. They are often strongly organized and act as experts as well as pressure groups within and across state frontiers. They are conspicuous in the copyright field. Much of the work here is in fact carried out by a number of 'epistemic' communities which maintain close relations at the governmental and nongovernmental level but are often surprisingly isolated from other similar groupings in the information and communications field. The intellectual property communities have almost no contact with, say, the technical-regulatory experts whose work and contacts focus on the ITU or with the sets of diplomatic-legal experts who are mainly involved in UN activities. It is altogether typical that when copyright and telecommunications experts were brought together in the early stages of the discussions concerning piracy of satellite television transmissions, they did not manage more than a dialogue of the deaf.

Whether by chance or design, this situation has led to copyright being regarded and treated as a specialist esoteric domain largely separated from other issue areas in communications. It seems that the increase in politicization of issues necessarily implies a widening of these epistemic communities and the beginning of 'cross-epistemic' relationships.

Very little has been done to map and analyse the role, interrelationship or efficiency of these 'epistemic' communities, whether in communications generally or in copyright. Beyond any doubt they play an important role in the copyright field. But exactly which role or roles beyond such obvious functions as the defence of common interests or lobbying for favourable treatment in policy, law or negotiation? What is their relative strength and efficiency in different countries and how effective are they internationally? How do they relate to the different and sometimes contradictory functions of copyright? Such questions require thorough study before the various aspects of the activities and roles of these epistemic communities can be fully assessed.

The next level in this model is represented by 'international regimes'. This term refers to sets of generally agreed rules, regulations and plans, organizational energies and financial commitments accepted by a group of states. The regimes are differentiated according to purposes, instrumentalities and functions. These three features are seen as the axes of a three-dimensional policy space within which international organizations operate. International organization thus represents the most concrete of the three levels of institutionalization.

These concepts appear most useful for locating copyright regimes and organizations in the overall international relations space as well as in the international communications space.

At the level of international regimes, the communications field is characterized by two main features: the wide dispersal of regimes, and the inconsistencies, even contradictions, between these dispersed regimes. Even a superficial look at the existing regimes proves the point. Among the most important may be mentioned the technical-regulatory regime for telecommunications; the general politico-juridical regimes for freedom of information and the special regimes for different kinds of information flows (news, meteorology, remote sensing from satellites, trade and commercial information, cultural and educational materials, technical and scientific information, etc.). Other regimes are concerned with issues ranging from satellite broadcasting to customs procedures, and to the new international economic order. This, then, is the context for the regimes covering copyright and neighbouring rights.

In general, each regime or set of regimes is associated with a particular international organization. For telecommunications it is the ITU; for freedom of information, the UN; for culture and education, Unesco, etc. The copyright field shows a comparatively complex structure with the division of responsibility between Unesco, WIPO, the ILO and other bodies.

The scope of acceptance of regimes and associated organizational structures varies considerably from one issue area to another. It is virtually global in the case of telecommunications, but controversial about freedom of information. In the copyright field the characteristic feature is once again a complex scenery of varying degrees of adherence to the regimes attached to the concerned organizations.

2 Issues of communications

It has become a truism to speak of the communications revolution or the information explosion. However, the expressions themselves are significant in that they point to a profound change in our attitudes to the entire communications/information complex. All through history communications issues have received their fair share of attention. But communications and information were largely taken for granted and seen as processes functioning in support of other social activities and goals which were judged to be more fundamental, whether they were expressed in religious, economic or political terms. It is only in recent years that there has occurred a change in perspective so that, for the first time, communications *per se* have become an issue in society.

So far, efforts to deal with communications and information issues in a comprehensive, coherent manner are rare at all relevant levels: in terms of the development of technologies and the introduction of new services, in terms of policy, in terms of the institutional and legal framework: 'most countries find it difficult to sort out their own policies, to weigh the demands between different services, to relate telecommunications to other systems used for the transport of ideas and people, and to choose efficient social instruments for formulating policy and for running the different systems' (International Institute of Communcations, 1977, p. 13).

One effect of recent technical and social developments is the beginning of a break-down, or rather break-up, of the traditional, mainly technology-bound, legal and institutional categories into which systems and services have been fitted. This trend is reflected in the recurrent, sometimes continuous, changes in legislation and structure which appear not so much as an expression of coherent public policies but as temporary reactions to insufficiently understood technnological and social pressures.

Characteristic of the present situation is the absence, at the national and international level, of an agreed conceptual framework. In fact, there is not even agreement on what we are talking about: there is neither an agreed terminology, nor a basic taxonomy. A recent count of definitions of 'communications' arrives at a total of well above one hundred. Not only do conceptual approaches vary according to political, socio-economic and ideological differences, but engineers, social scientists, communications practitioners and lawyers operate with different concepts without a common language. Even within the legal field there is no shared discourse since telecommunications, copyright, computer or information lawyers have each developed a separate, specific universe of discourse.

One obvious cause for this state of affairs is that legal concepts and principles in the communications field generally have been linked to a particular technology or level of technology. Relevant legal rules and law-making institutions are therefore often inadequate when faced with a rapidly changing technology. In general, the legal framework antedates the 'communications revolution'. Concepts that have been developed for one mode of communication, such as the press, are stretched beyond their inherent capacity to cover new situations. The adaptation to changing circumstances is mainly patchwork. This piecemeal approach has resulted in the adoption of legislation covering limited aspects of communications, often in the interest of particular institutions or social groups and without due consideration of larger policy issues.

Consequently the present image of policy, structure and regulation in communications is one of rapid change and great confusion. Communications systems and information services have generally developed without coherent policies or overall planning. Neither national legislation nor the international legal framework provides for a coherent 'communications' or 'information' law. Such law is pluralistic, unco-ordinated and based on certain limited, functional objectives. Communications and information are the concern of various branches of law which are of varied origin and separate evolution, drawing upon different concepts and legal approaches, and resulting in legal rules that are, to varying degrees, deficient and often contradictory.

The lack of consistency and coherence in legal concepts and applicable provisions is also conditioned by historical circumstance: important branches of international 'communications law', particularly telecommunications and copyright, first developed in the mid-1800s, while others are based on more modern legal concepts. In this historical perspective it should also be noted that, in such early areas as telecommunications law and copyright law, the original concepts were formulated by a limited number of mainly European nations; other applicable branches of law, such as space law, have evolved in a wider international context.

The need for reconsideration of 'communications law' also arises from current challenges to traditional policies and legal regimes which used to be largely taken for granted. At the international level, the discussion of issue areas such as 'freedom of information' and 'free flow of information' has reached a virtual impasse.

These challenges are an expression of the transformation of the international system. The struggle for political independence has been followed by demands for a new international order, starting with the economic world order, to which was soon added the world information order. Such concepts as freedom of information and free flow of information are under attack by the developing countries as instruments used to maintain the present patterns of dependence and dominance in the communications and information sector. In particular, they have reacted against the imbalances in the international flow of news and cultural products whether in the form of magazines, books, films, radio or television programmes. To a large extent, the demands for a new international information order can be expressed in terms of access by developing countries: access on reasonable terms to technology and services; access to the mechanisms of information flows to make their views better known; and access to the information and knowledge required for development purposes. Copyright is therefore directly and indirectly affected by these issues.

The debates on the new international information order, even though conducted with a great deal of conceptual confusion, represent one instance of the attempts to reach more coherent approaches to the communications/information complex. There are others. Communications is now seen as crucial in social life, even as the one characteristic feature of organized communities. There is a new sense of the relationship between social structures and patterns of communication, between information and power. Communications and information are analysed as a resource in society with reference to national economies or in terms of societal and individual needs.

Some observers consider the advent of electronic communications to be a fourth communications revolution, alongside and equally important as the three earlier ones: the invention of speech, the invention of writing and the invention of printing. Other analysts postulate a new communications and information environment, whose invisible and largely transnational networks constitute a radically changed global context for economic and cultural life. The changes in the information environment are seen to go beyond the increase in the quantity of data and information that is now being made available. The perceived changes bring about a new phenomenon: transformations of a qualitative nature which affect fundamental aspects of society (see McHale, 1976; de Rosnay, 1975).

In this view the changes of modalities of communication are crucial in their impact on cultural forms and identities. Inherent in these changes is a shift from the traditional paradigm of linear communication from sender to receiver to modes of communication that are multi-modal, interactive and more participatory in their potentials. The fusion of technologies amplifies the relationships with the social and physical environment and, more important, reshapes the information content and perceptions of society. The effect on society has therefore been compared with the impact of the invention and diffusion of the printed book and its effect on the older cultural traditions. Its larger impact would be upon the symbol systems which sustain all cultures. Through these new technologies and capacities, we are dealing with the signals and messages which change us, as well as those through which we change the environment.

These approaches share one characteristic: they concern all forms, processes and products that may be included in such terms as information, knowledge, communications of whatever kind, and thus include the arts and other forms of cultural expression. They represent a re-orientation of perspectives, a new way of perceiving not only communications but society as well.

From another perspective the analysis has been conducted in economic terms. The computer, telecommunications and other electronic information industries take on a continuously increasing global importance. According to one evaluation, this complex of industries has already developed to a level where it is the third largest in the world economy. Related analyses point to what has been termed the shift from an industrial to a post-industrial society.

According to this analysis, while a pre-industrial society is essentially based upon raw materials, an industrial society is organized primarily around energy and the use of energy for the production of goods. A post-industrial society is largely organized around information and the utilization of information and is characterized by an economy particularly concerned with information, data and service-based activities. One recent study suggests that, by 1980, some of the industrialized societies will spend between 4 and 5 per cent of their gross national product on the information sector. In another study which analyses the US economy, information is seen as a collection of many hetero-geneous goods and services that together comprise an activity; this information activity includes all the resources consumed in producing, processing and distributing information goods and services. According to this broad definition, 46 per cent of GNP is bound up with information activity and nearly half the labour force does some sort of 'informational' work and earns 53 per cent of labour income (Porat, 1977a). Similar figures have been advanced in Canada. 'The information content of Canada's output of goods and services today is between 40 and 50 per cent, while about half today's manpower can be classified as "information workers". Tomorrow the microprocessor and the electronic chip will give further impetus to the replacement of non-information activities by information activities' (Sauvé, 1979, p. 2).

In economic terms there seem to be two different questions concerning information: should it be dealt with as a commodity or as a resource, or, rather, in what circumstances should the emphasis be on one or the other of these approaches? Each of these attitudes results in very different implications for policy and regulation.

The concept of information as a commodity has, as could be expected, evolved in countries with a market economy. Even though the concept was not formulated in terms we now use, it represents one of the fundamentals on which copyright legislation has been constructed. In recent times, this approach to information has been strengthened and is applied in numerous ways. As a typical example may be mentioned those new professions which function as information-brokers (consultancy firms, film sale agents, news agencies, etc.), and whose activities consist of the collection (and sometimes also the production) and sale of information. Major businesses, including industries, now recognize information, not material goods, as their most precious asset; if proof were needed one has only to consider the security measures taken to protect computerized data, which in Italy have gone so far as to include special legislation on attacks against data banks. Information handling has thus become an industry and a trade in its own right, and also a crucial aspect of public and private administration. In fact, recent studies have introduced such new concepts as the 'primary information sector' which includes those firms which supply information goods and services exchanged in a market context, and the 'secondary information sector' which comprises all the information services produced for internal consumption by government and non-information firms. To the former belong industries which produce information hardware or other information for distribution or sale as a commodity, including management, consulting and legal services, education, libraries and information services, and the mass media. The latter include most of the public bureaucracy and all of the private bureaucracy; bureaucracy in this context is described as an information-producing, distributing and consuming organization (Porat, 1977a).

Most of the studies based on this approach have concerned the US economy, and warnings have been voiced against an indiscriminate application to other economies. However, studies undertaken in other industrialized countries seem to confirm the general picture.

According to another economic analysis, the production and transfer of information is not only a commodity, but can almost be likened to a burden – indispensable to be sure – that has to be supported by the rest of the economy. Information, in one perspective, thus has a market price; in another perspective, it constitutes a growing part of the national economy.

In this kind of approach, copyright as traditionally perceived would seem to have a given place, whichever way its role is defined and the details of its functioning regulated.

A different perspective is provided by the other approach in which information is seen as a resource in society, even as the key resource. This attitude is supported by the argument that information and organized knowledge, which includes the arts and other forms of cultural expression, have several unique properties.

The first unique property is that all other resources depend on information and knowledge: it is the perception and evaluation of resources which make their use possible. Thus the extent of information determines the availability of other resources. Obviously, information seen in this perspective has a great economic value, but even more important is its social value, since all activities in society are conditioned by available information.

The second unique characteristic of information refers to the concept that, as a resource itself, information is not reduced or diminished by wider use and sharing. On the contrary, its value tends to gain in the process – 'value' seen here both in economic and social terms. The concept of 'value added' through various communications transactions has been mentioned as a valid factor in analysing the 'information economy'. Less attention has been paid to the idea of added value from a social point of view, one reason probably being that we still do not have adequate intellectual tools for the analysis of this aspect.

A further aspect concerns the use of communications and information resources, in particular of the modern electronic kind, to reduce or replace the consumption of other resources. This aspect has not been sufficiently explored and still remains controversial. However, there is already an obvious trend towards the replacement of paper by electronic methods in public and private administration, and also in such information enterprises as newspapers and news agencies. In a larger and longer term perspective, the partial replacement of physical transport by electronic communications has been suggested. The interest in such issues originated with the recognition that electronic communications, both in manufacturing and use, have the characteristic of being much less resource-depletive than traditional industrial processes, are economical in energy use and have a relatively low impact on the physical environment (see McHale, 1976).

In comparison with the commodity concept, the resource characteristics of information would lead to a different approach to the production and distribution of information in society. The emphasis would tend to be on a wide and unhampered dissemination and flow of information which is seen as essential for the economic, social and cultural activities of a society. The concept of information as a resource in society raises a number of fundamental issues which go beyond the market approach and involve wider social and political aspects: How should this resource be allocated in order to respond to social requirements and individual needs? Who controls and retains power over this resource? Which policies, structures and rules are the most adequate in this perspective?

These analyses and observations have so far mainly concerned the situation in industrialized societies which are seen as being in a transitional stage in their transformation to 'information societies'. It is recognized, though, that such areas as informatics, defined as the fields related to the construction and use of mainly electronic information processing systems as well as to their social impact, are of equal importance to industrialized and developing countries and will play an essential role in relation to such objectives as achieving a new international economic order.

With regard to developing countries, recent changes in development thinking have led to a reappraisal of the role of communications and information. In emerging new paradigms and models for development, the trend is towards similar comprehensive approaches as those which have developed for industrialized countries.

Thus analyses of implications of the so-called 'basic needs model' have resulted in conclusions that are relevant in this context. The basic human needs approach grew out of the search for a development strategy which could deal more effectively with the problem of continuing poverty in the world. It constitutes a direct attack on world poverty by meeting the basic needs for food, nutrition, health, education and housing, as well as through employment and income-gathering activities among the lowest 40 per cent income groups. The basic needs model requires an appropriate macro-policy framework for development and a reallocation of total investment in favour of the lowest income groups. It also means a balance between centralization and decentralization and a commitment to development from the bottom up, to local self-reliance, community and grass-roots organization and participation in planning, decision-making and implementation.

This approach obviously requires an unprecedented inflow of new information into the village; information that will reach even the poorest villagers. It will be necessary to develop programmes designed to help increase agricultural production, to stimulate and guide adjustments to new production methods and to new consumption patterns. Also needed are programmes which increase the farmer's understanding of his dependence on and responsibility for environmental quality, and of changing social and economic circumstances.

Thus 'what is essentially called for is the transformation of the village from a traditional society to an information community, capable of acting and responding creatively to relevant information reaching it, capable also of reaching out for that information' (Soedjatmoko, 1978a, p. 13).

This thought has been expanded into one of the few concepts

that manages to provide a perspective including both developing and industrialized countries. This approach can, therefore, be seen as the application to all countries of the concept of an information society in a perspective wider than that of an information economy. Today all societies face the challenge of adjusting to rapid techno-economic, socio-cultural and political changes on a scale which makes it possible to speak of social transformation. The capacity of a nation to manage this adjustment depends crucially on its collective capacity to generate, to ingest, to reach out for and to utilize vast amounts of new and relevant information. Soedjatmoko has called this capacity for creative and innovative response to changing conditions and new challenges 'the learning capacity of a nation' (Soedjatmoko, 1978b). The need for this capacity as a means to manage orderly transformation requires all societies to become information societies in this larger and deeper sense.

What can be said, then, about the required policies in an information age, particularly as they relate to intellectual property rights? On the basis of experience, almost nothing. The concepts and approaches mentioned above are very recent and still evolving. They have not yet penetrated policy. Communications or information policy exists only in isolated sectors, for specific media or in response to limited urgent problems. Only a few countries have made efforts to develop coherent policies in the telecommunications sector. Most countries are grappling with policies for their media, but have generally concentrated on each medium in isolation. All recent reports in the field of informatics decry the lack of national policy; this might be understandable but no less harmful when the basic list of issues includes the development of systems, the procurement of hardware and software, trade, the impact on employment, education and training, research, government applications, transborder data transmission and international co-operation.

3 Flows of information: policy, organization and control

In the light of the concepts and approaches mentioned in the previous section, copyright issues take on a new complexion. They become one aspect of information issues generally, protected works being one element of overall information flows and processes. Inevitably, this perspective raises a series of new questions. Two sets of issues are particularly relevant: copyright in relation to the organization of information flows and copyright in relation to the control over information.

The organization of information flows has become one of the most controversial – and one of the most confused – issues facing national societies and the international community. To a large extent public debate has crystallized around such concepts as freedom of information, the free flow of information and demands for a new international information order. The debate on these issues is no different from the discussion of other communications issues. It is controversial through the clash of different and often opposing concepts, ideologies and interests; it is confused in the absence of an agreed conceptual framework and even lack of agreement on the subject of discussion. There is more reaction than analysis.

It is revealing that the debate on a 'new international information order' is conducted without any clarity as to what is to be covered by the expression 'information'. Much of the debate and controversy has focused on 'news'; i.e. on the 'journalistic' dimension of information often conceived in a relatively narrow manner. Even a cursory look at current patterns of organizing the flow of news makes it clear, though, that we deal differently with news of political events, of commodity movements or of the weather. In discussing information in a larger sense, we encounter a series of different information flows with a diversity of patterns in terms of purposes, content, structures and legal regimes. It is therefore necessary to relate copyright issues to the diverse flows of information.

There is no generally accepted approach to the identification or categorization of information flows in society. They may be analysed in terms of geographical scope; functions and purposes; the communicators involved and their relationships; economic and social importance; or the direction of information flows, whether one-way, two-way or multiple.

By combining functional and content factors it is possible to identify a series of 'specialized' information flows and to analyse the corresponding systems of control and regulation.

The first and most obvious category refers to the flow of news and other material of a 'current affairs' interest mainly in relation to the mass media. This is in fact the information flow which so far has been at the centre of the international debate. In comparison, the other information flows to be mentioned appear more specialized, even if they can easily be seen as equally, if not more, important to the conduct of modern societies. They are specialized in that function, urgency and impact are distinctly perceived. Among these specialized information flows, the most important include the following areas:

—environmental monitoring and information flows: the collection, treatment and distribution of information on the environment. The methods used range from the most traditional methods for weather observation to the most sophisticated remote sensing of the earth via satellites. The information serves a host of different purposes: meteorology, navigation, surveillance of crops, forests, water and other natural resources, etc.;

—information concerning disasters, catastrophes and relief operations, epidemics and other health hazards, etc.;

—trade, financial and commercial information flows on which national economies and the international economic system are totally dependent;

—security and military intelligence;

—educational and cultural materials, including entertainment;

—administrative information, which here is taken to include information flows between national administrations, international organizations in such areas as diplomacy, negotiation, legal disputes.

Obviously, these categories are interrelated and partly overlapping. They may, though, be used as a first approximation of the kind of approach required.

This attempt to identify specific information flows in society can also serve the purpose of establishing their relationship to communications systems and channels. Each information flow, if it is specific enough, is associated with special communications systems in society. Thus, for example, not only military intelligence but also trade and financial information is transferred over specially established networks which generally are not available for other purposes.

Copyright is a method for providing regulation and control over information flows. It must therefore be seen in the context of other methods of achieving such control. The question of control over information immediately raises the question of fundamental attitudes towards the role of information in society. Is information a resource, a commodity, a right, a duty? Or rather, in what circumstances should information flows be organized and controlled according to each of these criteria?

There is, of course, no one answer to these questions. Each kind of information flow identified above requires its own organization. Disaster and health warnings can be seen as a public resource only, and not as a commodity which can be bought and sold. The other categories are less clear cut. Different societies have decided differently on the relative weight to be given to the resource and the commodity aspects, or in another perspective to the balance between the public sector and the private sector. The focus on the issues involved thus varies with different socio-economic systems.

To some extent, the organization of information flows revolves around an axis which may be defined as access versus protection and other forms of control. However, this perspective is too simplistic. Two cases may be used to clarify some of the issues and position taken.

The first example concerns the formation of international legal rules concerning remote sensing of the earth by satellites. This technology has advanced far enough to enable the collection of precise information on natural resources, even underground or underwater, conditions of crops and forests, water flows and fishing resources.

The basic issue as discussed in the Legal Sub-Committee of the UN Outer Space Committee does not so much concern the collection of data as the use, access to and distribution of information deriving from these data. Some countries maintain that such information should be freely available to whoever requests it – and, it has been added, is prepared to pay for it. Other countries vehemently object to this view: it would be inequitable and unacceptable if third parties were able to obtain vital information on a nation's natural resources and other environmental features which might not be available in the concerned country itself. A third position seems to imply that the information collector should keep total control over the information and be able to do with it what he wishes. It might be possible to locate, according to present rules, a copyright claim in the remote sensing information chain according to any one of these attitudes. However, the issue has never been discussed in those terms but in political and international public law terms.

In this case the assumption seems to have been that copyright policy would not provide the right level for solving the issues involved. This would thus be an example of the phenomenon which in international relations theory has been called the politicization of issues: the trend towards including an increasing number of activities and issues within the area of conscious social choice and public, as opposed to private, decision-making.

The second issue area involves the current changes in the organization and control of information flows. The information explosion has caused a new concern: the identification, processing, storage and retrieval of vast quantities of information, some of which may quickly become obsolete.

A primary need of present day society is accessibility to information, past and present, copyrighted as well as in the public domain . . . ways and means will have to be found to disseminate this information and still protect the developers' interests . . . But the private creators who are seeking protection for their works also need to have immediate and unlimited access to the information that is being developed . . . in order to continue creating (Marke, 1967, pp. 88–9).

The problem arising from this situation cannot be solved by reference only to the access versus protection axis. One effect of the information explosion is a tightening of the timescale which is translated into a need for rapid access and treatment of information, whether protected or in the public domain. Another related effect concerns the sheer volume of information which is on the point of overwhelming both decision-makers and the private citizen. One response is the development of a new approach that may be subsumed under the expression 'information management' and the emergence of a new category of 'information works'.

The volume and speed of present information flows requires information-brokers or mediators beyond the traditional journalists. To some extent this need could be met by changes in the library and documentation sector. However, other needs are met by an information-broker community which assembles, orders and disseminates information in highly specialized subject areas. Sufficient attention has so far not been paid to the implications and practices of this broker community which comprises consulting firms, news agencies, data service bureaux, etc. A characteristic feature of these practices is that they deal with information as a commodity to be sold and bought as any other. The form given to this commodity is often the specialized report prepared on commission or for sale. The content may consist of publicly available information which is awkward of access and collection. It is processed and presented in a form which may be protected by unfair trade practices, and by confidentiality as much as by copyright, but which certainly takes it out of the public domain. Not unexpectedly these reports are offered at prices which make them accessible only to the strongly organized and already information-rich elements in society: government and other public authorities, industry and business, and to some extent universities and research institutions.

The two cases represent interesting contrasts. In the case of remote sensing, control and access are discussed in politico-juridical terms and agreed rules will be in the area of international public law. In the second case the implications of present practices are unclear. That copyright protection in this case serves to enhance private economic values is obvious. It is more debatable whether it also serves others of its stated functions such as the encouragement of knowledge and intellectual production.

One possible method of achieving reasonable and practicable solutions would be to analyse copyright rules in relation to the purpose and function of different information flows as mentioned above.

Another approach could be based on the analysis of information law as proposed by the American researcher Marc Porat. He divides information law according to a horizontal and a vertical perspective (1977b, p. 10). The vertical view of information law concerns the statutes, regulations and court decisions that affect the structure of information industries: publishing, postal service, telephone, telegraph, radio, television, satellites and new emerging services. The horizontal view treats those legal issues which involve the flow of information from party to party. In order to provide a conceptual framework for the analysis of social and economic information flows, Porat draws upon the work of the economist

Wassili Leontif and organizes information flows according to an input–output matrix showing the origin and destination of these flows. Column 2 thus indicates the flow from individuals to business and would, from a legal point of view, include privacy law and the assignment of intellectual property rights. Copyright would also appear in the regulation of information flows from business to business (column 5).

		To		
		Individuals	Business	Government
From	Individuals	1	2	3
	Business	4	5	6
	Government	7	8	9

Such a model is similar to other concepts mentioned earlier: they represent a definite change in attitude to communications away from a fragmented, gadget-based approach. Advanced thinking in this field takes it for granted that all societies face new opportunities and challenges through the changes in economic and cultural life brought about by the 'information explosion'. For the first time there is a focus on the overall configurations, on the organization of major communications systems. There is a growing realization that we must look at all major social systems for the transfer of information if we are to deal intelligently with any one of them.

In this perspective the development of communications systems will be seen in relation to the information flows between the individual and his total environment, physical as well as social. The emergence of a more systemic approach to communications and information has led to a new interest in communications policy and planning as an area of study, reflection and action.

At this stage, at least, these new developments provide the only possible framework for evolving a coherent approach to copyright: to consider all the various networks and services as components of the total communications system that is available and under continuous development in a given society.

The application of this systemic approach implies an analysis of how works, in various guises and transformations, flow through the available channels and media within the total communications system. Messages or works are generally originated within and for a specific medium, but are then transferred from one medium to another and from one area of protection to another, whether functionally or geographically defined.

A flow- or process-oriented approach based on a systemic conceptual framework provides a new method for dealing with a number of almost intractable problems relating to copyright. First, it could serve to identify the works in their different transformations and locate, in the communications processes and flows, the points where mechanisms for the protection, authorization and remuneration can be placed. Second, it could serve to identify and locate, in the production/manufacturing/multiplication/distribution chains, the contributions and functions of the 'author', 'performer', 'manufacturer' and 'publisher'. The possibility of a new approach in this area appears particularly important in a situation where the functions traditionally ascribed to each of these categories are changing and also combined in novel ways. It would, therefore, be possible to analyse the nature and role of the new kinds of authors/creators/contributors and publishers/producers/distributors as participants in the creation/production/distribution and flow of works.

Third, it could serve to find new solutions to the issues raised by changes in the nature of 'performance', 'publication' and 'making public' in a situation where the traditional distinctions between 'public' and 'private' are no longer adequate.

Fourth, this method could be used to determine the flow of money within the communications system: the nature of financing and remuneration at different stages in the flow and transfer of works; how added value is created as supplementary 'exchange value' in this process; the way in which this added value is redistributed and paid for and what benefits accrue to authors, performers and other participants in creation/production.

Finally, it could provide a means for clarifying the conditions for increased access by the individuals who together make up the 'public', but also need to be participants. The unprecedented problems that now face all countries also demand support for widespread creativity and for new levels of knowledge throughout society.

Bibliography

Amri, Aberrahmane (1977), 'Commentary', *Performing Right Year Book*, London, pp. 51-2.

Asimov, Isaac (1970), 'The fourth revolution', *Saturday Review*, 24 October, pp. 17-20.

Berger, John (1972), *Ways of Seeing*, British Broadcasting Corporation, London; Penguin Books.

Bloom, Harry (1974), 'Outline of Computer Research Project', unpublished.

Breyer, Stephen (1970), 'The uneasy case for copyright: a study of copyright in books, photocopies and computer programs', *Harvard Law Review*, vol. 84, no. 2, pp. 281-351.

Briggs, Asa (1978), 'The Historian and the Future', *Futures* (London), December.

Cerf-Weil, Annie (1979), 'L'audiovisuel et les droits voisins', *Film Echange*, no. 5, winter, pp. 5-19.

Chakroun, Abdallah (1969), 'What attitude should the developing countries adopt following the Paris Copyright Conference, February 1969?', *EBU Review*, no. 115 B, May, pp. 50-4.

China Policy Study Group (1979), 'China's new laws', *Broadsheet*, vol. 16, no. 10, October.

Ching, Puig, and Bloodworth, Dennis (1976), *The Chinese Machiavelli*, Secker & Warburg, London.

Cohen, Saul (1964), *Fair Use in the Law of Copyright and Related Topics*, Los Angeles Copyright Society and UCLA School of Law, University of California Press, Berkeley and Los Angeles.

Commission of the European Communities (1978), 'Community action in the cultural sector', *Bulletin of the European Communities* (Brussels), Supplement 6/77.

Copyright Office (1977), *General Guide to the Copyright Act of 1976*, Library of Congress, Washington, DC.

Covarrubias, Miguel (1972), *Island of Bali*, Oxford University Press/Indira, Kuala Lumpur (first published in 1937).

Crawford, Francine (1975), 'Pre-constitutional copyright statute', *Bulletin of the Copyright Society of the USA*, vol. 23, no. 1, October.

de Freitas, Denis (1977), 'New United States copyright law', *Performing Right Year Book*, London, pp. 52-6.

de Rosnay, Joël (1975), *Le Macroscope*, Editions du Seuil, Paris.

Department of Commerce, National Bureau of Standards (1977), *Copyright in Computer-Readable Works: Policy Impacts of Technological Change*, Special Publication 500–17, US Government Printing Office, Washington, DC.

Department of Trade (1977), *Copyright and Designs Law* (Report of the Committee to consider the Law on Copyright and Designs), Cmnd 6732, HMSO, London.

Dietz, Adolf (1976), *Le Droit d'Auteur dans la Communauté Européenne: analyse comparative des législations nationales relatives au droit d'auteur face aux dispositions du Traité instituant la Communauté Economique Européenne*, Commission of the European Communities, Brussels.

Dock, Marie-Claude (1963), *Etude sur le droit d'auteur*, Librairie Générale de Droit et de Jurisprudence, Paris.

Dock, Marie-Claude (1974), 'Radioscopie du droit d'auteur contemporain', *Il Diritto di Autore*, vol. 45, no. 4, pp. 415–40.

Escarra, Jean (1936), *Le Droit chinois*, Librairie du Recueil Sirey, Paris.

Fleishits, Y., and Makovsky, A. (1976), *The Civil Codes of the Soviet Republics*, Progress Publishers, Moscow.

Freegard, Michael (1977), 'The future of the author's copyright', *Performing Right Year Book*, London, pp. 42–9.

Gotzen, Frank (1977), *Performers' Rights in the European Economic Community*, Commission of the European Communities, Brussels.

Hauser, Arnold (1962), *The Social History of Art*, vol. 1, Routledge & Kegan Paul, London.

Hazan, J. (1970), 'The origins of copyright in ancient Jewish law', *Bulletin of the Copyright Society of the USA*, vol. 18, no. 1, October.

Hunnings, Neville March (1979), 'Copyright as a hindrance to free movement of thoughts', *European Intellectual Property Review*, vol. 1, July.

ICA (1979), Report of Conference on the Arts and the European Community, Institute of Contemporary Arts, London.

International Institute of Communications (1977), Telecommunications: National Policy and International Agreement (briefing paper in preparation for the World Administrative Radio Conference, 1979), London.

ILO/Unesco/WIPO (1979), Intergovernmental Committee of the International Convention for the Protection of Performers, Producers of Phonograms and Broadcasting Organisations and its Subcommittee on the Implementation of the Rome Convention, *Reports of the Secretariat*, documents ICR 6/6 and 6/7, ICR/SC.1/IMP 2 and 5.

International Telecommunication Union (1968), *Radio Regulations and Additional Radio Regulations*, Geneva.

International Telecommunication Union (1977), Final Acts, World Administrative Radio Conference for the Planning of the Broadcasting-Satellite Service on Frequency Bands 11.7–12.2 GH2 (in Regions 2 and 3) and 11.7–12.5 GH2 (in Region 1), Geneva.

Kase, Francis (1967), *Copyright Thought in Continental Europe: its development, legal theories and philosophy*, Rothman S. Hackensack, NJ.

Keohane, R. O., and Nye, J. S. (1977), *Power and Interdependence*, Little, Brown, Boston.

Klaver, Francesca (1975), *The Legal Problems of Video-Cassettes and Audio-Visual Discs,*, Unesco/WIPO document DA/34.

Krishnamurti, T. (1967), 'Protocol regarding developing countries appended to the Stockholm Act of the Berne Convention', *EBU Review*, no. 106B, November, pp. 59–68.

Legge, James, ed. (1972), *Shu Ching: Book of History* (rev. C. Waltham), Allen & Unwin, London.

Levenson, Joseph (1964), *Modern China and its Confucian Past: the problems of intellectual continuity*, Anchor Books, New York.

Li, Dun (1971), *The Ageless Chinese*, Scribner, New York.

Liu, Alan (1971), *Communications and National Integration in Communist China*, University of California Press.

Lo, Man Hung (1979), *Country Report: Hong Kong*, Proceedings of Regional Seminar on Copyright and Neighboring Rights for Asian and Pacific States and Territories, Unesco/WIPO document ND/1978.

Lokrantz, Bernitz A. (1969), 'Telesatelliterna och upphovsrätten', *Nordiskt Immateriellt Rättsskydd*, Stockholm.

McHale, John (1976), *The Changing Information Environment*, Elek, London.

Marke, Julius (1967), *Copyright and Intellectual Property*, Fund for the Advancement of Education, New York.

Masouyé, Claude (1968), *The Berne Convention: its principles, development and administration* (Symposium on practical Aspects of Copyright), Bureaux Internationaux Réunis pour la Protection de la Propriété Intellectuelle, Geneva.

Masouyé, Claude (1971), 'Towards a system of international protection of programme-carrying signals transmitted via satellite', *EBU Review*, no. 128B, July, pp. 61–7.

Masouyé, Claude (1972), 'The gestation of a new international convention regarding space satellites', *EBU Review*, vol. 23, no. 5, September, pp. 51–63.

Masouyé, Claude (1973), 'The distribution of signals transmitted by satellite (or the "Nairobi turning-point")', *EBU Review*, vol. 24, no. 5, September, pp. 40–9.

Masouyé, Claude (1974), 'International protection of intellectual property', *EBU Review*, vol. 25, no. 2, pp. 53–69.

Masouyé, Claude (1977), 'The protection of international works and the activities of WIPO in this field', *EBU Review*, vol. 28, no. 1, pp. 31–7.

Masouyé, Claude (1978), 'Current international copyright problems', *EBU Review*, vol. 29, no. 2, pp. 48–52.

Meyer, Christopher (1977), *Computer-related Activities of the National Commission on New Technological Uses of Copyrighted Works in the*

United States, document WIPO B/EC/XII/10 – Unesco IGC (1971)/II/14, 1 October.

Monta, Rudolph (1959), 'The concept of "copyright" versus the "droit d'auteur"', *Southern California Law Review*, vol. 32, no. 2, winter.

Neary, Stephen (1978), *Copyright in Sound Recordings with Special Reference to Problems of Unauthorised Reproduction*, Proceedings of Regional Seminar on Copyright and Neighboring Rights for Asian and Pacific States and Territories, Unesco/WIPO document ND/1978.

Nomura, Yoshio (1971), 'The new Copyright Act in Japan', *EBU Review*, no. 126B, March.

Oliver, Robert (1971), *Communication and Culture in Ancient India and China*, Syracuse University Press.

Olsson, Agne Henry (1975, 1978), *Copyright: Svensk och internationell upphovsrätt*, Liber Förlag, Stockholm.

Patterson, Lyman Ray (1968a), 'Copyright and author's rights: a look at history', *Harvard Library Bulletin*, vol. 16, no. 4, October.

Patterson, Lyman Ray (1968b), *Copyright in Historical Perspective*, Vanderbilt University Press.

Pepinsky, Harold E. (1975), 'Reliance on formal written law, and freedom and social control in the United States and the People's Republic of China', *British Journal of Sociology*, vol. 26, no. 3, pp. 330–42.

Plant, Arnold (1934), 'The economic aspects of copyright in books', *Economica*, May, pp. 167–95.

Poole, James (1978), 'Piracy: TV treasure, record gold', *Sunday Times*, 1 October.

Porat, Marc (1977a), *The Information Economy: Definition and Measurement*, US Department of Commerce, Office of Telecommunications (OT Special Publication 77-12 (1)).

Porat, Marc (1977b), 'Information Law: Defining the Field and Providing a Legal Research Tool', unpublished, Stanford Research Institute, Menlo Park, California.

Porter, Vincent (1974), 'The law on copyright', *Journal of the Society of Film and Television Arts*, vol. 1, no. 1, summer.

Porter, Vincent (1978), 'Film copyright: film culture', *Screen*, vol. 19, no. 1, spring, pp. 90–109.

PRS (1977), *The Performing Right Year Book*, Performing Right Society, London.

Püscher, Heinz (1976), 'Copyright in the German Democratic Republic', *Copyright Bulletin*, vol. 10, no. 3.

Putnam, George Haven (1962), *Books and their Makers During the Middle Ages, 1476-1600*, vol. 1, Hillary House, New York.

Radack, Shirley (1979), 'Copyright and the computer', *Information Hotline*, vol. 11, no. 1, January, pp. 15–17.

Rao, C. H. Ramakrishnan (1978), *Country Report: India*, Proceedings of Regional Seminar on Copyright and Neighboring Rights for Asian and Pacific States and Territories, Unesco/WIPO document ND/1978.

Recht, Pierre (1969) *Le Droit d'auteur: une nouvelle forme de propriété*, Librarie Générale de Droit et de Jurisprudence, Dulculet, Gembloux, Paris.

Ringer, Barbara (1969), 'Relationship between the two texts of the Universal Copyright Convention', *EBU Review*, no. 125B, January, pp. 42-6.

Ringer, Barbara (1977), 'Origin and evolution of the Universal Copyright Convention', *Copyright Bulletin*, vol. 11, no. 4.

Risset, Jean-Claude (1979), *Problems Arising from the Use of Electronic Computers for the Creation of Works*, Unesco/WIPO document GTO/3.

Ruggie, John Gerard (1975), 'International responses to technology: concepts and trends', *International Organization*, vol. 29, no. 3, pp. 557-83.

Sauvé, Jeanne (1979), *The Telecommunications Revolution: Canada must play to win*, Press release, Department of Communications, 21 March.

Siebert, Fred S. (1971), 'Property rights in materials transmitted by satellites', *Journalism Quarterly*, vol. 48, no. 1.

Soedjatmoko (1978a), 'National Policy Implications of the Basic Needs Model', slightly revised version of paper presented at seminar on Implications of the Basic Needs Model organised by Dutch National Advisory Council for Development Co-operation, The Hague, 24 February.

Soedjatmoko (1978b), *The Future and the Learning Capacity of Nations: the role of communications*, International Institute of Communications, London.

Sprenkel, S. van der (1966), *Legal Institutions in Manchu China*, Athlone Press, London (1st ed., 1962).

Strange, Susan (1976), 'The study of transnational relations', *International Affairs*, vol. 52, no. 3, pp. 333-45.

Straschnov, Georges, Bergstrom, Svante, and Greco, Paulo (1958), *Protection internationale des droits voisins*, Emile Bruylant, Brussels.

Thomas, Denis (1967), *Copyright and the Creative Artist*, Institute of Economic Affairs, London.

Thompson, Edward (1973), 'International protection of performers' rights: some current problems', *International Labour Review*, vol. 10, no. 4, April.

Thomson, J. B. (1979), Notes on the Law of Copyright, paper presented at Seminar on Broadcasting and the Law, Asia-Pacific Institute for Broadcasting Development, Kuala Lumpur.

Ulmer, Eugen (1971), 'The revisions of the copyright conventions', *EBU Review*, no. 130B, November, pp. 86-98.

Ulmer, Eugen (1977), *Copyright Problems Arising from the Use of Copyright Materials in Automatic Information and Documentation Systems*, document WIPO/B/EC/XII/9, Unesco IGC (1971)/II/13.

Ulmer, Eugen (1979), *Problems Arising from the Use of Electronic Computers and Related Facilities for the Storage and Retrieval of Copyright Works*, Unesco/WIPO document GTO/1.

Unesco (1963), *Intergovernmental Copyright Committee*, document IGC/VII/5.

Unesco (1972), General Conference, Item 25 of Provisional Agenda: 'Advisability of adopting an international regulation concerning the photographic reproduction of copyright works', document 17 C/23.

Unesco (1975), *Intergovernmental Copyright Committee (1971)*, document XR 1.

Unesco/WIPO (1974), International Conference of States on the Distribution of Programme-carrying Signals Transmitted by Satellite, Report of the General Rapporteur, document CONFSAT/42.

Unesco/WIPO (1977), Working Group on the Problems in the Field of Copyright and Neighboring Rights Raised by the Distribution of Television Programmes by Cable, Report presented by the Secretariat and adopted by the Working Group, document WG/CTV/I/6.

Unesco/WIPO (1978), Working Group on the Legal Problems Arising from the Use of Video-cassettes and Audiovisual Discs, *Report*, document WWG/1/8.

Voronkova, M. A. (1978), *Country Report: Soviet Union*, Proceedings of Regional Seminar on Copyright and Neighboring Rights for Asian and Pacific States and Territories, Unesco/WIPO document ND/1978.

Weston, Jeremy (1977), 'The un-photocopiable journal', *New Scientist*, London, 17 March.

Whitford Report, *see* Department of Trade.

WIPO (1978), *Guide to the Berne Convention for the Protection of Literary and Artistic Works (Paris Act, 1971)*, Geneva.

WIPO (1979), *General Information*, WIPO publication no. 400, Geneva.

Wolfers, Arnold (1959), *Discord and Collaboration: essays in international politics*, Johns Hopkins Press.

Index

Abstracts and copyright, 171
Actors in international relations, 204, 206
Addresses, 32
Administration of rights, 40-6, 188-9; *see also* individual countries
African Model Law, *see* Model Laws for developing countries
Agreements, European, 75-6, 87
Aldus Manutius, 9
All-Union Copyright Agency (VAAP), 41, 128-9, 162-3
'Alternative' media, 184-5
American Television and Radio Archive, 41
Amplification systems, 35
Amri, A., 129
Anglo-American copyright law: author, nature of, 34, 92-3; and motion pictures, 54; philosophy of, 14, 17, 26-7, 108, 176, 192, 193, 196
Anne, Queen, Statute of (1709), 12-13, 14, 15, 30, 90
Anonymous works, 39
Archives, 39
Art, and new media, 186-7; signed works, 5
Artijsus, 41
Artists: performing, *see* Performers; status, 22, 28, 187
Asimov, Isaac, 148
Assimilation of foreign works, 49, 58-9
Austria: administration of rights, 40; educational use, 196

Authors: collaborative, 33, 110; definition, 33-5, 92, 114, 126, 137, 183, 185, 187, 229; as employees, 34, 93-4, 110, 114, 126-7, 134, 193; joint, 33; nationality, 53, 58; nature of, 33-4, 111, 114; as publishers, 190; rights: and cable TV, 158, categories, 37, 66, 108, 114, 122-3, contractual, 43, different approaches to, 26-7, 28, 92-3, 122-3, 182-3, 185-6, 191-2, 197, early definition, 11-13, 14, 17-18, 36-7, exercise of, 182, 188-9, principle of, 182, remuneration of, 197, transferability, 92-3, in unpublished work, 10; and Rome Convention, 71-2; societies, 43-6; working conditions, 34

Bali, art in, 4-5
Basic needs development model, 221
Beaumarchais, P. de, 17-18
Beckett, *see* Donaldson *v.* Beckett
Belgium: administration, 40; educational use, 196; fair use, 196; piracy, 19, 20; works, definition, 31
Beneficiaries of copyright, 34-5
Berger, John, 186
Berlin, Berne Convention revision (1908), 51
Berne Convention for the Protection of Literary and

For Product Safety Concerns and Information please contact our EU
representative GPSR@taylorandfrancis.com
Taylor & Francis Verlag GmbH, Kaufingerstraße 24, 80331 München, Germany

* 9 7 8 1 0 3 2 8 5 8 2 4 1 *